Ancient Peoples
of the American Southwest

STEPHEN PLOG

Ancient Peoples of the American Southwest

SECOND EDITION

Drawings by Amy Elizabeth Grey

With 150 illustrations
17 in color

Thames & Hudson

Ancient Peoples and Places
FOUNDING EDITOR: GLYN DANIEL

**In memory of Fred
who was always much more than a brother**

Frontispiece: A 15th-century mural from a kiva at Pottery Mound
in the Rio Grande Valley, depicting a female wearing a tunic with
a characteristic design and carrying a small pot in her left hand.

First published in 1997 in hardcover in the United States of America by
Thames & Hudson Inc., 500 Fifth Avenue, New York, New York 10110

thamesandhudsonusa.com

Second edition 2008

Library of Congress Catalog Card Number 2007901209

ISBN 978-0-500-28693-7

Printed and bound in Slovenia by MKT Print d.d.

Contents

Preface

This book is intended to provide an up-to-date introduction – for students and travelers alike – to the ancient peoples and places of the American Southwest, a region famous for its mysterious cliff dwellings as well as its extensive pueblo towns, some still inhabited today by the descendants of the ancient Southwesterners. My own interest in the Southwest has deep roots. I was born in Roswell, New Mexico and spent my youth in El Paso, Texas. My grandmother and mother regularly attended Edgar Hewett's lectures on New Mexico archaeology and decorated their house in Roswell with Navajo rugs and the garden with manos and metates found on their property near Ruidoso, New Mexico. My initial exposure to the region's archaeology came in Paul Martin's field camp at Vernon, Arizona, where my (late) brother, Fred, was on the staff. Fred loved to play the role of 'big brother' and during his first summer in Vernon he arranged for me to visit for a week (a very unusual event in Paul Martin's tightly run camp) and then to be offered the position of dishwasher and camp photographer for the next two field seasons. During those years, several notable archaeologists were among the students and staff at Vernon: Tim Earle, John Fritz, Mark Leone, Craig Morris, Charles Redman, and Michael Schiffer. My occasional trips to the Hay Hollow Valley to photograph the excavations, the opportunity to choose a research topic like the students in the field school, and the chance to hear such visiting scholars as Robert McC. Adams, Ned Danson, Emil Haury, Thomas Kuhn, Watson Smith, Leslie White, and Nathalie and Dick Woodbury, all fueled my interest in the prehistory of the region.

I have always been heavily influenced by Fred's perspective, to the point where I often find it hard to separate his ideas and mine. Although I have not cited any of his publications in the text (something I did not realize until compiling the list of references), the entire book could have the endnote, 'Fred Plog 1944–1992.' I regard *The Archaeology of Arizona*, co-authored with Paul Martin, as the best overview of the Southwest, the most complete presentation of both theory and data. And I have always agreed with his arguments that Southwestern archaeologists must expand their understanding of the past by choosing more appropriate methods and by asking broader questions.

To many prehistorians the Southwest is – or should be – an archaeological Garden of Eden. Thousands of sites have been excavated, dating is precise because of dendrochronology, preservation is excellent because of the arid environment, and the clear connection between the native peoples of prehistory and history allows us to trace the evolution of cultures for thousands of years. Moreover, this is a region where so many innovations in method and theory have occurred that it is impossible to discuss the history of American archaeology without a focus on the Southwest. More than any other part of the world the Southwest gave birth to the 'new' or 'processual' archaeology[1] which attempted to demonstrate that archaeology has no limits, that it is possible to 'know' prehistoric social organization and religion in the same way that we can 'know' technology and chronology. Yet, despite these favorable conditions and good intentions, studies of the Southwest too often epitomize the primary shortcomings of processual archaeology – an overemphasis on climate, technology, and economy; a lack of attention to internal cultural dynamics; a neglect for social organization, ritual and cosmology. For these reasons, I have tried to write a summary of Southwestern prehistory that focuses as much on social relations as on environmental change, as much on ritual and exchange as on pottery and projectile point types.

For this second edition I have focused primarily on updating two sections of the book, the chapter on the Archaic and the section of Chapter 5 on Chaco Canyon. Our knowledge of the Archaic period is changing perhaps more rapidly than is the case for any other time period, and the revisions attempt to incorporate research over the last decade. In the case of Chaco, new publications appear almost yearly, reflecting the importance of the area from AD 1030 to 1115.

I should note here too that some Native Americans of the Southwest object to the term "Anasazi" for a variety of reasons, preferring "Ancestral Pueblo" (which also encompasses the "Mogollon"); this edition, however, keeps to the traditional terminology.

Several people played a key role in crafting the manuscript and all deserve a special thanks: Michael Adler, Wesley Bernadini, Emily Cubbon, Jennifer Dieudonné, Gary Dunham, Jillian Galle, Michelle Hegmon, Abby Holeman, Carrie Heitman, Maripat Metcalf, Paul Minnis, Julie Solometo, Adam Watson and Chip Wills. In addition to my brother, Dick Ford, Kent Flannery, Henry Wright, and Joyce Marcus all must be acknowledged for their role in shaping my approach to archaeology. Joyce has been influencial not only over my thinking, but in spurring me to put pen to paper. And Bill Frank has helped keep me working late at night, though with one eye on the baseball game or the email wire. Finally, Amy Grey prepared all the superb illustrations and, most importantly, made working together fun.

Archaeologists often divide the last two millennia of Southwestern prehistory into a sequence of phases or periods. The earliest of these schemes was developed for the northern Southwest and is referred to as the Pecos

TIME SCALE	PECOS CLASSIFICATION	MESA VERDE	CHACO CANYON	RIO GRANDE VALLEY	MIMBRES	CASAS GRANDES	PHOENIX BASIN
1800							
1700	Pueblo V			Historic			
1600							
1500				Classic		Robles	
	Pueblo IV					Diablo	
1400					Cliff	Paquimé	
1300			Mesa Verde	Coalition		Buena Fé	Classic
1200	Pueblo III	Mesa Verde	Abandonment		Black Mountain		
						Perros Bravos	
1100		McElmo	Late Bonito		Classic Mimbres		
			Classic Bonito	Developmental			Sedentary
1000	Pueblo II	Mancos	Early Bonito			Pilon	
		Ackman					Colonial
900							
800	Pueblo I	Piedra	Pueblo I		Late Pithouse	Convento	
700							
600	Basketmaker III	La Plata	Basketmaker III				Pioneer
500							
400					Early Pithouse		- - - - ? - - - -
300							
200	Basketmaker II		Basketmaker II	Preceramic			
100							
AD 1							

Classification. It is still employed today, although with modifications to account for the varied temporal patterns in different areas. More typical are phase sequences with names and dates that are unique to each province, as illustrated above. These phase names are not used in the text because their use assumes that the reader already has some familiarity with the ancient peoples of the Southwest.

OVERLEAF 1 White House Ruin, a 13th-century cliff dwelling in Canyon de Chelly National Monument, northeastern Arizona, is nestled in a small opening near the base of a sandstone cliff.

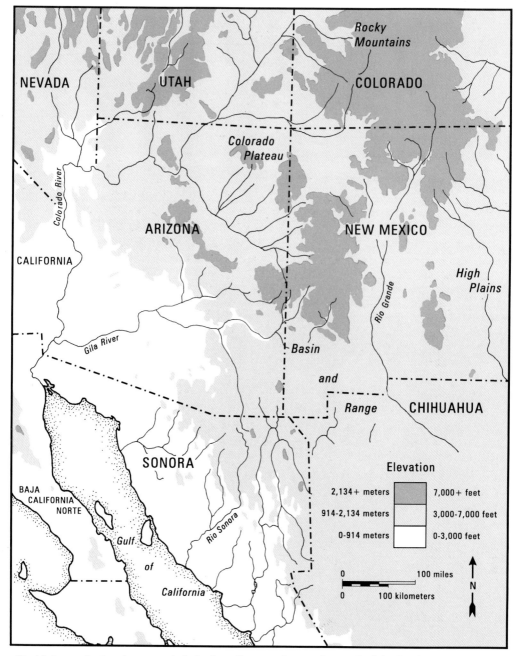

2 Rapid changes in elevation over relatively short distances characterize much of the Southwest, creating a mosaic of landforms and vegetation patterns.

3 RIGHT An extremely sparse vegetation cover of mesquite, creosote, and a variety of cacti is typical of much of the arid Sonoran desert in southern Arizona and New Mexico and northern Mexico.

1 · Introduction: People and Landscape

The American Southwest as typically defined includes all of Arizona and New Mexico; the southern reaches of Colorado, Utah, and Nevada; and the northern Mexican states of Chihuahua and Sonora. It is a region that evokes a wealth of images and myths. Many might picture harsh deserts dotted with cacti and rattlesnakes. Others think of Hollywood versions of the colonization of the West in which nomadic Apache warriors attack a wagon train of American settlers, but beat a hasty retreat when the U.S. cavalry thunders to the rescue. Anyone familiar with the Southwest, however, knows that such stereotypes are at best only half truths, and at worst totally false. Juxtaposed with the starkly beautiful Southwestern deserts are resplendent mountains and plateaus covered by forests of juniper, pine, or Douglas fir. The majority of the indigenous peoples were not nomadic warriors, but settled farmers, hunters and gatherers, traders and craftsmen. For every modern city, such as Albuquerque, Tucson, or Phoenix, there are hundreds of small villages and homesteads inhabited, in some cases for centuries, by Native Americans. And, for each of these villages, we find thousands of ruins of native settlements. Many of these define spectacular national parks and monuments – Chaco Canyon in northwestern New Mexico, Mesa Verde in southwestern Colorado, Canyon de Chelly in northeastern Arizona, or Casa Grande near Phoenix in southern Arizona.

The landscapes

4–7 LEFT Canyon de Chelly National Monument in northeastern Arizona exemplifies the spectacular canyon landscapes of the northern Southwest. The ancient Southwesterners farmed the floodplains of the canyons and built pithouses and pueblos in alcoves in the cliff walls. BELOW LEFT Monument Valley, northeastern Arizona, one of the more arid parts of the region. The numerous prehistoric settlements in Monument Valley illustrate the ability of the native peoples to adapt to a wide range of environments. ABOVE The fruit of the prickly pear cactus (*Opuntia sp.*) was harvested and eaten by native groups, and the pads were also consumed after first burning off the large thorns. BELOW Rugged and occasionally snow-capped mountain ranges with forests of pine, spruce, and fir rise high above nearby valleys or mesas with deeply cut canyons in many sections of the Southwest.

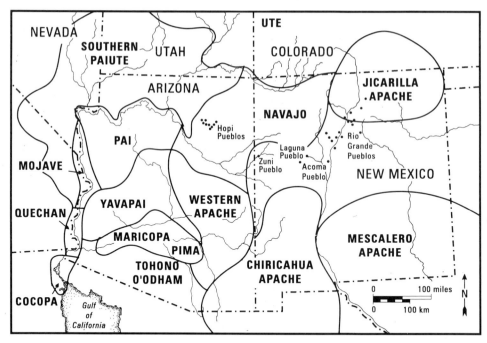

8 Tribal territories in the 18th and 19th centuries. Native Americans inhabited most areas of the Southwest at European contact and some groups, particularly the Navajo, expanded their settlement area through the 17th and 18th centuries.

Studies of these ruins have revealed early towns inhabited by hundreds of people – some of the largest prehistoric settlements in North America. Complex irrigation canals, dug without the aid of metal tools, are associated with several of these towns. Despite the lack of horses or other means of transport, the ancient Southwesterners journeyed south into Mexico and east to northern Texas and Oklahoma to trade for such exotic materials as copper, buffalo hides, the feathers of the brightly colored macaw, or shell for use as ornaments or in ceremonies. These people were constrained by their environment, but not controlled by it. Their technology was limited, but their diligence and ingenuity were not.

8   Native Southwesterners today comprise descendants both of those who inhabited the region before European contact, and of those who arrived in the late prehistoric period or early historic era. Members of the former group include the Pueblo peoples of the northern Southwest and several more southerly peoples who lived in villages that the Spanish called *rancherías*. Relative newcomers to the region include the Navajo and Apache, who only entered the Southwest in the late 15th century or early 16th century. Important though they have been to the life of the region in historic times, they played no part in the story of the ancient Southwest to be told in the following pages.

9 The pueblo of Santo Domingo in the Rio Grande Valley is referred to in some of the earliest Spanish accounts of the 16th century and is still a thriving settlement today.

The Pueblos of the north and east

The modern Pueblo peoples of New Mexico and Arizona are unquestionably descendants of the ancient Southwesterners. Many of them still dwell in villages constructed during the prehistoric era, the oldest continually inhabited settlements anywhere in North America. We group these people together – the Hopi of northeastern Arizona, the towns of Zuni, Acoma, and Laguna in the Cibola region of west-central New Mexico, and the many communities of the Rio Grande Valley – because of clear similarities in economy, architecture, and religion. Multi-story, apartment-like blocks of contiguous dwellings built using shaped sandstone blocks or adobe serve as residences and storage rooms for groups ranging in size from a few hundred people to a few thousand. In AD 1599, the Spanish settler Don Juan de Oñate described them as follows:

9, 10

> Indians, settled after our custom, house adjoining house, with square plazas. They have no streets, and in the pueblos, which contain many plazas or wards, one goes from one plaza to the other through alleys. They are of two and three stories ... and some houses are of four, five, six, and seven stories.[1]

10 Pueblo groups of the northern and eastern Southwest constructed multi-story, contiguous residences of adobe and masonry.

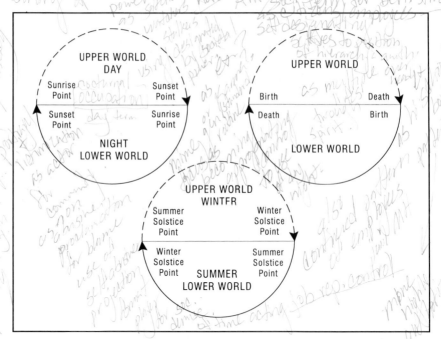

11 Pueblo thought emphasizes the cyclical nature of time, with space structured by a division between the upper world and the lower. The Hopi view birth and death (above right) as a continuous cycle. Individuals who die in the upper world return to the lower world through the *sipapu* and are then reborn in the lower world. Ultimately the re-embodied spirits of the dead return to the upper world in newborn babies. Seasons are reversed in the two worlds (below), as are night and day (above left) as the sun moves from one world to the other.

These villages are the focus of activities throughout the year, but small groups also make numerous short and long trips to hunt and gather, to obtain resources such as salt or clay, or to visit religious shrines.

The various Pueblo groups share many ideas about the nature of the cosmos, including the belief that their people first emerged from an opening in the underworld and then, over the years, migrated to their current villages. The dichotomy between the underworld and the upper world is one that organizes Pueblo thought in a variety of ways. The Hopi, for example, believe that night occurs when the sun passes into the underworld; night and day are thus reversed in the two realms. Seasons are also reversed, so when it is winter in one realm, it is summer in the other. Death in the upper world is followed by birth in the underworld, and vice versa.[2] This series of daily, yearly, and unbounded cycles between different states creates a strong degree of dualism in Pueblo society.

The Pueblos produce most of their food through farming (with corn as the primary crop), but with important supplements from hunting animals and gathering wild plants. The growing season allows only one crop a year, the alternation between farming and non-farming periods reinforcing the

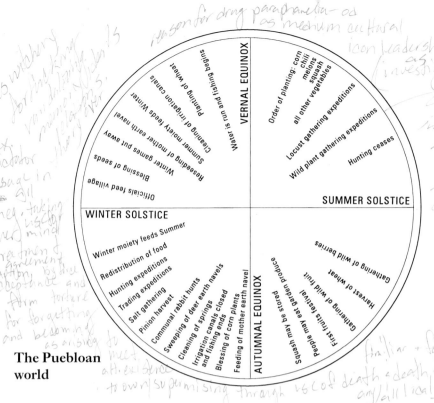

The Puebloan world

VERNAL EQUINOX

Water is run and fishing begins
Planting of wheat
Cleaning of irrigation canals
Summer moiety feeds Winter
Cleaning of mother earth navel
Reseeding of mother earth navel
Winter games put away
Blessing of seeds
Officials feed village

Order of planting: corn
chili
melons
squash
all other vegetables
Locust gathering expeditions
Wild plant gathering expeditions
Hunting ceases

SUMMER SOLSTICE

WINTER SOLSTICE

Winter moiety feeds Summer
Redistribution of food
Hunting expeditions
Trading expeditions
Salt gathering
Piñon harvest
Communal rabbit hunts
Sweeping of deer earth navels
Cleaning of springs
Irrigation canals closed and fishing ends
Blessing of corn plants
Feeding of mother earth navel

Gathering of wild berries
Gathering of wild fruit
Harvest of wheat
First fruits festival
people may eat garden produce
Squash may be stored

AUTUMNAL EQUINOX

12 For the Tewa, one of the Pueblo groups of the Rio Grande Valley, a wide range of activities related to agriculture, hunting, or plant collection are distributed throughout the yearly cycle. They cultivate the native crops of corn, beans, and squash during the late spring, summer, and early fall, and hunt on a regular basis primarily during the late fall and winter.

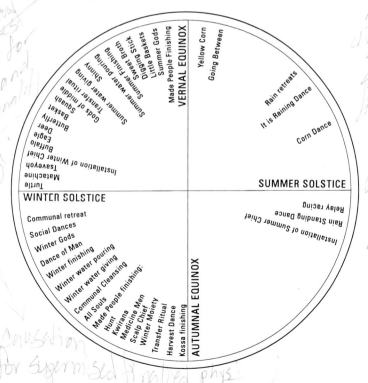

VERNAL EQUINOX

Little Baskets
Summer Gods
Made People Finishing
Buttering Stick
Summer Broth
Sweet Finishing
Summer water pouring
Summer water ritual giving
Transfer of middle
Gods of middle
Squash
Basket
Butterfly
Deer
Eagle
Buffalo
Installation of Winter Chief
Tsayevoh
Matachine
Turtle

Yellow Corn
Going Between

Rain retreats
It is Raining Dance
Corn Dance

SUMMER SOLSTICE

WINTER SOLSTICE

Communal retreat
Social Dances
Winter Gods
Dance of Man
Winter finishing
Winter water pouring
Winter water giving
Communal Cleansing
All Souls
Made People finishing:
Hunt
Kwirana
Medicine Men
Scalp Chief
Winter Moiety
Transfer Ritual
Harvest Dance
Kossa finishing

Relay racing
Rain Standing Dance
Installation of Summer Chief

AUTUMNAL EQUINOX

13 The annual cycle of Tewa ritual reflects and reinforces the economic pattern. Summer ceremonies seek to increase rainfall and promote fertility and crop yields, while rituals that focus on war and game animals occur during the fall and early winter.

14–16 ABOVE Hopi men leave the Snake kiva in the village of Oraibi in August 1900 to begin the hunt for rattlesnakes that will be needed for the snake ceremony. BELOW Some kivas consisted of a large room with a smaller antechamber where altars were often erected. Kiva floors were sometimes covered with thin sandstone slabs with a central hearth, the *sipapu* or *sipofene*, and embedded wooden slabs or stones that served as lower loom anchors. Beams to anchor the upper part of the loom were hung from the ceiling or fastened to the walls. RIGHT The *sipapu*, a small hole in the floor of both historic and prehistoric kivas, symbolizes the location where Pueblo people first emerged from the underworld to build villages in the upper world.

Kivas and kachinas

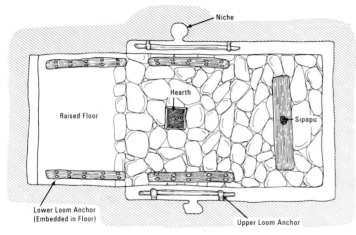

Niche

Hearth

Raised Floor

Sipapu

Lower Loom Anchor
(Embedded in Floor)

Upper Loom Anchor

dualism in Pueblo thought. The solstices or the equinoxes tend to be significant points dividing the calendar into two primary periods. Among the
Hopi, ritual activity is concentrated during the late spring, summer, and
early fall, whereas among some of the Rio Grande communities the most
intense period of ceremonies falls between the autumnal and vernal
equinox.[3] Astronomical observations – often made by simply noting the
location of the sunset or sunrise along the horizon – are thus important to
the scheduling of many activities, ranging from farming to ceremonies.

Ceremonies are organized by special societies and directed by leaders or
priests who have memorized complex rituals. Most rituals have public, communal components conducted either in open plazas or in *kivas* – subterranean religious structures – as well as sessions in kivas restricted to ritual
specialists. Many Pueblo groups symbolize the place of emergence from the
underworld, the *sipofene* or *sipapu*, by a small hole in the floor of their kivas.

A well-known aspect of Pueblo religion, particularly in the western
groups, are the public kachina dances. The Pueblos believe kachinas to be
ancestor spirits who mediate between the living and Pueblo deities, and
bring rain and other benefits to the communities. They live in the underworld for half the year, then emerge and remain in and around the villages
between the winter and summer solstices. The numerous types of kachina –
ranging from owls and bears to butterflies – are represented by dancers
believed to be imbued with the spirit of the kachina when they wear the req-
uisite mask and costume.

17 A group of kachina dancers at the Hopi village of Oraibi sometime during the 1930s.

Despite the similarities in religion, economy, and village architecture among the various Pueblo groups, many clues suggest disparate origins. Village organization, patterns of kinship, and details of ritual all show considerable variation. Among western Pueblo groups, for example, ceremonies focus mostly on efforts to produce fertility and rain, while in the east the emphasis is on medicine and curing.

The Pueblo peoples also speak a range of languages belonging to several different language families. The Hopi language, for example, is part of the Uto-Aztecan language family, an extremely large group that also encompasses non-Pueblo peoples of the Southwest and Great Basin, as well as others who now live as far away as central Mexico and Central America. The Zuni, on the other hand, speak a tongue subsumed within the separate Zuni language family, while residents of nearby Acoma speak a dialect belonging to the Keresan family. Among the many Pueblo communities of the Rio Grande Valley can be found representatives of the Kiowa-Tanoan and Keresan language families.

Linguistic anthropologists use the differences among the various languages as an index of how long it has been since the ancestors of the modern groups interacted enough to share a common language. Based on these estimates, it appears that a separation of some of the groups occurred several millennia ago. Within the Uto-Aztecan family, divergence probably began about 5,000 years ago, whereas differences among the various Tanoan branches suggest separation about 2,500 to 2,000 years ago. All these estimates indicate that cultural and linguistic differences began to emerge during the prehistoric era.[4]

Rancherías of the south and west

The early Spanish explorers contrasted the compact villages of the Pueblos with the *rancherías* – diffuse communities of scattered dwellings – of the native peoples of western and southern Arizona and northern Mexico. Typically constructed with a framework of poles covered with brush, woven mats, or mud daub, the residences within a single village were sometimes as much as half a mile apart. The *ranchería* pattern had precursors during the prehistoric era, but, as we shall see in later chapters, more compact communities comparable to the Pueblos also existed here prior to the arrival of the Spanish.

The *ranchería* people include the Yavapai, Walapai, and Havasupai of western Arizona, and the Mohave, Quechan (or Yuma), Cocopa, and Maricopa of the lower Colorado and Gila Rivers – all speaking dialects of the Yuman language family. The Pima and Tohono O'odham (formerly Papago), Tarahumara, Concho, and Opata of southern Arizona and northern Mexico, have dialects belonging to the Uto-Aztecan family. Significant differences in group organization and religion also separate the *ranchería* people from the Pueblos. Typically a Pueblo ritual leader is a prominent

18

18 A traditional Pima house with a wooden framework was first covered with arrowweed, wheat straw, cat's-tail reeds or other plant material and then a layer of earth.

person within his social group and village; ritual, political, and social leadership are closely intertwined. Among the *ranchería* peoples ordinary men, rather than priests, perform ritual songs and speeches in a cycle of communal ceremonies focusing on rain and fertility. The well-defined hierarchy of offices found in the Pueblos is lacking here. Kivas and kachinas are also absent.

In addition to the communal ritual cycle, shamans conduct more individualized ceremonies among the *rancherías*. Shamans are prophets and diviners who can cause and cure illness and who possess magical powers in hunting, rainmaking, and warfare. They acquire these powers through dreams or visions, in which an individual travels to a sacred place where he encounters a spirit who imparts songs and other knowledge to the dreamer. Curing rituals, still common today,[5] usually involve the removal of a spirit or foreign object by brushing the patient with particular objects or by sucking his body.

Most *ranchería* groups depended to some extent on farming, but the degree of dependence varied. Those who were mainly farmers resided in riverine areas such as the Colorado, Sonora, or Gila Rivers, inhabiting a single village or moving between two villages during the course of the year. Other people, such as the Havasupai, consumed wild plants and animals, or, like the Navajo, herded flocks of sheep and goats after they were introduced by the Spanish. Such groups were more mobile, often inhabiting primary villages in different ecological zones during the summer and winter, and establishing secondary camps for the collection of different resources or to move herds to new grazing areas. The hunting and gathering Tohono O'odham moved several times each year as local resources became exhausted, relying on a widespread network of kin to obtain information on the availability of resources in different areas.

The low rainfall of the southern and western Southwest generally limits agriculture to valleys where irrigation is possible, or where periodic floodwaters provide sufficient moisture for crops. In contrast to the north, the

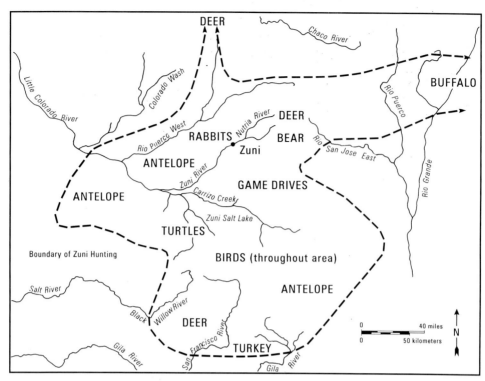

19 Pueblo people lived in one primary village throughout the year and generally farmed land in the immediate vicinity of that village, but they ranged over a sizeable area to collect plant foods and minerals, to hunt, or to worship at religious shrines. This map illustrates the vast area over which the Zuni ventured as they hunted rabbits, birds, turkey, deer, antelopes, bear, and buffalo.

growing season is often long enough potentially to allow more than one crop a year. Lower winter precipitation and the nature of native cultigens, however, appear to have limited that option, and double cropping only became common when the Spanish introduced wheat which thrived under the climatic conditions typical of the late fall and winter.

An active trade in a variety of materials cross–cut the cultural differences between the southern and northern parts of the Southwest in prehistoric times. During his travels through the *ranchería* region in 1539, Fray Marcos de Niza reported that he saw 'more than two thousand skins of cattle, extremely well tanned,'[6] obtained from the city of Cibola (Zuni). These buffalo hides had in fact been traded all the way from the plains of eastern New Mexico and northern Texas. Other valued goods included shell from the Pacific Ocean and the Gulf of California, parrot and macaw feathers from the Gulf Coast region of Mexico, and cotton. Pueblo groups also mined turquoise in several areas, most notably the Cerrillos region of the Rio Grande Valley, and hunted or collected a variety of animals, plants, and minerals over a substantial area encircling their villages. Travel over long distances was thus common, creating an intricate pattern of contacts among the different groups.

'The snow and cold are unusually great': the environmental setting

Few of us would attempt to live off the land in the Southwest for a year or even a week, because of its aridity and perceived barrenness. Yet native peoples have survived and even thrived here for centuries, exploiting the diverse environments of desert, plateau, and mountain, using a knowledge accrued over many generations that has allowed them to predict where farming would be successful and when and where wild plants could be gathered or animals hunted.

Of crucial importance are vegetation, rainfall, and temperature. Natural vegetation includes edible plants ranging from the nuts of piñon pines to the small seeds of a variety of grasses and forbs to the fruits of cacti. These plant foods also sustain animals, and therefore influence the types and densities of fauna that can be hunted. Temperature and rainfall not only affect natural vegetation, but are also critical in determining the success or failure of farming. When many people think of the Southwest it is the torrid high summer temperatures that come to mind. But winters can be equally severe. During his initial encounter with the Zuni in west-central New Mexico in 1540, Francisco Vásquez de Coronado wrote that 'The snow and the cold are unusually great, according to what the natives of the country say.'[7] The best-known chronicler of the Coronado expedition, Pedro de Castañeda de Nájera, later wrote that it was the beginning of December and 'it snowed every afternoon and nearly every night, so that, in order to prepare lodgings, wherever they camped they had to clear away a cubit of snow.'[8] These frigid conditions can begin early in the fall and linger into late spring, if not early summer, as many an archaeologist can attest. I still vividly recall the early June morning on Black Mesa in northeastern Arizona when I awoke to find icicles hanging from my tent. The growing season over much of the northern Southwest is thus only long enough to raise one crop. The Hopi plant some corn as early as the middle of April, sow their main crop around the middle of May and then harvest it in late September or early October, but frosts can occur in that area as late as early June and as early as the middle of September.

20 Nuts encased in the cones of piñon pine (*Pinus edulis*) are rich in calories and served as an important food source for the prehistoric and historic peoples of the Southwest. Gum from the tree was also used to waterproof baskets and to prepare some dyes.

Preservation and precipitation

21–23 ABOVE Anasazi cliff dwellings remain so dry that the original wood frame of a wattle-and-daub structure wall is still preserved at the Anasazi dwelling of Kiet Siel, Navajo National Monument, northeastern Arizona. LEFT Ceramic storage jars were often hung from the ceilings of pueblo rooms using ropes or fiber straps. This jar with the fiber straps still intact was recovered by Neil Judd at Betatakin in Navajo National Monument. BELOW Average precipitation by season for Phoenix in the Sonoran desert and Keams Canyon in the plateau country of northern Arizona. Heavier summer rainfall sustains farming, but the dry springs hinder seed germination and may kill crops before the summer rains arrive.

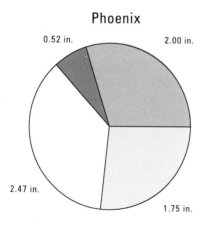

Phoenix

0.52 in.
2.00 in.
2.47 in.
1.75 in.

Keams Canyon

1.39 in.
2.26 in.
3.73 in.
2.74 in.

January-March Precipitation
April-June Precipitation
July-September Precipitation
October-December Precipitation

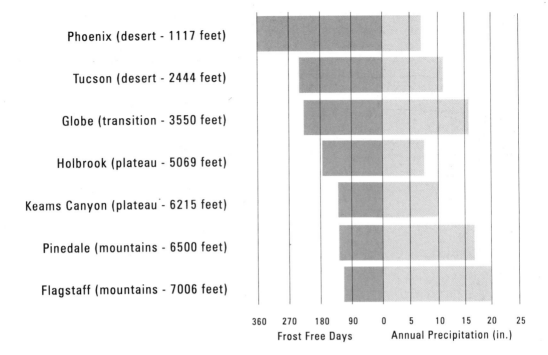

		Frost Free Days				Annual Precipitation (in.)				

Phoenix (desert - 1117 feet)

Tucson (desert - 2444 feet)

Globe (transition - 3550 feet)

Holbrook (plateau - 5069 feet)

Keams Canyon (plateau - 6215 feet)

Pinedale (mountains - 6500 feet)

Flagstaff (mountains - 7006 feet)

360 270 180 90 0 5 10 15 20 25

Frost Free Days   Annual Precipitation (in.)

24 Annual precipitation and the average length of the growing season for several cities and towns in the Southwest. The general pattern is for precipitation to increase and growing season to decrease as one moves to higher elevations.

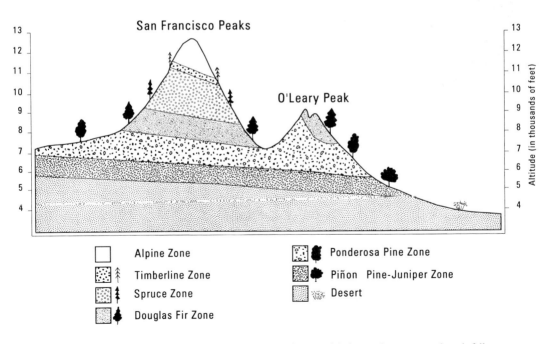

San Francisco Peaks

O'Leary Peak

Altitude (in thousands of feet)

Alpine Zone   Ponderosa Pine Zone

Timberline Zone   Piñon Pine-Juniper Zone

Spruce Zone   Desert

Douglas Fir Zone

25 Vegetation zones on the San Francisco Peaks in north-central Arizona. As one ascends, rainfall increases and thus vegetation changes. The most common tree changes from piñon to ponderosa pine and then to Douglas fir and spruce.

Another year-to-year concern is whether or not there will be sufficient moisture for plants to germinate and mature. Although numerous rivers and streams are shown on maps of the Southwest, many watercourses are ephemeral, carrying run-off only during particular seasons or after heavy rains. Farmers in historic as well as prehistoric times have often therefore had to depend exclusively on rainfall, and that rainfall has frequently been insufficient. A small part of the region may average as much as 25–30 in (64–76 cm) of precipitation a year, but 5–15 in (13–38 cm) is more typical. Such aridity does at any rate benefit the archaeologist: food remains, clothing, and wooden structures and implements are all well preserved in the dry conditions.

Also significant is the pattern of rainfall through the year. Particularly critical is the late spring to early summer period when fields are planted. In both the southern and northern Southwest, that period from April to June is the driest of the year. If winter rains and snows do not recharge soil moisture sufficiently, germination will be hindered and yields reduced. July through September is the wettest part of the year, but storms tend to be so localized that rain may fall on one area, while other nearby fields remain bone dry. Unpredictable temperature and precipitation mean unpredictable farming.

Altitude is another important environmental factor. Rainfall increases and temperature and growing season decrease as one climbs to higher elevations. Given the diversity of topography and elevation in the region – from about 300 ft (100 m) in some areas to over 12,000 ft (3,600 m) in mountainous zones – we find a wide range of climatic conditions and plant zones.

Perhaps the most important characteristic of the Southwestern environment, therefore, is its diversity. Sizzling summer temperatures, mild winters, and rainfall of less than 10 in (25 cm) a year characterize the arid Sonoran desert to the south, where the Hohokam site of Snaketown is found. Here the dominant vegetation includes cacti such as cholla, prickly pear, saguaro, and ocotillo; shrubs such as saltbush, greasewood, and creosote; and low trees like mesquite along drainages. The modern city of Phoenix lies in this zone.

North of the Sonoran desert, through the middle sections of Arizona and New Mexico, run beautiful mountain ranges. Below the timber line, ponderosa pine forests or woodlands of piñon and juniper cover ridges and slopes, with grassy meadows or sagebrush in valley bottoms. Temperatures may be 10–15°C (18–27°F) lower than in the Sonoran desert, rainfall 2–3 times higher. The city of Flagstaff lies in this zone.

In between are transition zones, often sharing characteristics of both mountain and desert. They feature rapid changes in topography, and broad areas of plateaus and mesas. Such zones vary greatly in both vegetation and environmental conditions, presenting both challenges and opportunities to prehistoric settlers.

For example, the extensive Colorado Plateau of the northern Southwest, where the sites of Mesa Verde and Chaco Canyon are located, lies mostly at

26 Intense summer rainstorms in the Southwest often drench some localities while leaving nearby residents frustrated and dry.

elevations between 4,000 and 8,000 ft (1,200 and 2,400 m), but some sections are as arid as parts of the Sonoran desert. Holbrook, for example, in east-central Arizona is 4,000 ft (1,200 m) above Phoenix in the southern desert and almost 2,000 ft (600 m) below Flagstaff in the mountains. While summer temperatures in Holbrook are intermediate between the two other cities, as would be expected from their respective elevations, average annual precipitation in Holbrook barely exceeds that of Phoenix, while winter temperatures are almost as low as those at Flagstaff. Average maximum temperatures for January are 46, 42, and 65 °F (8, 6, and 18 °C) for Holbrook, Flagstaff, and Phoenix respectively, while average annual rainfall is 7.4, 19.8, and 6.7 in (18.8, 50.3, and 17 cm). These transition zones and plateaus are thus a formidable challenge for people relying on hunting and gathering or agriculture.

The rapid changes in elevation in many parts of the Southwest make it possible to travel only 20 or 30 miles and move from the heat and aridity of the desert to the cooler, more luxuriant mountains. For thousands of years, therefore, people have been able to exploit a wide variety of environments with minimal movement. Many groups, both historic and prehistoric, took advantage of that opportunity.

Dating ancient sites, reconstructing past environments

For the prehistoric period – the period before written records – archaeologists generally have to rely on several different scientific methods of variable accuracy to date the past, in particular (since the 1950s) radiocarbon dating. In the Southwest, however, the dry environment has furnished archaeologists with one exceptionally accurate dating method: dendrochronology, or tree-ring dating. The technique – now applied in many different parts of the world – was pioneered here in the 1920s by an astronomer, A. E. Douglass. He exploited the fact that each year trees such as the Douglas fir and piñon pine produce an outer ring or layer of new wood, which builds up into a sequence of rings over the lifetime of the individual tree. Crucially the rings vary in thickness from year to year, largely because of annual fluctuations in climate. By matching and overlapping ring sequences in living trees with those in old wood, Douglass and his successors built up a master chronology for the Southwest over the last 2,000 years. Beams recovered from archaeological sites are dated by matching the beams' ring sequences with those of the master chronology. By 1930, Douglass could assign calendar dates to many major sites, such as the cliff dwellings of Mesa Verde and Pueblo Bonito – the first true dates for prehistoric sites anywhere in the world.

In the Southwestern deserts of the Hohokam, however, tree-ring dates are unavailable because of the scarcity of trees and the presence of different species which lack the regular growth patterns of the northern ones. As a result, radiocarbon dating, a less precise dating method, is used to date Hohokam sites on the rare occasions that charcoal is recovered. Conclusions about how processes of culture change in the Southwestern deserts parallel patterns in the north ultimately will depend upon an improved Hohokam chronology, but the most recent interpretations have suggested some strong correlations.

Tree-ring width patterns, determined as they are by variation in precipitation and temperature, also provide relatively precise reconstructions of past climates. These dendroclimatic reconstructions are particularly important in discussions of the last two millennia. But there are also other methods of investigating ancient environments, especially pollen analysis, research into packrat nests, and geomorphology (the study of past landforms).

Pollen grains produced by different plants can be distinguished by their shape, size, and other characteristics. They also preserve well in the types of soils found through much of the Southwest. Pollen recovered from archaeological sites can thus be analyzed, revealing the types and frequencies of plants present at the time the site was occupied. Because pollen from some plants is blown over many miles, however, pollen analysis provides more information on the region in which the site is located than on vegetation patterns in the immediate vicinity of the site.

Paleoenvironmental research has also discovered that nests made by packrats survive for thousands of years under certain conditions, and consist largely of organic matter collected by the packrats within a short radius of the nest. Thus, nests found near archaeological sites provide excellent information on the types of vegetation that grew in the area. The organic material can be dated through radiocarbon methods, aiding our understanding of how vegetation patterns changed over time.

Another method of looking at past environmental conditions focuses on weather and landforms. Geomorphologists have found that patterns of erosion (degradation) and soil accumulation (aggradation) in rivers and streams are caused by changes in the amount of annual precipitation or in seasonal precipitation patterns. By examining stratigraphic profiles – the layers of soils exposed in the banks of drainages – that document the history of degradation and aggradation, they have been able to develop models of how climatic conditions changed over time in the Southwest.

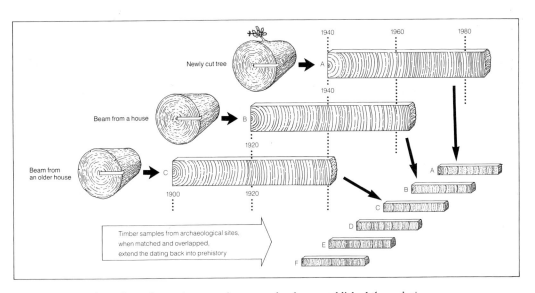

27 A master chronology of tree-ring growth patterns has been established through the overlap of living trees with those from historic and prehistoric settlements. Beams recovered from archaeological sites are compared against that master chronology to date the death of the tree.

28 Neil Judd's cook, Tom, stands in front of the kitchen tent after late April snows blanketed the area.

Studying Southwestern archaeology: from Model T's to models of the past

In 1924 I thought I knew a good deal about the Southwest.... But, I flatter myself, I was not nearly as wrong as was he who advised me, just 50 years ago, to take up work in another field because, he said: 'The Southwest is a sucked orange.'

I only wish I could return to that wonderful country and wet my aged lips once again in the rich juice of a fruit which a half-century of research has little more than begun to tap.[9]

Alfred Kidder, one of the founding fathers of Southwestern archaeology, penned the above testimonial in 1958 after a long and distinguished archaeological career that began in the Southwest and ended in the Maya region. Nearly 40 years later, the statement still captures the appeal and the challenges of research in the region (see box p. 34). Despite the tons of earth removed by shovel and trowel to expose the villages and camps where the ancient Southwesterners once lived, many unanswered questions remain.

Intensive archaeological studies of the Southwest began in the late 19th and early 20th centuries. It often required several days of arduous travel on horseback and horse-drawn wagons for pioneering scholars such as Kidder to reach the many remote areas of the Southwest in order to begin answering basic questions such as who settled Mesa Verde and Chaco Canyon and when were the large cliff dwellings and great pueblos built and then

29 A summer thunderstorm filled Chaco Wash and ensnared a Model T during Neil Judd's work at Pueblo Bonito in Chaco Canyon in 1921.

deserted. The journey of Neil Judd, a contemporary of Kidder's, to north-eastern Arizona in March 1917 illustrates some of the difficulties:

> I boarded a train at Washington, D.C. on March 16, 1917. I reached Flagstaff, Arizona, three days later, hired five chance laborers from a street corner, and left with them on the twentieth by automobile for Tuba City, seventy-five miles distant, western agency for the Bureau of Indian Affairs. Sheltered from winds by the old octagonal trading post at Tuba, we transferred to John Wetherill's four-horse freight wagon, driven by his faithful Navaho teamster, Chischili-begay. From Tuba it was seventy-five or eighty miles to the Wetherill trading post at Kayenta with two nights in the open on snow-covered ground, and from Kayenta by saddle horse and pack mule another fifteen or twenty miles to Betatakin, our first objective. Thus, within a week, I utilized four means of transportation – the best the country offered – to reach my destination.[10]

By the 1920s the automobile made travel easier and the Model T quickly   29
became the transportation method of choice. Judd remembered that 'Model T's were everywhere in the 1920's. Kidder's 'Old Blue' and Morris's 'Old Black' were only two of a long and faithful lineage.... Like Navaho sheep they stood well off the ground; they were designed to straddle high centers, to go where any other four-legged creature could go.'[11] But while the early pioneers found travel easier, putting together the pieces of the archaeological puzzle has proven to be more complicated than some initially anticipated.

The seduction of archaeological fieldwork in the Southwest

Travel in the Southwest may be much easier today than it was for pioneer archaeologists like Kidder and Judd, but the remoteness of many field camps still creates the same sense of isolation and necessitates a spartan lifestyle. During the three summers I participated in archaeological research in the mountains south of Winslow, our field crew lived in tents with no running water or electricity, and we cooled our drinking water by filling a burlap water-bag and hanging it from a tree. The highlight of the week was a two-hour round-trip drive along dusty roads to devour an ice cream or, even better, the weekend trip to the nearest motel and a hot shower. Like Kidder and Judd and many others before us, we learned the hard way that scorpions have a fondness for unoccupied shoes, that the sting of the harvester ant (a ubiquitous resident of archaeological sites) is just as painful as the scorpion's, and that if your tent isn't closed tightly you may awake during the night to discover that you are virtually nose-to-nose with a skunk in search of food!

The many pleasures of life in the field more than outweigh such inconveniences, however. There is little that parallels the camaraderie that develops in such field camps, or the anticipation of what will turn up with the next scrape of the shovel or trowel – pottery, the wall of a dwelling, a storage pit, or simply heightened expectations. And nothing is more enjoyable than walking through the pine forests of the Southwest, absorbing the aroma of pine needles and scouring the ground for the broken pottery or stone tools that are always the first tantalizing signs of a nearby archaeological site. Experiencing the isolation and seemingly limitless vistas of the Southwest also elicits a range of thoughts and emotions that stay with you for the rest of your life. Recalling his initial summer of fieldwork in 1933 in southwestern Colorado, Watson Smith wrote:

To one committed to a life on that windswept mesa, all of this grandeur might have seemed a mockery against the harsh and bitter realities of dragging a living from the soil beneath one's feet. But to me it was breathtaking and uplifting. I had never known so vast and so seemingly empty a world as this. Perhaps in this respect I was one with the Anasazi people who had gone before; I cannot read their minds, but it is almost impossible not to wonder with what awe and emotion they had witnessed that vastness in their own time.[12]

There were continuities between past and present, but also significant discontinuities. The clear differences among native groups that we observe today become much more indefinite and obscure as one looks further back in time. Much of the early research by Kidder in northeastern Arizona and at the pueblo of Pecos in New Mexico, and by Judd at Betatakin and then at Pueblo Bonito in Chaco Canyon, therefore concentrated on basic questions of chronology (see box p. 30) and cultural similarities and differences.

Excavation, survey, and interpretation
These fundamental questions were answered through careful study of the many clues – pottery, baskets, architecture, burials, food remains – left by the ancient Southwesterners. Pottery designs, weaving patterns, and mortuary rituals were described and classified in order to allow comparisons of sites and to trace patterns of change through time that could be exploited as clues to the dates of occupation. Several aspects of the Southwestern landscapes enhanced this research. A favorable consequence of the aridity is that conditions for preservation of a variety of materials are excellent, particularly when those materials are further protected through deposition in caves or rockshelters. Excavations may thus uncover food remains, clothing, implements made from wood or plant fibers, and construction materials, in addition to the more durable pottery and stone tools recovered from the typical archaeological dig.

Another product of the dry environment and the consequent low density of vegetation is that most prehistoric villages and camps can be located by simply searching for fragments of pottery or other artifacts that typically litter the surface of most sites. These characteristics make it productive to complement intensive excavations of individual villages with broader surveys of whole regions. During one of my field projects in northeastern Arizona, for example, our crew of 10 people spent 3 months systematically walking back and forth over a 46 square mile region, identifying site locations from the presence of artifacts. We mapped the distribution of almost 800 places where the ancient Southwesterners lived, collected food, or simply dropped a ceramic pot while carrying water back to the village. After dating those sites using our knowledge of how painted ceramic designs varied over time, we estimated the number of people who lived in the region at different periods and examined what types of locations were favored for villages. If our studies were restricted to only a small number of excavated sites, the conclusions would be much more limited and less accurate.

Analogies between past and present
The opportunity to learn from the modern descendants of the prehistoric peoples has also proved invaluable in attempts to reconstruct and explain the development of prehistoric societies. Studies of how they make their tools and construct their dwellings provide models of similar practices in the past. By examining Hopi or Pima farming practices, we gain an understanding of

the agricultural methods that earlier peoples could have employed in similar environments. Perhaps more importantly, through analogy with modern native groups we can develop ideas about prehistoric life that are more difficult to infer from archaeological remains, including details about religious practices and beliefs and kinship relationships.

Connecting history and prehistory in the Southwest so closely, however, also creates dangers and dilemmas. The danger is that we will be unaware of, or insensitive to, the concerns and beliefs of the people whose ancestors are the immediate focus of our studies. These people regard some archaeological sites as ancestral homes, if not religious shrines, that may be desecrated through archaeological study. Burials are of particular significance and often have not been treated appropriately by archaeologists.

The dilemma is to learn how we can take advantage of the knowledge gained from contemporary Native American groups without simply imposing the present on the past, or romantically creating myths and images that lead to a distorted view of prehistory. When we marvel at the ability of people to live without modern technology in what is to us an inhospitable and formidable environment, we can encourage the belief that such groups have always been on the verge of starvation and that it is only through a harmonious relationship with the environment that they have survived. Such a view may be correct for many times and places, but is clearly false for others. Ancient farmers in the Southwest often produced sizeable agricultural surpluses, belying the notion of persistent economic crises. Equally, they occasionally degraded their environment to such a degree that certain areas sometimes had to be abandoned.

When we examine the entire prehistoric time span, the archaeological record reveals a striking amount of cultural change. Given that our goal is to learn how prehistoric peoples transformed their culture and responded to changing conditions over periods of millennia, we subvert that goal by assuming that the present is simply a clearer, more detailed image of the past. In the following chapters, as we discuss the prehistory of the region from the first human occupation at the end of the ice age through the arrival of the Spanish explorers in the 16th century, we will focus on both similarities and differences between the prehistoric and historic peoples as a means of understanding the changes wrought during different time periods.

2 · Paleo-Indians: Early Hunters and Gatherers 9500 to 7000 BC

The first humans to enter the Southwest encountered a very different environment from the one we are familiar with today. Their ancestors had entered the Americas at the end of the last ice age, the Pleistocene, when ice sheets still covered much of North America. Sea levels were lower because water was locked up in the ice, and this exposed a land bridge between Asia and Alaska, allowing the first Americans to cross what is now the Bering Strait. Archaeologists still hotly debate the exact timing of the crossing. Evidence from a variety of sites document first settlement of central Alaska by 10,000–9500 BC and widespread human occupation of North America by 9500–9000 BC.[1] But radiocarbon dates from sites as far apart as Meadowcroft Rockshelter in Pennsylvania and Monte Verde in southern Chile provide intriguing hints of human settlement several thousand years earlier, if not more. With the substantial number of sites dating to the period from 9500–9000 BC, it would be surprising if humans were not present in at least some parts of North America a few thousand years prior to that period, but unequivocal proof has remained stubbornly elusive. In the Southwest, the Lucy site some miles east of Albuquerque, and Hermit's and Pendejo Cave in the south have yielded possible indications of very early occupation, including radiocarbon dates ranging from 33,000 to 15,000 BC. But questions exist about the association between the dated material and the cultural deposits. The oldest generally accepted settlement of the Southwest therefore belongs to the period after 9500 BC.

The North American ice sheets never reached the Southwest, but they influenced the local environment greatly. Deserts and desert grasslands had not yet formed; instead plant communities varied much more than today, with complex localized mosaics of many different types of plants.[2] The animals available for the early hunters to pursue included not only the modern trio of rabbit, deer, and antelope, but also magnificent big-game species that are now extinct: the American camel (*Camelops* sp.), Shasta ground sloth (*Northrotheriops shastensis*), horse (*Equus* sp.), lion (*Panthera leo atrox*), and mammoth (*Mammuthus columbi*). And these were indeed 'big game.' The American lion, for example, weighed perhaps 50 percent more than modern forms, with a body length of 5–8 ft (1.6–2.5 m); mammoths were as tall as 10–11 ft (3.2–3.4 m) at the shoulder with large, incurved tusks, and may have been two or two-and-a-half times the weight of modern elephants.[3] Precisely why this megafauna, as it is known, came to die out remains a matter of considerable debate, as will be discussed below.

The earliest periods: Clovis and Folsom

After 9500 BC, and for the remaining four millennia of the Paleo-Indian period, there is ample evidence of human presence in the Southwest. Throughout that period, the places where Native Americans camped or butchered animals are distinguished by distinctive stone tools, in particular splendid projectile points that were skillfully crafted from stone and then mounted at the ends of spears. The two most famous Paleo-Indian sites in the region, Clovis and Folsom, discovered in the 1920s, have given their names to the oldest spearpoints found widely across North America. Clovis points, the initial type, characteristic of the period 9500–9000 BC, are identi-

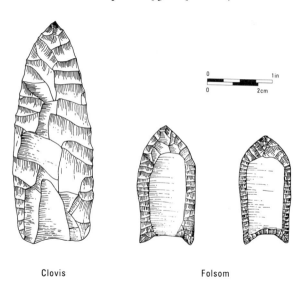

30, 31 RIGHT Clovis (left) and Folsom (center and right) fluted points recovered from Paleo-Indian sites in the central Rio Grande Valley. BELOW RIGHT Mainshaft and foreshaft of a Paleo-Indian spear. The weight and the more streamlined nature of the point and foreshaft, particularly at the location where the shaft and point were bound together, enhanced their penetration into the animal being hunted, a significant assistance given the extremely tough skins of some large animals.

Clovis   Folsom

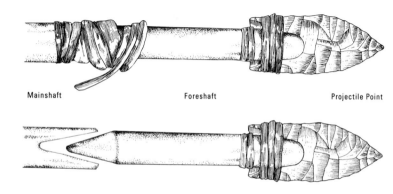

Mainshaft   Foreshaft   Projectile Point

32 Excavation at Naco in southeastern Arizona by John Lance (upper left) and Emil Haury (lower right) revealed the remains of a mammoth in association with eight Clovis projectile points. The lower jaw of the mammoth lies near the center of the photograph, with the ribs and vertebrae in the foreground.

fied in part by a long indentation (referred to as a 'flute' by archaeologists) running from the base part of the way to the tip. The flute allowed a large, heavy stone point to be more easily wedged and bound into the split fore-shaft of the spear.[4] The next, younger point type, Folsom (9000–8500/8000 BC), has a proportionally longer flute on a considerably shorter spearpoint. Other point styles distinguish later stages of the Paleo-Indian period.

Few of the early sites have many tools or much debris. Naco and Lehner Ranch in the San Pedro River Valley of southeastern Arizona are typical. Naco was discovered when run-off from heavy summer rains eroded part of the stream bed, exposing part of the skull and tusk of a mammoth. Clovis hunters left behind eight of their spearpoints in dispatching the animal. Cultural deposits at Lehner Ranch, also discovered in the side of an eroding stream, were slightly more substantial. Here archaeologists found 13 Clovis points and 8 cutting or scraping implements in association with 9 mammoths (all either calves or young adults, which may have been easier to isolate and kill) and single instances of horse, bison, and tapir. Two hearths could have been where the hunters cooked some of the meat.[5] The hearths, bones, and artifacts lay in different stratigraphic levels, indicating that the Lehner Ranch materials represent several hunting episodes.

Clovis points appear to be consistently associated with remains of large, now-extinct Pleistocene animals. At Folsom sites, in contrast, we find high frequencies of smaller animals, as well as a smaller type of bison, characteristic of the Holocene (post-Pleistocene) geological period. Clovis and Folsom point forms thus span a period of transition during which their makers witnessed – and had to adapt to – significant change in the Southwest environment. From the Folsom era to the end of the Paleo-Indian period, the frequency of known sites decreases in the west and parts of the south, a trend probably due to the drier climatic conditions which caused a deterioration in large animals' habitats, and a reduction in the number of permanent watering holes where such animals could be successfully discovered and hunted. In short, the Southwest was rapidly becoming less and less suitable for the way of life pursued by the first Native Americans who entered the region.

Point styles, social organization, and economy
The Clovis and Folsom points found in the Southwest are remarkably similar to projectile points of a comparable age from other parts of the continental United States. Later Paleo-Indian artifacts, on the other hand, and artifact assemblages from even more recent time periods, show much greater regional differences. How can one account for this initial homogeneity and later diversity? The likely explanation is that the Clovis and Folsom peoples – primarily hunters – lived in highly mobile groups which maintained extensive social networks across large areas, whereas their successors – more dependent on a greater variety of foods, especially plants, in smaller areas – lived in less mobile groups. Inevitably, the artifacts of the later groups will show greater variation, since their owners had less contact with contemporaries in distant places than did their predecessors.

Both theoretical studies and research on groups who depend more heavily on either hunting or gathering suggest that the efficient collection of different types of resources requires different modes of organization. When the collection of plants whose locations are more predictable is the focus of food gathering, as was likely the case in the Southwest after the Folsom period, they are more efficiently gathered by small groups dispersed within the area in question, with each group controlling a limited territory. In contrast, animals that move about the landscape and thus are unpredictable in location, such as the megafauna and bison of the Clovis and Folsom periods, are hunted more effectively by larger groups of people concentrated in fewer and larger settlements whose locations may frequently change with the movement of the animals. Groups that gather plants will therefore be more restricted in their movement across space and the resulting distributions of artifact styles may be comparably restricted. It is also possible that groups who control limited territories will use artifact styles to signal ownership and such behavior would also produce more limited distributions of point styles.

Although there are few firm estimates of population densities during the Paleo-Indian period, when one considers: *1*, the small number of known sites relative to the area of the Southwest region and the length of the time period being considered; and *2*, the evidence of dependence on mobile animals such as mammoths and bison, it appears likely that population densities were low and thus social networks could have been extensive. An indication of the far-flung nature of social networks in the early Paleo-Indian period comes from the site of Lindenmeier, on the northern plains of

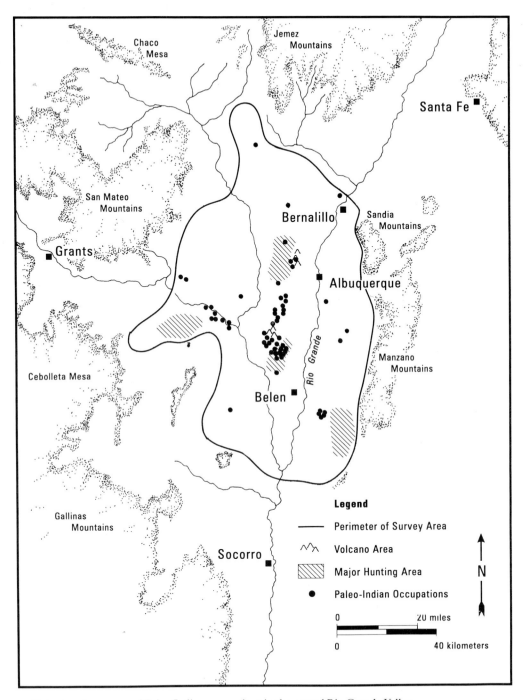

Legend

— Perimeter of Survey Area

︿︿ Volcano Area

▨ Major Hunting Area

● Paleo-Indian Occupations

0   20 miles

0   40 kilometers

33 Major hunting areas and Paleo-Indian occupations in the central Rio Grande Valley.

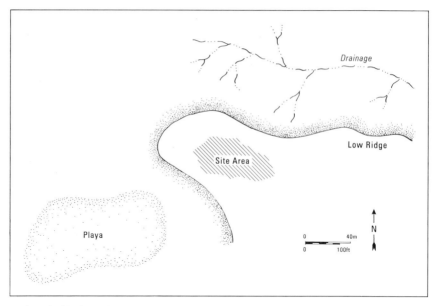

34 A typical Folsom site location in the central Rio Grande Valley. Folsom sites tend to be found on ridge tops to the north of major hunting areas and near sources of water such as *playas.*

Colorado, just south of the Wyoming border and outside the Southwest region. Folsom bison hunters here made their butchering tools from types of stone whose natural sources lie 300 miles or more from the site.[6] The stone was probably obtained through trade ties that were important in creating social bonds between groups, thus maintaining large social networks that helped ensure survival.[7]

In the Southwest, the Paleo-Indian occupation was less intense than in nearby regions. Archaeologist James Judge examined a survey area of roughly 3,000 square miles around Albuquerque and found a total of 59 occupation areas and 1,513 Paleo-Indian artifacts.[8] He discovered the densest site concentrations in four 'hunting areas' with relatively unbroken terrain where grasses would have been abundant, numerous shallow lakes or *playas* would have been characteristic, and thus large animals would have gathered.[9] Folsom groups typically located their campsites on ridges down-wind from and overlooking the hunting areas, prime locations for watching the animals feeding on the grasses or drinking at the *playas.*[10] Similar patterns occur with the sparser Paleo-Indian remains found in other parts of the Southwest.[11]

When all such sites are considered together, however, Judge found that only 72 weeks of occupation by a single band (72 'band-weeks' to use Judge's phrase) of 25–30 people, as is typical in modern hunting and gathering groups, could have created all the Folsom sites and artifacts. In contrast, he

33

34

estimates that the single site of Lindenmeier represents 630 'band-weeks' of occupation.[12] When we consider that there is more evidence of Paleo-Indian occupation in Judge's survey region than in most other parts of the Southwest, these data imply sporadic use of the region by mobile populations who were either hunting and gathering over a much wider range of Southwestern environments than occurred within Judge's study area, or were primarily exploiting neighboring areas outside the Southwest.

The vanishing ice age megafauna

One of the most fascinating and enigmatic episodes in early human history is the extinction of the big-game species at the end of the Pleistocene in North America, as well as many other areas of the world. Associated with these extinctions was a concurrent trend toward dwarfing – a decrease in the average body size of many large North American mammals that managed to survive the Pleistocene-Holocene transition. Explanations of these phenomena range from interpretations suggesting they were caused by environmental change, to proposals that it was the rapid colonization of North America by efficient Paleo-Indian hunters that was responsible.

The close association between the appearance of Clovis points across North America and the rapid process of megafaunal extinction, gave rise to the idea that humans were a primary cause for these species' destruction. At many Southwestern sites, however, it is not clear whether the associations of Clovis tools and mammoth remains were created when Paleo-Indians killed and butchered mammoths, or when they scavenged mammoths that had died from other causes. Experiments have shown that hunters equipped with a spearthrower or *atlatl* and spears tipped with Clovis points are capable of mortally wounding animals as large as a modern elephant.[13] However, many Clovis sites like Naco and Lehner Ranch have artifact assemblages with several complete Clovis points and few butchering tools, suggesting unsuccessful kills, a significant contrast with sites in later periods in which large numbers of the smaller, Holocene animals occur in association with high frequencies of butchering tools. It has been suggested, therefore, that the people of the Clovis period may have scavenged mammoth remains more often than they actually killed the animals.[14] Moreover, the faunal remains recovered from Clovis sites show that these people hunted a variety of animals, yet some of the species became extinct while others did not. Hunting pressure is thus not likely to have been the primary reason for the disappearance of Pleistocene big-game animals, though as we shall see it may have been a contributory factor.

If humans were not the key factor, then the Pleistocene-Holocene climate change becomes the most plausible agent. Recent studies have revealed that there was less seasonal variation during the Pleistocene than there is today.[15] With the transition to the Holocene, summers became warmer and winters colder relative to each other. This new pattern could have caused both the

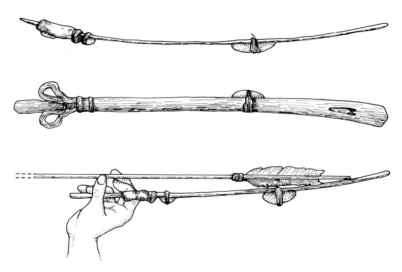

35 Side (upper drawing) and top (middle drawing) views of an *atlatl* or spear thrower from Broken Roof Cave in northeastern Arizona. The *atlatl* was made of oak with finger-loops of animal hide. A groove or notch in the end of the *atlatl* (middle drawing) helped to hold the spear in position and the stone added weight and increased the force of the throw. The lower drawing shows how the *atlatl* was held in the hand.

extinction of some plants and animals and reductions in body size among the animal species that managed to survive. Body size is a determinant of many physiological characteristics of animals, ranging from birth rate to life expectancy.[16] As body size increases, so does the age at which reproduction begins and the length of the gestation period, and as reproductive age and the length of gestation increase, it becomes more difficult for populations to replace individuals who die.[17] The 1.8-year gestation period of the modern elephant is significantly longer than almost all other animals, yet it may have paled in comparison with the estimated 2.5-year-long period of *Mammuthus*.[18] The large Pleistocene megafauna may thus have been more vulnerable to extinction. As climates became more seasonal, larger animals with long gestation periods and long intervals between the birth of their young could not adjust. A decline in the diversity of vegetation, with only those plant species which were able to cope with the seasonal variations in climate surviving, also made it more difficult for large animals to obtain a diet with sufficient nutrients, decreasing overall fitness and fertility and reducing the ability of the population to maintain itself.[19] The result was that animals with gestation periods in excess of one year survive today only in the tropics where the lack of seasonal extremes is comparable to the Pleistocene conditions in North America.[20]

We should not regard climatic and human overkill explanations as mutually exclusive, however; decreases in fitness or fertility would have been exacerbated by hunting pressure.[21] Similarly, as smaller streams became more ephemeral and *playas* dried up at the Pleistocene-Holocene transition, the number of available watering places declined, possibly making the locations of animals more predictable and hunting more successful.[22]

Some animals were better adapted to the environmental conditions of the Holocene, and the growth of their populations changed the mix of species available to human hunters and thus influenced human behavioral and cultural patterns. Large ruminants (animals that chew the cud and have complex stomachs), such as bison and deer, which were less numerous in the Pleistocene, flourished in some parts of Holocene North America because they could successfully exploit the more limited number of plant species characteristic of the new, more seasonal environment.[23] It is not surprising, therefore, to find greater numbers of bison bones at later Paleo-Indian sites than at Clovis sites.

Folsom groups were more abundant than Clovis in the Southwest, but fewer sites survive for the later Paleo-Indian period. Thus, in the central Rio Grande Valley region surveyed by Judge, he found a decrease in site frequencies after the Folsom era, with sites increasingly located near more constant sources of water, such as streams, rivers, and springs, as the small *playas* began to dry up and disappear.[24] The decline in the number of Paleo-Indian sites is not, however, a clear-cut indication of a reduced intensity of human occupation, because groups that are moving less often during the course of the year will inevitably create fewer sites.

The post-Folsom era also saw a shift in hunting and gathering, from an emphasis on a limited variety of big-game species, supplemented by smaller animals and wild plants, to a broader focus on a range of foods, in particular a much greater reliance on the collection of plants.[25] Coincident with these changes, as we saw above, went a shift in projectile points from similar, broadly based styles to more diverse, regional styles as later Paleo-Indians moved around less and had fewer contacts across large areas. These developments set the stage for the next several millennia of Southwestern prehistory.

36 Paleo-Indians used the *atlatl* (see ill. 35) to hunt large animals. Use of the *atlatl* following the steps illustrated increased the power and thrust of the spear. Experiments have shown that this weapon is capable of mortally wounding large animals such as elephants.

3 · The Archaic: Questions of Continuity and Change 7000 BC to AD 200

The Archaic was an era of subtle and perhaps episodic, but significant, culture change that established the foundation for the more visible and rapid shifts in subsequent decades. Spanning the millennia from roughly 7000 BC to AD 200, it encompassed a decline in the frequency of big-game hunting, the widespread establishment of an economy based on plant collection, and the beginning of a dependence on domesticated plants. These crops included corn (maize), squash, and perhaps beans, but there are also hints of native cultivation of such local plants as pigweed (*Amaranthus sp.*). Archaeological evidence, however, is tantalizingly slight compared to more recent time periods, although new fieldwork over the last 10–15 years has begun significantly to augment the available information. Known sites are relatively few in number, perhaps because they are difficult to locate due to the low density of artifacts found on them, or due to the layers of soils deposited on top of them during subsequent periods. A renewed focus on the period, in part the melancholy result of fieldwork prior to the construction of roads and housing developments, has begun to suggest answers to some key questions about the area.[1]

The gathering gourmets

Archaic peoples undoubtedly lived off a wider range of resources than their Paleo-Indian predecessors, and ate more plant foods. Evidence comes not only from the actual plant and animal remains found on the few sites excavated, but also from changes in where sites were located in the landscape. Studies from northern and northwestern New Mexico to northern Mexico demonstrate that Archaic settlements are situated in a greater diversity of environments, often in areas where a variety of plants and animals were accessible.[2] Such settings range from the sides of canyons to the margins of small lakes (the *playas*), to boundary zones where plants characteristic of better-watered habitats, as well as those present in drier upland regions, were available within short distances. Thus, while most Paleo-Indian sites appear to be located near areas that were optimal for the hunting of large animals, Archaic sites were chosen to take advantage of a more diverse set of foods.

The diet was indeed varied. Archaic peoples ate the seeds of a variety of grasses, protein-rich walnuts, and nuts extracted from the cones of piñon trees; they also enjoyed the fruits and pads of various types of cactus such as cholla, saguaro, and prickly pear; the beans and berries from mesquite and juniper trees, respectively; and the seeds and greens of several types of annual plants that are characteristic of areas with disturbed soil, such as pigweed, goosefoot, and tansy mustard. Animals hunted included deer, bighorn sheep, antelope, some bison, carnivores such as coyote, badger, and bobcat, and many types of small animals such as rabbit, gopher, and ground squirrel. Not surprisingly, the precise animals hunted varied from site to site, but we find one consistent pattern from southern Utah to south-central Arizona: small mammals, particularly rabbits, make up a large majority of the animal remains (although it is likely that the less numerous larger animals still provided a significant proportion of the total meat consumed).[3]

The Archaic economy marks an important adaptive change as plant collection became the focus of subsistence. Grinding stones for processing seeds were thus in abundance. In addition, new 'scheduling' decisions were required as groups had to make choices about which foods to gather in different seasons. All groups that live off the land must plan their activities and movements according to when foods become available. In temperate environments with a limited growing season such as the Southwest, different resources often mature at the same time in widely scattered locations, making it impossible to collect all of them at the same time. Decisions must constantly be made about which resources to gather and which to ignore.

Hunting certainly continued during the late fall and winter when few plant foods could be collected, but in the spring, summer, and early fall when

37 Rope snares were made using cordage of yucca fibers or other plant fibers.

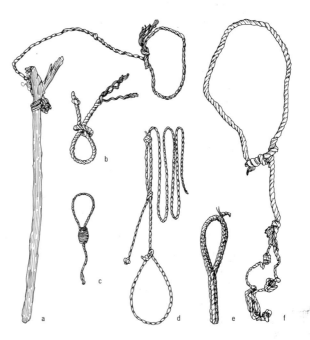

everyone participated in the harvest of seeds, nuts, greens, and fruits, hunting only focused on smaller animals that could be pursued without conflicting with gathering activities.[4] Thus, during the periods of peak abundance of wild plant foods everyone participated in the harvests and, instead of hunting deer or other large animals, they set traps in the vicinity of their camps.[5] Snares recovered during excavations at the sites of Tularosa and Cordova Caves in west-central New Mexico illustrate the importance of such hunting methods.[6] Made of rope fashioned from plant fibers, most likely yucca, such snares could be set and left by hunters while they pursued other activities, and are most appropriate for trapping small animals that tend to live in restricted areas. Such small animals also reproduce rapidly, so even frequent trapping does not significantly reduce their numbers.[7]

37

Continuity or change: examining the evidence

Given the contrast between the Paleo-Indian and Archaic ways of life in the Southwest, to what extent was there cultural continuity between the two periods? Did the same groups adapt as their social and natural environment changed, or did newcomers arrive during the Archaic? Some scholars have argued that the climatic conditions of the Archaic were unfavorable, with much of the Southwest being arid and inhospitable, and that there was little or no human occupation of many areas until they were re-populated near the end of the Archaic, when climatic conditions became more suitable. From this point of view, Paleo-Indian and Archaic groups were culturally different, with Paleo-Indian groups part of a Plains-based culture while Archaic groups originated to the west or south. Other archaeologists, however, have maintained that there was no significant cultural discontinuity and that population densities gradually increased through the Archaic. To resolve this debate requires consideration of several types of evidence.

Of initial importance is the nature of the Holocene environment during the period, as the climatic fluctuations were substantial enough to affect where and how Archaic groups chose to live. Our reconstructions of environmental conditions (from geological studies of patterns of soil build-up and soil erosion in drainages, examinations of packrat nests, and analyses of pollen deposited by vegetation) identify two important transition points at approximately 5500–5000 BC and 2500–2000 BC, bracketing a period that archaeologists refer to as the Middle Archaic or Altithermal. During the first period, there appears to have been a change in patterns of storm movement associated with the reduction in the glacial shield covering the northeastern United States. Circulation patterns that had previously brought cool, dry air masses during the summer were replaced by a more westerly flow in the summer, and a south-to-north circulation in the winter that carried generally drier air from the Pacific Ocean.[8] Associated with this change – for reasons that are still being debated – was the initiation of a process of soil erosion (arroyo cutting), producing narrow and deeper valleys rather than shallow, broad alluvial floodplains. The end of the period is marked by a transition to the opposite pattern, with climatic conditions favoring the formation of floodplains and creating soil and moisture conditions more favorable for cultivation and irrigation. Interpretations differ as to the likely rainfall and temperature patterns caused by these climatic changes, and their impact on vegetation.[9] The consensus view is that temperatures during the period were slightly higher, with winter precipitation lower and summer rainfall higher, but overall a greater aridity. These modifications were significant enough to alter vegetation patterns, with plants that tolerated drier conditions replacing thirstier species.

But these changes did not reduce food availability throughout the Southwest as has sometimes been suggested. There was an expansion of piñon-juniper woodlands and grasslands that offered a variety of edible plant foods, including the nutritious piñon nut. But such generalizations neglect both shorter-term climatic changes and differences among the various areas of the Southwest. For example, while piñon woodlands increased in the northern Rio Grande valley where they replaced stands of spruce and fir that provided few edible resources, they declined in the southern part of the valley. But even here in the south, the loss of piñon nuts may have been balanced by increases in desert plants such as agave, sotol, and yucca, which were all important food sources throughout Southwestern prehistory. Thus, although the Altithermal may have been a period of greater aridity, it was not necessarily a period of decreased food availability in all parts of the Southwest.

These changes in vegetation patterns likely caused some modification in group movements through the year, since stands of piñon nuts or agaves have patchy distributions. In addition, many of these plants must be gathered within a few weeks of ripening or they will be eaten by animals. Because plants ripen at different times depending on altitude, South-   38
westerners could exploit a wide range of foods simply by moving up and

38 Some plants such as yucca grow over a wide range of elevations. Because average temperature generally drops with increasing elevation, yucca will flower earliest in the year at its lowest range and latest at its upper limit. This pattern allowed plant collectors to move from the lowlands to higher elevations from spring through to fall, harvesting these plants as they successively matured at higher elevations.

down in the landscape over relatively short distances. Movements between stands of piñon nuts or from one elevation zone to another may thus have been a frequent aspect of life during this era.

The case for continuity

Turning now to the archaeological evidence, a variety of perspectives suggests that there is no need to postulate an influx of newcomers into the region during the Archaic to explain the differences from the Paleo-Indian period. In the first place, those differences may have been exaggerated. Plant foods are probably under-represented in the surviving Paleo-Indian evidence.

A related aspect of the Paleo-Indian evidence is the probability that there were people in at least part of the Southwest who were more dependent on gathering than on hunting at this early time. It is clear from archaeological research on the periphery of the Southwest, particularly the Great Basin to the north and the Colorado River drainage to the west, that groups with more diverse hunting and gathering adaptations, with little reliance on big game, were present during the Paleo-Indian period. Indeed it would be surprising if the Paleo-Indians had not adjusted their economic pursuits to fit the foods available in different environments and at different times. This being so, the Paleo-Indian to Archaic transition seems less abrupt, a conclusion supported by the marked similarity between the shapes of late Paleo-Indian projectile points and those made during the early Archaic.[10]

Some, however, have challenged the idea of cultural continuity,[11] arguing that there was little or no occupation of much of the northern and central Southwest until the end of the Altithermal, around 2000 BC.[12] To test this hypothesis, Wirt Wills examined radiocarbon dates[13] from the central Southwest, mainly the eastern half of Arizona and the western half of New Mexico. He concluded that hunter-gatherer populations were in fact present in the region throughout the Altithermal, although not in every area. There was thus regional continuity, but substantial fluctuations within individual locales.[14]

Archaic sites were usually established earlier in the more southerly areas and at lower elevations. Wills proposes that this trend is related to increasing summer rainfall, a pattern that would have favored a change in woodland vegetation from spruce and ponderosa to piñon pine and an expansion of open grasslands. These changes would have occurred earlier at more southerly latitudes and at lower elevations. Piñon-juniper woodlands and open grasslands have more edible resources than spruce and ponderosa forests. Interestingly, some of these resources require processing using grinding stones, roasting pits, and other devices which increase the archaeological visibility of sites on which they are found as well as the likelihood of finding charcoal that can be radiocarbon dated. Wills therefore suggests that there was both a tendency toward gradual population increase through the Archaic, and changes in artifact assemblages that increase our ability to find and date Archaic sites. Together these produce increasing frequencies of radiocarbon-dated sites within the region as a whole.

The trends of the Archaic thus can best be explained as adjustments made largely by descendants of people present in the region at the beginning of the period. However, because hunting and gathering groups were mobile and trade and information exchange networks existed, we should recognize that the geographic boundaries employed by archaeologists are arbitrary, and it would be surprising if there had not been some movement of groups between the Southwest and the surrounding regions.

Social groups and regional networks

Up to this point, the discussion has focused on the economic basis of Archaic society and cultural continuity. But how closely integrated was that society? Most noteworthy is a shift toward geographically less extensive networks of social contacts. At least, that is what the evidence from projectile points and raw materials seems to tell us. Similarities in the shapes of spearpoints from different sites allow us to group them into distinct 'style zones.' As we saw above, Paleo-Indian point styles stretch across vast areas of the United States. By the early Archaic those zones have shrunk considerably, but still show surprising uniformity over 12,500 square miles of the north-central Southwest. During the middle Archaic, however, there is a proliferation of point styles covering smaller areas. We thus see a trend that will continue for several centuries toward regional stylistic distributions. Associated with the reduced extent of style zones was a significant increase in the proportion of stone tools that the Archaic people made from locally available raw materials. A similar pattern of change occurs in both the Plains and the eastern United States.

Stylistic patterns seem to have been one means by which social information could be communicated both within and outside the group. Possession of tools and weapons of a certain design or shape helped indicate membership of a group.[15] Such communication would have been invaluable as regional population density increased, mobility declined, and groups became more tied to a particular area, increasingly relying on plant foods that were more predictable in location. There was thus less need to maintain far-reaching social networks as population increases allowed individuals more frequent contact with the socially (but not geographically) distant members of different groups.[16]

Beginning the transition to agriculture

It is within this context of reduced mobility and greater ties between social groups and resources in specific areas that plants began to be cultivated during the late Archaic. Corn (maize) and squash appear to have been used first, with beans grown later. None of these plants – ultimately so central to farming in the Southwest – were originally domesticated in the region; those processes unfolded several hundreds of miles south in the central highlands of Mexico beginning about 4500–4000 BC. Southwestern populations simply acquired seeds from areas to the south after cultigens had diffused northward through group movement and trade. But in all parts of the world, including the Southwest, it seems that groups knew how to grow plants from seeds, and likely had access to some seeds such as corn, well before they cultivated them.

Although we once thought that the ancient Southwesterners practiced some corn agriculture as early as 3000 BC,[17] re-examination of the evidence has shown that this was not the case. There is now widespread evidence of cultigens (maize and squash) – almost as widespread as in the later pueblo period when farming was firmly established – by 1000 BC, with evidence of initial utilization of maize by 2000 BC. Two of the most interesting recent discoveries have been at the Old Corn Site in west-central New Mexico, where multiple dates demonstrate maize cultivation sometime between 2500 and 1800 BC,[18] and at Las Capas near Tucson, where irrigation canals appear to date as early as 1000 BC.[19] Nevertheless, it is important to note that there is considerable evidence of economic diversity within and between regions; while some groups invested more in farming, others were less reliant.[20]

Like many other questions considered in this chapter, the issue of why cultigens began to be used by groups has provoked different answers. Rather than a response to improved environmental conditions,[21] as some have suggested, it is more likely that farming was adopted to increase the efficiency of food collection at a time of expanding population and reduced access to certain resources.[22] Thus, farming was not initially the focus of the economy, but an important supplement to the continued emphasis on gathering and hunting as it increased the probability that Archaic groups would be able to find sufficient food in an area. It nevertheless required compromises, as it constrained the movement of groups. Maize and squash were originally tropical plants ill-suited to the aridity and short growing seasons of the Southwest, and therefore had not only to be planted, but cared for and protected through at least part of the growing season in order to achieve a successful harvest. Once planted in the spring, the farmers also had to anticipate returning to the same area for the fall harvest. The addition of farming, even as a supplement, thus required a repetitive pattern of seasonal movement in and around a particular locality each year, a locality where gathering would also be possible.[23] Farming may also have increased the division of labor within late Archaic society, with some of the population, possibly older individuals, remaining near the fields during the growing season while others collected resources elsewhere.[24]

Thanks to the growing predictability of the food supply achieved through agriculture and the fact that corn and squash could be stored for winter, year-round occupation of upland areas may have become possible. Previously such high ground had been inhabited only in the late summer and early fall when piñon nuts and grass seeds could be gathered in abundance.[25] Another possibility is that Archaic groups may have continued to live at lower elevations during the leaner winter months, but spent much of the spring, summer, and fall in the uplands. In either case, these people made the decision to farm in order to enhance the effectiveness of their gathering and hunting way of life, and not because they saw agriculture as an alternative to it.[26]

The first steps toward village life

Once Southwesterners began to move around less and tend crops in specific areas, they stayed longer at some settlements or revisited them annually. This in turn made it worth their while to construct permanent dwellings to live in and pits to store food. At the site of Milagro along Tanque Verde Creek in Tucson, three pithouses, several subterranean storage pits, and a midden deposit 131 ft (40 m) long and 1 ft (0.3 m) thick occur with some of the earliest evidence of cultigens found anywhere in the Southwest.[27] Maize seeds or fragments were recovered from 85% of the features (hearths and storage pits) at Milagro. Residential architecture is even more extensive at Cerro Juanaqueña in northwest Chihuahua, Mexico, at about 1250 BC. Occupants constructed roughly 500 terraces covering 10 hectares of the summit of a steep-sided hill. Many of the terraces had rock rings that appear to have been footings for brush structures. Hundreds of ground stone tools cover the summit and maize is the most abundant plant seed discovered during excavations, demonstrating the importance of farming here.[28]

At Bat Cave in the highlands of west-central New Mexico we find dramatic change in the cultural evidence associated with the first use of corn and squash: large storage pits, multiple hearths, rabbit-fur robes, wooden implements, and yucca fiber cordage all appear for the first time.[29] Thick, compacted occupation levels and superimposed hearths indicate frequent reoccupation of the site. The more intensive use of dry caves and rockshelters like Bat Cave during this period resulted in the deposition of a variety of materials that normally would not be preserved in the open sites. The handsome baskets, cradle boards, and sandals provide fascinating glimpses into 39–41 the lives of these people. A departure from earlier sites is the occurrence of burials in many of these caves and rockshelters, often placed in pits previously used for storage and occasionally preserved so well as to provide vivid insights into clothes and physical appearance. These discoveries indicate that feather- and fur-cloth blankets served as common winter garments, fitted clothing was made from cotton cloth and deerskin, and sandals woven from yucca leaves were the standard footgear.[30] Even variations in hairdressing are known, including partial head shaving and long, braided locks.[31] 42

Along with strong evidence for more intense and prolonged occupation of some settlements, these burials offer intriguing indications that group ownership of territory also increased. Although best known from the cave sites, burials have also been found at open sites such as Cienega Creek in eastern Arizona, Valley Farms (near Las Capas) in southeastern Arizona, and, in particular, L Playa along the Magdalena River in the Mexican state of Sonora.[32] Cienega Creek may have been reoccupied over a period as long as 1,000 years and for much of that time a single pit was used to bury the remains of 36 individuals who were cremated and placed in basket containers.[33] Seven cremations were also found near the pit. Cross-cultural studies of hunting and gathering and agricultural groups reveal that burials are

Fashion and style in the Southwest

39–42 LEFT Seamless woven bag with black and red decorative pattern recovered from a cave in northeastern Arizona. BELOW Front (left) and back (right) of a cradle board from White Dog Cave in northeastern Arizona. BELOW RIGHT Two warp wickerwork and multiple warp sandals from Tularosa Cave in west-central New Mexico. Sandals were made from yucca leaves, cordage made from yucca fiber, juniper bark, and hides. Human hair was occasionally used to make toe and heel loops. ABOVE RIGHT Styles of hairdressings revealed by mummified burials recovered from caves in northeastern Arizona: *a* and *c* were males, *d* was a female, and *b* indeterminate.

:::: Red

■ Black

0   2in

0   4cm

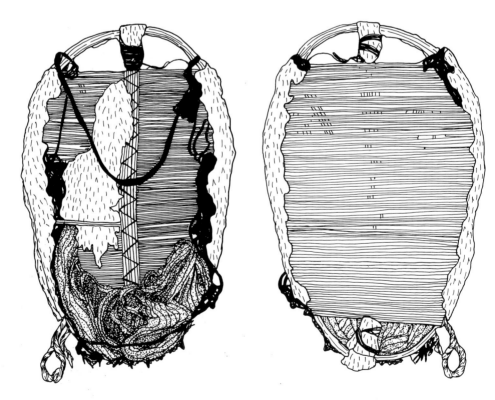

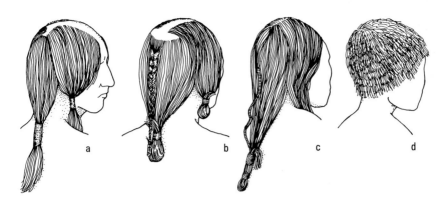

usually associated with more formalized ties between specific social groups and particular geographic areas, and that burials validate and reinforce rights of ownership and inheritance. Similar studies also indicate that the use of snares comparable with those found at Tularosa Cave are often linked with group ownership of trapping territories.[34]

Burials, storage pits, and dwellings were the first components of a set of processes that had a significant long-term impact on subsequent generations of ancient Southwesterners, marking the first steps toward village life. Those initial steps will be considered in more depth in the following chapter.

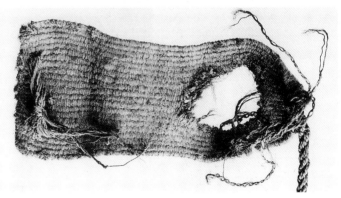

4 · The Rise of Village Life
AD 200 to 700

The development of villages – settlements where people reside in sturdy homes for much of the year, conduct ceremonies, and bury their dead – represents one of the most significant transitions in the evolution of human society.[1] Characteristics of modern towns which we take for granted – property ownership, communal religious buildings, high densities of people, symbols of differential social status, and elaborate technologies – generally appear to have developed with or after the establishment of the first villages.

Archaeologists searching for a universal single factor which led to village development have found that the process was far more variable from region to region than once thought. In the Near East, villages inhabited throughout the year were established before the domestication of plants and animals, whereas in highland Mesoamerica or the American Southwest, permanent villages followed domestication. Given our current level of understanding, we still have much to learn from studies of individual areas such as the Southwest. In the remainder of this chapter, we will conduct such an inquiry, examining some of the best-known sites, the types of challenges faced by people who chose increasingly to depend upon cultigens, and the solutions to those challenges. We will explore the key architectural, demographic, ideological, socioeconomic, and technological changes which occurred together with, and often because of, the development of villages.

Villages and the time lag: a millennium of change

By the end of the Archaic, around AD 200, people had already become less mobile, moving less often from place to place through the course of the year. However, the initial efforts to grow crops, and the associated settlement and organizational changes, mark only the first steps in the village process. Not until approximately AD 600–800 do we find evidence throughout most of the Southwest for groups residing in individual villages throughout the year. This sedentary way of life appears to have been the product of a long evolutionary process, not a radical change caused by the sudden introduction of novel ideas or new peoples to the region.

The time lag between the initial evidence of agriculture in Archaic settlements and the development of sedentary life in villages can be explained partly by the fact that agriculture brought with it new problems which often outweighed its benefits. Farming forces people to work harder and to face greater risks of malnutrition and starvation, as we shall see. Anthropological studies indicate that without some mechanism of encouragement – a set of laws, a political or religious authority, or at least some political or social incentives – few individuals will choose to work harder than necessary if options requiring less labor are still possible. No evidence of this degree of political and social compulsion has been found for the period in question. Perhaps as important, despite a rise in the density of population in the Southwest, individual groups still had the option to collect wild plant foods and hunt animals. A mixed strategy of hunting and gathering supplemented to a limited extent by farming was thus likely to have been followed by most groups until it was no longer possible.

Farming undoubtedly has the advantage of providing known locations for food, but dependence on a small range of cultivated plants brings its own problems. One basic dietary requirement for all humans is the consumption of sufficient protein. Proteins are made up of several types of amino acids and those we cannot synthesize in our bodies must be obtained from our diet. The initial cultigens in the Southwest, corn and squash, lacked the essential amino acid lysine, and were therefore an incomplete source of protein. Furthermore, the times of planting and harvesting may have conflicted with the optimal periods for hunting larger animals and thus decreased the time available for hunting.[2] These conflicts may have exacerbated nutritional problems, since animal meat was an important source of complete protein.

Malnutrition was one problem associated with farming, risk of starvation was another. Although agricultural fields can be very productive when environmental conditions are favorable, they can fail completely if conditions are poor. In contrast, natural plant and animal communities are relatively less productive in good times, but more productive in poorer ones. In the Southwest, indigenous plant communities include species that have evolved there over thousands of years, developing characteristics such as root systems that can tap water from deep underground and allow them to survive when rainfall is low or absent. By contrast the cultigens first used by Southwestern groups evolved outside the region, and could only survive through human manipulation of the environment. Thus, increased dependence on cultigens probably generated higher yields *on average*, but also greater *variation* in the food supply in any one locality from year to year.

There was a further difficulty for these nascent farmers. In Archaic times, if there was a food shortage in one area people could move to a better-endowed region. This became less and less possible once groups began to settle permanently in a particular area. In order to make the transition to a primarily agricultural economy further innovations were therefore required – in particular the introduction of storage pits to guard against food shortages.

Pithouses and houses in pits

Among the notable trends that characterize the centuries during which the village process unfolded are increases in the number, size, and frequency of various structures and facilities. Structures made by nomadic groups are often so simple that they leave little trace after the passage of hundreds of years. Well-defined dwellings become a more common characteristic of sites that postdate the introduction of cultigens and the associated changes in social organization described in the last chapter.

43   Dwellings in the Sonoran desert regions of southern Arizona were square to rectangular in shape, with walls formed of closely spaced wooden poles embedded in the ground (sometimes set within a shallow pit so that one stepped down to the floor upon entering the house), interwoven with smaller pieces of wood and reeds, and then covered with a veneer of dirt.[3] The roof of the structure was supported by a set of posts inside the structure and there was often a side entrance.

44   Typical in the northern Southwest were subterranean dwellings or pit-houses with floors that were excavated as much as 4–6 ft (1–2 m) below the surface of the ground and roofed with wooden beams, brush, and soil. These often had internal support posts and were entered either from the side or via a ladder placed through a hole in the roof. The size and depth of these dwellings, and the necessary use of wooden and stone tools to dig or fell timbers, suggest that construction required considerable effort – an impression confirmed by experimental studies demonstrating that hundreds of hours are needed to construct a typical pithouse.

In the Mogollon and Anasazi regions these dwellings may have been occupied primarily during the colder parts of the year, when their subterranean nature would have minimized heat loss from the hearths inside.[4] Stored foods cached in pits both inside and outside the structures allowed sizeable groups to remain in one location for much of the cold season, thus justifying the additional effort required to construct such dwellings. At other times of the year, groups may have fragmented, spreading out so that they could exploit more efficiently the scattered patches of wild foods. At smaller sites

43 Floor plan and probable framework of a Hohokam house. Houses were typically erected within a shallow pit, with the walls and roof constructed using timbers covered with a matting of reeds, grass, and finally earth.

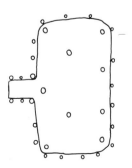

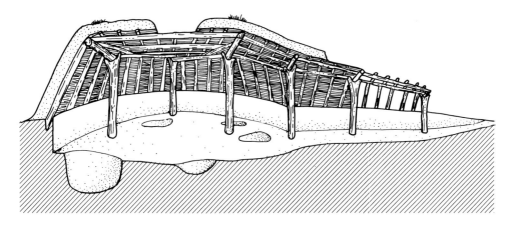

44 Cross-section of a typical Mogollon pithouse with a side (as opposed to roof) entrance. Vertical posts embedded in the floor supported a framework of large and small beams overlain by a layer of earth.

we find evidence of less substantial dwellings, requiring less labor for construction, which may have been used during warmer periods. Many settlements, both large and small, have external subterranean storage pits with narrow openings that limit the amount of oxygen available to bacteria and insects that can destroy stored foods. Some scholars have proposed that these unobtrusive pits may have been built when sites were abandoned for a period and it was necessary to leave stored foods behind while collecting food in other areas.[5]

Storage and personal property at Shabik'eschee Village and the SU Site
We find pithouses at numerous sites and in many different parts of the Southwest during the period *c*. AD 200 to 700. In addition, although the size of the typical settlement may have changed little, the largest communities saw a significant rise in the number of dwellings. Also evident at both small and large sites was an increase in storage volume. These characteristics are best exemplified by two sites, Shabik'eschee Village and the SU (pronounced 'Shoe') Site, originally excavated in the second quarter of this century and then restudied decades later. Both Shabik'eschee and SU were occupied around AD 500, but they have somewhat different storage patterns that suggest organizational differences between the two resident groups.

Shabik'eschee Village in northwestern New Mexico is one of over a hundred settlements in Chaco Canyon (an area known best for spectacular pueblos constructed primarily in the 11th and 12th centuries as discussed in Chapter 6) inhabited between AD 500 and 700. It was partially excavated by archaeologist Frank H. H. Roberts in the 1920s and again by the National Park Service in the 1970s.[6] Larger than most contemporary settlements, where typically between 1 and 12 dwellings are found, the inhabitants of

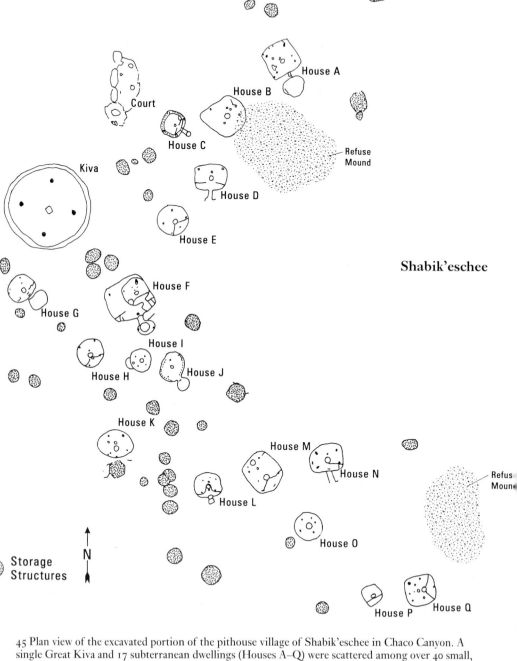

0   15 m

0   50 ft

House A

House B

Court

House C

Kiva

Refuse
Mound

House D

House E

Shabik'eschee

House F

House G

House I

House H

House J

House K

House M

House N

Refus
Moun

House L

House O

Storage
Structures

N

House P

House Q

45 Plan view of the excavated portion of the pithouse village of Shabik'eschee in Chaco Canyon. A single Great Kiva and 17 subterranean dwellings (Houses A–Q) were scattered among over 40 small, subterranean storage structures.

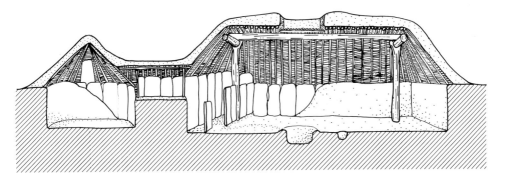

46 Cross-section of a typical dwelling at Shabik'eschee. The floors of Shabik'eschee dwellings averaged about 190 square ft (18 square m). The volume of the sub-surface storage structures averaged around 56 cubic ft (1.6 cubic m), and they were circular to rectangular in shape. Structure walls were lined with sandstone slabs and the roofs were made of wood overlaid by twigs, bark, and earth and supported by four posts planted in the floor of the structure.

Shabik'eschee constructed over 60 shallow pithouses, with 19 excavated in   45–47
the original study. The floors of these dwellings had been excavated below the ground surface and were circular to rectangular in shape. Structure walls were lined with sandstone slabs and the roof was made of wood overlaid by twigs, bark, and earth and supported by four posts planted in the floor of the structure.

Associated with, but exterior to, the 19 excavated pithouses are 45 storage 'bins' constructed in a manner similar to the pithouses, with slab walls and dome roofs with small openings in the top. Even if many of the pithouses and storage structures were not used contemporaneously, the volume of the storage structures is considerable in relation to the number of dwellings.

Sites like Shabik'eschee were probably established by groups that came together in the fall to collect piñon nuts and perhaps other wild resources.[7] If conditions for agriculture were favorable the following spring and summer, settlers may have remained at the site and farmed nearby areas, but if not, small groups of a few families likely moved to settlements elsewhere. The large storage structures would have allowed stored resources to be watched and protected by a small group remaining at the site throughout the year.

47 House F at Shabik'eschee after excavation. Stone slabs covered with a coat of plaster formed the walls of the dwelling and four internal posts supported the roof. The floor of the house was 11 to 12 ft (3.3 to 3.6 m) across and had a central hearth pecked into bedrock.

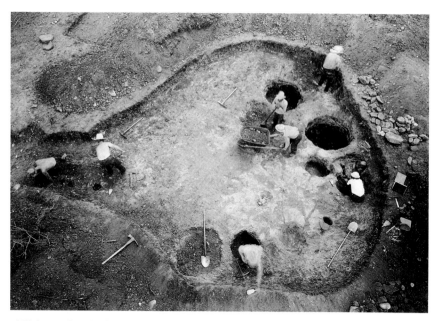

48 Pithouse C at the SU Site during excavations in 1939. The SU pithouses were significantly larger than those at Shabik'eschee, with an average floor area of 415 square ft (38.6 square m). Here pits inside the structures served as the primary storage areas, with an average volume of 95 cubic ft (2.7 cubic m) per structure.

The SU Site in west-central New Mexico was excavated in the late 1930s and the 1940s by Paul S. Martin.[8] He dug 28 out of the roughly 40 pithouses here. Probably constructed in a manner similar to those at Shabik'eschee, though lacking slab-lined walls and antechambers, the SU pithouses were 48 nevertheless significantly larger.[9] Here substantial numbers of pits *inside* the structures served as the primary storage areas. Given the large size of individual dwellings, goods may also have been stored on the floors of the houses.

These characteristics of Shabik'eschee Village and the SU Site are noteworthy for several reasons. A change from communal ownership of food (with clearly defined rules for sharing of resources) to individual ownership (which allows the accumulation of wealth) appears to be one of the key transitions in the development of sedentary, agricultural villages. While the pattern of specialized external storage structures at Shabik'eschee is more suggestive of group sharing where goods are stored in open, visible areas, the abundant storage pits inside pithouses at the SU Site and the less numerous ones in Shabik'eschee dwellings suggest some private ownership by families of both villages. These communities may thus represent somewhat different points along the evolutionary paths from mobile hunter-gatherers to sedentary farmers, and are indicative of the dynamic, variable nature of Southwestern communities during this period.

Public buildings and collective ritual

Together with family ownership and control of resources, the construction of communal buildings typifies the development of sedentary villages. Noteworthy at some of the larger settlements, such as SU and Shabik'eschee, are unusual structures that have been interpreted as communal religious structures or 'public buildings.' The clearest example is a Shabik'eschee structure that was unusual in having a low bench that encircled the building and a floor area over fives times as large as the average pithouse. There is some evidence that the structure was not completely roofed. Many have proposed that this was one of the earliest examples of a 'Great Kiva' – a larger-than-average religious structure more typical of later periods in Chaco Canyon, built to serve much larger social groups than lived in a single settlement. At the SU Site, one pithouse was also much larger than the others. The structure, Pithouse A, had characteristics not found in other houses, including horizontal beams placed at several points around the interior walls as possible supports for the roof posts and a lack of interior pits. Similar variation in the size of houses has been discovered in southern 49 Arizona at Snaketown and Pueblo Patricia where large square houses, supported by four substantial internal posts and by sturdy walls, date to the same time period as much smaller dwellings. The presence of hearths and domestic artifacts in these larger houses may indicate that they were also the dwellings of community leaders who could recruit large numbers of followers, or who used their homes for both public and private functions.[10]

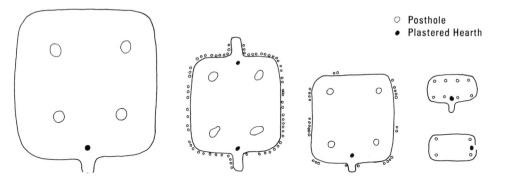

49 Houses that served as the dwellings of leaders or as community meeting places (left three) were considerably larger than the average house (right two).

At first, these structures were by no means common, but by AD 700–900 they had become a regular feature of a standardized settlement plan. In many agricultural societies, such structures are the focus of ceremonies performed at particular times of the year, such as those described for the Pueblo peoples in Chapter 1. Dependence on agriculture brought with it an increased need to understand and predict seasonal and longer-term environmental fluctuations in order to farm successfully. Archaeological evidence from the Southwest shows that humans spent increasing amounts of time trying to direct and placate the forces and spirits that they believed controlled their environment. For Pueblo people today, Alfonso Ortiz (himself a native of San Juan Pueblo) tells us that: 'the undulating rhythms of nature govern their whole existence, from the timing and order of ritual dramas to the planning of economic activities.'[11] Moreover, 'everything in the cosmos is … knowable and, being knowable, controllable' through 'letter-perfect attention to detail and performance, thus the Pueblo emphasis on formulas, ritual, and repetition revealed in ritual drama.'[12]

The evolution of these calendrical rituals also seems to be strongly associated with the greater potential for social conflict as village size increased and control of food production or distribution by individual families developed. Communal rituals may have been necessary to create and reinforce the sense of identity and community that had been weakened by placing family welfare ahead of the well-being of the entire village.

But calendrical ceremonies may have also had an immediate economic effect as well. Among the Pueblo today, considerable amounts of food are redistributed within villages during rituals, enough to assist needy households.[13] It is also possible that trade occurred not only within, but between groups. As dependence on agriculture increases, one way of reducing the greater risks of starvation is for groups in different areas to share food. In that way, a shortage in one area can be reduced by the surpluses available in another. Such cooperative relationships, however, can be difficult to maintain between people without close kinship ties, so they are therefore conducted in a ritual setting in order to 'sanctify' the relationships and reduce the possibility of conflict.

Nevertheless, conflict there was at this time, to judge by the inaccessible locations of some large villages from the period. Settlements such as the Promontory Site, the Bluff Site, and the Connie Site all lie on top of steep ridges or mesas. Considerable daily effort would have been required simply to transport food and water back to each site. Some sites are also surrounded by what appear to be stone walls of considerable size. Though there are few other indications of social tensions, the absence of sites in similar settings during later periods, when public buildings and other characteristics of village societies were very common, suggests that complex ritual sanctions were needed – and indeed were eventually successful – in establishing peaceful relationships between groups once the control of resources passed to specific individuals or families.

More villages, more people

A rise in population may have exacerbated social tensions as villages developed. What caused the populations to increase? The reasons are unclear, but several factors have been identified – factors concerned with female fertility and individual mortality. Seasonal fluctuations in food, for example, are known to affect female fertility among modern hunting and gathering groups.[14] Fertility levels among !Kung San women in southern Africa fall during seasons when food is scarce. More stable or more abundant food supplies can therefore be expected to lead to higher fertility. Two possible sources of more stable food supplies can be proposed for this period in the Southwest. First, ecological data suggest climatic conditions were more favorable until at least the last few centuries prior to the Christian era. And a second critical change may have been the increases in storage facilities, allowing food abundant in one season to be exploited in a less productive season.

Population growth was not, however, simply a byproduct of changes in environment and technology, but also resulted from conscious decisions that affected family size. Ethnographers have observed that hunter-gatherer women must carry their offspring while gathering plants or moving from place to place. Infants are also breast-fed for as long as 3–4 years. It would be nutritionally and physically impossible for a woman to carry and suckle two very young infants while actively gathering plant foods for her family. Studies have also shown that intense and prolonged breast feeding – through a little-understood biological mechanism – reduces a woman's chances of conceiving another child, thus limiting the number of children a woman will have and keeping a large birth interval between infants. By the time a child is 4 years old it will be able to walk and consume the solid food which it will now be able to gather for itself.

Sedentary women no longer had to limit the number of children to the number they could carry and feed; in agricultural societies there were also more appropriate weaning foods available so that breast-feeding did not have to be prolonged. These limitations being lifted, it may now have become desirable to conceive more children so that they could help with a variety of agricultural tasks, whether weeding or keeping small animals out of the fields.[15] Cultural norms – age at marriage, periods when intercourse is prohibited, and the definition of reasonable birth intervals – that can inhibit population growth, may therefore have been modified.

A less nomadic lifestyle would also have diminished the physical impact of year-round mobility on all individuals, probably increasing the average life-span and further increasing rates of population growth. Burials from this period are few, however, and this hypothesis requires rigorous testing.

Diet, nutrition, and technological innovation

Among the many changes that helped maintain the evolution toward village life, two innovations stand out. The first was the addition of a new cultigen – beans, initially domesticated in Mexico – during the last few centuries BC.[16] Beans complement maize and squash because they contain high amounts of lysine, the amino acid missing from the other two cultigens; together the

Ceramics: a technological revolution

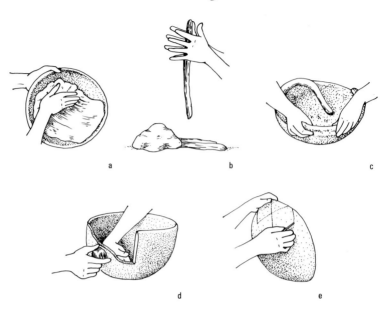

50 Steps in manufacturing a vessel: a) the clay is kneaded until it has the right consistency; b) strands of clay are formed by rubbing the clay between the hands; c) successive strands are added to form the walls of the vessel; d) the vessel's walls are thinned using a scraper or a paddle and anvil; and e) the vessel is painted using a brush made from yucca fibers.

Suitable clay for making ceramic vessels can be found throughout the Southwest, but it was only in the first few centuries AD that the ancient Southwesterners began to fashion it into pots. Studies of native potters have helped us understand the steps their ancestors took to turn clay into container.[17] The first step was for women (native potters are almost exclusively female and that was likely the case in prehistory as shown by burials of some women with their pottery production kits) to collect the raw material in outcrops common along arroyos or the escarpments of mesas, pulverize it using a mano and metate, and then clean it by separating clay from small stones and other impurities. The potter then added water and began to knead the material until it could be rolled into balls. The balls were covered with a damp rag or wet grass and then left for a few days so that the plasticity of the clay increased.

Vessels were created first by making a base, either by using the bottom of an inverted container or simply by kneading and molding a lump of clay by hand into the shape of a shallow bowl. Ropes of clay were then formed by rolling the clay between the palms and these were then used to build the walls of the vessel, with the clay rope or coil placed on top of the base and then on earlier coils, pinching the line of contact to bond each addition to the growing vessel. After a vessel of the desired size had been made, the vessel was then smoothed and shaped further. Potters of southern Arizona and northern Mexico used a paddle-and-anvil process at this stage, beating the exterior of the vessel with a paddle, while bracing the interior with an anvil of stone or other material, in order to thin the vessel walls and increase the height of the container. Pueblo potters instead used the coil-and-scrape method, employing a fragment of gourd rind or a broken piece of pottery to shave and smooth the vessel walls while supporting the opposite side of the vessel with the hand. Once the shaping process was complete, the vessel was left to dry.

Decoration could be applied once the vessels were dry, using brushes made from maguey or yucca leaves that were cut and chewed until the plant fibers formed bristles. The containers were then ready to be fired. The potters first dried the vessels further by placing them around the perimeter of a burning pile of brush or dung, but this step was not universal. The primary firing was then accomplished in one of two ways, at a location and time where there would be little wind: *1*, a shallow pit was dug, the bottom of which was lined with stone, and the vessels were placed upside down on the stone platform and covered with wood, animal dung, or other fuel which could be ignited; or *2*, burning dung, placed on the ground, was covered by a platform of sandstone slabs and sherds of pottery. The vessels were then placed upside down on this platform or on top of each other to form a rounded pile. The pile was covered first with large fragments of pottery sherds and finally with a layer of animal dung.

51 Hopi potters at work in the village of Hano in 1893.

three plants provide a complete protein source.[18] The introduction of beans may have meant that less time had to be devoted to gathering wild foods, thus reducing the need to exploit as broad an area and contributing to the trend toward more permanent settlements.[19]

52   The second innovation also improved nutrition, and involved changes in the way foods were processed. Ceramic vessels appear for the first time at about AD 200 and become widespread by AD 500 (see box p. 66). Bulky and fragile, they demonstrate the increasingly sedentary nature of life. (Ceramic characteristics also change more rapidly than attributes of stone tools, allowing cultural changes to be delineated more precisely and dated more accurately.) Such vessels allow food to be boiled more efficiently and for longer intervals since they can be placed directly over a fire. Previously, heated stones had to be placed in pitch-coated baskets to boil foods briefly. Boiling is important in reprocessing dried foods, particularly corn, which is not only a good source of protein, but also high in carbohydrates. If eaten raw, only half of the carbohydrate can be metabolized into glucose, but if boiled, more than 90 percent can be converted because the starch is made accessible to digestive enzymes. Ceramic vessels also allow beans to be dried, stored, and cooked later without significant nutritional loss.[20] Increased food storage was a critical component of the village process, but it was a workable strategy only if methods of food preparation allowed groups to extract nutrients from dried and stored foods. Boiled cereals also provided suitable foods for weaning young children, potentially reducing the amount of time that children were breast-fed, and thus increasing female fertility as discussed earlier.[21]

Two additional modifications in technology are noteworthy. Tools employed to grind plant material during the initial part of the period included stone slabs (metates) with shallow basins and oval stones (manos) that were small enough to be held in one hand and rubbed against the
53   metates to pulverize plant material. Toward the end of the period, larger

52 An Alma Plain vessel, one of the earliest types of Mogollon ceramics, with *Mentzelia* (blazing star) seeds from Cordova Cave, west-central New Mexico. Historically *Mentzelia* was a food, a toothache medicine, and a substitute for tobacco.[22]

53 A Hopi woman grinding corn using a mano and metate, *c.* 1902.

metates with deeper troughs and large, rectangular manos that were probably held in both hands became more common.[23] The changes resulted in a more efficient set of grinding tools, allowing more plant material to be ground more quickly. These new forms of grinding stones most probably indicate an increase in dependence on cultivated plants. Although coprolites – preserved human feces – recovered from sites in the Four Corners region unambiguously demonstrate that the inhabitants there consumed a variable diet, corn was nevertheless the main constituent.

Hunting tools also changed. Smaller projectile points were manufactured, perhaps associated with the first use of the bow and arrow. James Judge has suggested that the spear is most useful when game is trapped through group drives, while the bow and arrow is better when individuals are hunting, as might occur when more effort is being devoted to agriculture.[24] The bow and arrow may also have been more effective when hunting the types of small animals that are often the focus of groups that give priority to the collection of plant foods.

The emergence of Hohokam, Mogollon, and Anasazi groups

Along with modifications in technology, we also find evidence for changing regional social relationships. There is some indication of increasing trade, involving items such as turquoise and marine shells, toward the end of the period. In most areas, however, tools were still generally made of local materials in a manner similar to the Archaic but different from the Paleo-Indian period, when widespread social networks and alliances existed. We see little change in the degree of stylistic variation of projectile points, but ceramics show the initial hints of emerging regional traditions in methods of production. Archaeologists have assigned names to the groups of people residing in the northern, central, and southern sections of the region where these different manufacturing patterns are characteristic. These names – Hohokam, Mogollon, and Anasazi – are central to discussions of cultural change in the following chapters. At this early time, however, sharp boundaries in artifact styles appear to be absent, suggesting major social boundaries were lacking as well.

Change and innovation in various aspects of social relationships, site architecture, or tools cannot thus be understood in isolation, but must be viewed in the context of alterations in all aspects of a group's way of life, from demography and technology to religion. Such apparently different developments as the production of ceramic vessels, the expansion of storage facilities, the construction of special buildings for rituals, and increased reliance on cultigens went hand in hand. All were interrelated, intersecting processes critical to the evolution of the village-centered way of life that prevailed through the Southwest during the centuries that followed.

5 · From Village to Town: Hohokam, Mogollon, and Anasazi AD 700 to 1130

The nearly four-and-a-half centuries from AD 700 to 1130 must be regarded as one of the most dynamic and intriguing periods of the prehistoric Southwest, characterized by unparalleled and precipitous change. Most noteworthy are the exceptional rise in population and the great range of landscapes now inhabited. Sparsely settled regions at AD 700–900 experienced such dramatic increases in numbers of settlements that by AD 1075–1100 there were more people in more areas of the Southwest than at any other period of prehistory. Equally striking are the large towns with several hundred rooms and commanding public architecture that developed amidst a landscape dotted with small villages. Snaketown in southern Arizona and Chaco Canyon in northern New Mexico are just two of the famous communities that flourished during this period. Yet by AD 1130–1150 many of these towns were vacant shells, devoid of the sounds of daily life, and certain areas were completely abandoned as their occupants packed their belongings and joined their kin elsewhere. We must now examine this turbulent epoch to try to understand these abrupt fluctuations.

We tend to name groups of people according to where they live, or by their cultural affiliations: on a global scale, for example, we speak of Americans, Italians, and Japanese. With a more local outlook, we identify individuals as Southern or Northern or, even more specifically, as New Yorkers or Bostonians. Archaeologists often attempt to group prehistoric peoples in much the same way, but they face many problems in deducing cultural groups from the dust and debris of prehistory (see box p. 72). In previous chapters we have abstained from such classifications because cultural differences were not sufficiently pronounced or critical to the discussion. Now, as we turn to the period of full village life, it becomes necessary to partition the Southwest on the basis of cultural characteristics and to examine the prehistory of various areas separately.

The three primary cultural divisions recognized by most Southwestern archaeologists are the Hohokam – almost certainly the ancestors of the O'odham – and the Mogollon and Anasazi, the forebears of contemporary Pueblo peoples. Although other divisions have been proposed, they are not central to the general discussion that follows. We will therefore begin with descriptions of the three primary divisions.

What mean these terms?

Although archaeologists use such terms as Hohokam or Mogollon to denote cultural differences among prehistoric peoples of the Southwest, it is important to emphasize three aspects of these distinctions. First, archaeological research tends to focus on the most enduring aspects of people's lives – the fragments of broken pottery vessels or the evidence left from the construction of dwellings. We know little about the languages spoken by these people and must attempt to decipher their beliefs and behavior from the material remains they left behind. Cultural divisions created by the archaeologists should therefore not be equated with those that may have been recognized by the ancient Southwesterners themselves. As noted in Chapter 1, there is far more linguistic diversity in the region than we would expect based on the cultural divisions of the archaeologists, suggesting a much greater number of groups than we can discern today.

Second, some of the ways that pottery or architecture differ among various groups of people are stylistic, that is, they are different ways to accomplish the same end such as the alternative styles of clothing that characterize older and younger generations in America. Some of these differences may be unconscious choices that simply reflect the ways that we have always been taught to do things. Other choices may be intentional efforts to distinguish a high-status group from a lower one, males from females, or alliances between groups of individuals. Yet other decisions may simply reflect the different resources available in a given area or time.

Finally, designating cultural groups such as the Hohokam, Mogollon, and Anasazi tends to create an image of group territories separated by clearcut boundaries. Prehistoric peoples traded, worshiped, and collaborated most often with other nearby groups. Cultural differences are often therefore clinal, increasing gradually as the distance separating groups also increases. Departures from these clinal patterns may occur because of social or political boundaries or simply because of geographical barriers that reduce the frequency of contact (one significant reason for the greater similarities between the Mogollon and Anasazi and their differences from the Hohokam). Even when such barriers do exist, 'boundaries' among groups are often fuzzy rather than discrete.

The Hohokam

The Hohokam inhabited the stark and arid desert areas of southern Arizona south of the Mogollon Rim, and extreme northern Mexico, with settlements extending northward toward Flagstaff during some periods. The cultural name means 'those who have gone' in the language of the O'odham who now live in the area. Distinguishing features of Hohokam settlements were ballcourts and platform mounds, both of which would have been associated with activities that carried ritual significance. Ballcourts provided the arena for a spirited game played with a small rubber ball. (One such ball was found inside a ceramic vessel recovered from a Hohokam site: it was made from Guayule, a rubber-bearing plant native to the desert regions of northern Mexico and southern Arizona.[1]) Little is known about the rituals conducted on the platform mounds, but the presence of palisades around a few mounds[2] suggests that parts of the ceremonies would have been closed to some members of the community.

The best-known and largest Hohokam site, Snaketown, lies in the Phoenix Basin at the confluence of the Gila and Salt Rivers. At its peak in the early to mid-11th century, it had a population of 300–600 and two impressive ballcourts. Hohokam families generally lived in wattle-and-daub (*jacal*) structures built around shallow pits in a manner similar to earlier periods. Sets of 2–4 dwellings typically clustered around a central plaza, each room cluster separated by several hundred meters, suggesting a distinct kinship group of 16–20 individuals, perhaps an extended family or a small lineage. Burial ritual differentiated the Hohokam from other Southwestern groups, in that they were the only ones before AD 1150 to habitually cremate their dead.

Hohokam families cooked and stored food in ceramic vessels that were generally buff or light brown in color, constructed using a small paddle-and-anvil to slowly form the container from the original ball of clay. Some vessels are plain and unelaborated, but others are decorated, most typically with a red paint, with designs that include both geometric forms and elegant life forms.

Hohokam groups living along major drainages such as the Gila, Salt, and Verde Rivers were pioneers in the use of extensive canal networks that they dug to irrigate their fields. As well as growing the typical Southwestern trio of corn, beans, and squash, they cultivated cotton, agave, and a few other native plants. They also hunted rabbits and deer and gathered wild mesquite beans, saguaro and cactus fruits to supplement the diet.[3]

The artifacts, architecture, and inferred religious practices of the Hohokam are in many ways much more similar to adjacent areas to the south in Mesoamerica than to the north in the Southwest, even during the preceding period of village development. Some scholars have suggested therefore that Mesoamerican groups migrated into the region and controlled or displaced the native Southwest peoples. Recent work shows, however, that

54

55

56

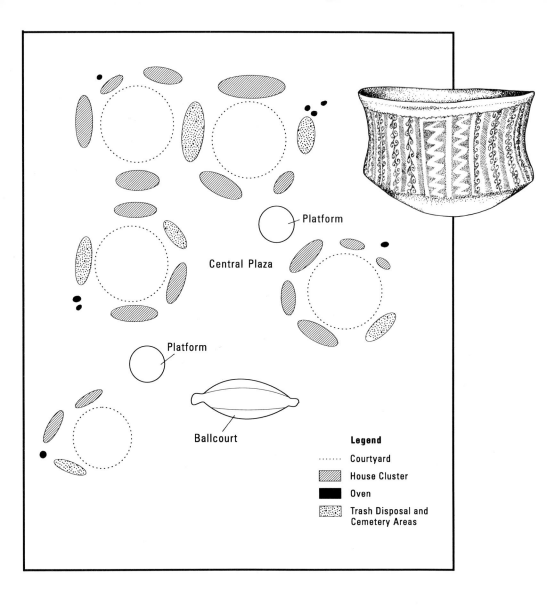

Platform

Central Plaza

Platform

Ballcourt

Legend

⋯⋯ Courtyard

▨ House Cluster

■ Oven

▨ Trash Disposal and Cemetery Areas

those features – such as ballcourts, platform mounds, and varied artifact assemblages – taken to indicate a sudden 'florescence' of Hohokam culture can be explained as one logical outcome of the village process and the increased importance of ritual and exchange. In any case, greater contact with peoples to the south would inevitably have been encouraged, if not dictated, by the physical geography of the region. With the Mogollon Rim to the north and east and rivers within the Hohokam region generally leading west and south, travel and trade would have been easier with peoples to the south than with groups to the north – which perhaps helps explain the similarities of Hohokam architecture to the cultures of northern and central Mexico.

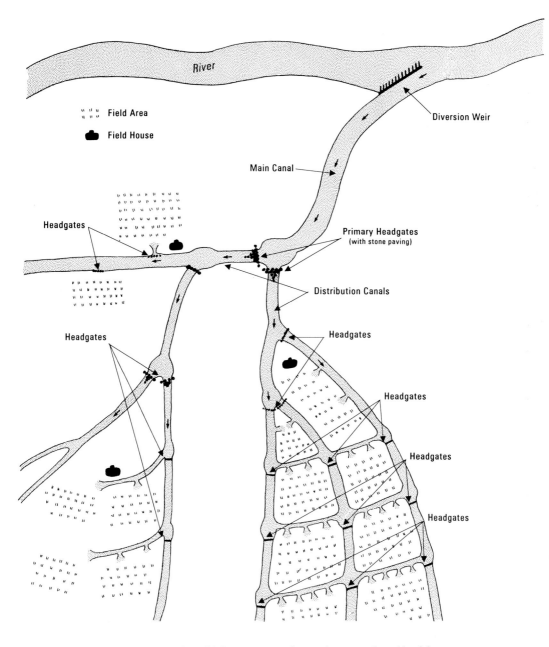

River

Diversion Weir

Field Area

Field House

Main Canal

Headgates

Primary Headgates
(with stone paving)

Headgates

Distribution Canals

Headgates

Headgates

Headgates

Headgates

Headgates

54 LEFT Hohokam community plan with houses grouped around courtyards and burial areas, middens, and ovens associated with each courtyard.

55 LEFT, INSET Buff-colored clay vessels painted with characteristic red designs distinguished the Hohokam of southern Arizona from the Mogollon and Anasazi to the north.

56 ABOVE The Hohokam diverted water from the Salt and Gila Rivers into large main irrigation canals that branched into smaller canals with headgates that were employed to allocate water to individual fields.

57–59 Mogollon potters produced a range of pottery vessels including ladles (RIGHT) and jars (FAR RIGHT), and canteens and pitchers in the shape of animals such as ducks (BELOW).

The Mogollon

The Mogollon people gained their name from the area in east-central Arizona and west-central New Mexico where this culture was first discovered – the Mogollon Rim and Plateau – which had been named after a governor of New Mexico, Juan Ignacio Flores Mogollon. Living to the north and east of the Hohokam, the Mogollon inhabited a markedly different landscape. Although their villages extended into some of the lower and drier regions of southern New Mexico, western Texas, and northern Mexico, it is their settlement of the colder, wetter, and more wooded mountainous parts of east-central Arizona and west-central New Mexico that has attracted the most attention from archaeologists. Here, small grassy meadows lying between hillsides covered with a canopy of pines created one of the most beautiful regions of the Southwest.

The earliest Mogollon lived in pithouses of the type described in the last chapter, but beginning in the late 10th and early 11th centuries they began to erect sets of contiguous, above-ground rooms comparable to the Pueblos that we see in the northern Southwest today. The earliest Mogollon pueblos, however, consisted of fewer than a dozen rooms and were probably the resi-

The art of the Mogollon

60 BELOW The residents of Higgins Flat Pueblo in the Mogollon region of west-central New Mexico adorned themselves with shell bracelets, shell necklaces, and pendants made from both shell and turquoise. Similar ornaments have been found at many other settlements in the prehistoric Southwest.

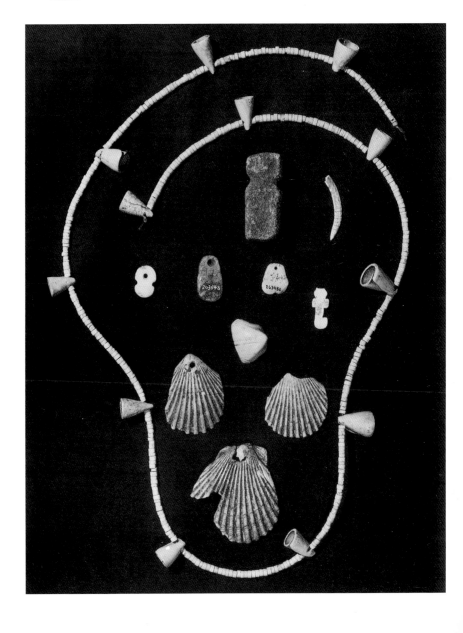

dences of only one or two families. Only later, in the 13th and 14th centuries, did they begin to construct settlements comparable in size to those of the historic period.

Mogollon ceremonies took place in subterranean kivas. Some of the kivas were small and circular, others larger and rectangular structures known as Great Kivas. In contrast with the Hohokam, the Mogollon interred individuals in shallow graves, with the body in an extended position. The similarities between the historic Pueblo and prehistoric ritual chambers (particularly their subterranean nature) and burial practices imply that the Mogollon, like their modern descendants, conceived of life as alternating between the upper- and underworld as discussed in Chapter 1.

The daily life of the Mogollon people was probably not all that different from the Hohokam, being centered around farming (though generally without the Hohokam reliance on irrigation), gathering wild plants such as piñon nuts, juniper berries, walnut, and various types of cactus fruits, and hunting a variety of animals. But no doubt there was considerable variation in diet among local groups given the wide range of environments inhabited.

The Mogollon stored and processed their foods using the characteristic Southwest assemblage of manos and metates, chipped stone tools, and 57–59   ceramic vessels. They manufactured brown-colored containers for cooking foods, as well as white and red vessels decorated with red and black paint that they used as serving and storage vessels. One subgroup of the Mogollon, the Mimbres people, produced the beautiful and world-famous Mimbres black-on-white ceramics discussed in detail later. Mogollon vessels were constructed from layers of clay coils placed one on top of the other and then smoothed with a scraper – the coil-and-scrape method. Rare on Mogollon 60   sites are the exotic stone palettes, worked shell, and copper artifacts that typify the Hohokam region.

The Anasazi

Close 'cousins' of the Mogollon were the Anasazi people who once lived in settlements throughout the plateau country of the Southwest, including much of northeastern Arizona, northwestern New Mexico, southeastern Utah, and southwestern Colorado (often referred to as the Four Corners region) and extending into southern Nevada during some periods. These people erected some of the most remarkable villages anywhere in the New World, the cliff dwellings in areas such as Mesa Verde National Park, Navajo National Monument, and Canyon de Chelly National Monument (all discussed in Chapter 6) and the Great Houses of Chaco Culture National Historical Park, to be discussed below. The excellent preservation of these once bustling towns and their setting – tucked away in isolated caves or rock shelters or suddenly arising from the middle of seemingly barren terrain – create vivid images that remain with visitors for a lifetime.

Such settlements, however, were the exceptions within the Anasazi

The Anasazi
unit-pueblo

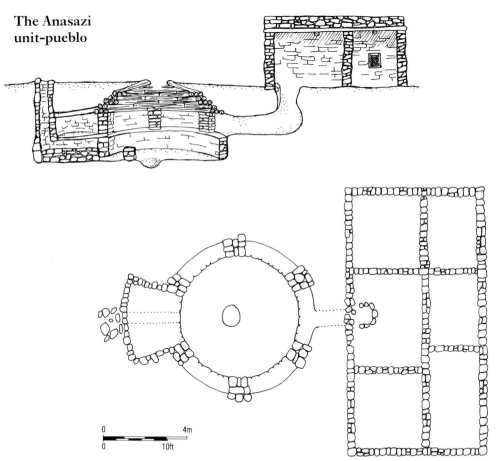

61 A typical Anasazi village or unit-pueblo of the 10th and 11th centuries. Many of these villages were composed of a small roomblock with 5–10 rooms and a single subterranean kiva to the south (top). The cross-section (center) and plan view (bottom) show the underground tunnel that sometimes connected the kiva with one of the masonry rooms. Stone pilasters on the bench of the kiva supported the roof timbers. Some kivas were key-hole shaped with a southern recess or banquette perhaps analogous to the antechambers in historic kivas.

62, 63 ABOVE Black-on-white painted bowls from Pueblo Bonito in Chaco Canyon, and (BELOW) black-on-white mugs from Lowry Ruin in southwest Colorado.

region. Like the Mogollon, through much of the prehistoric period the Anasazi lived in small groups of a few families rather than in the denser Pueblo towns of the historic period. Most Anasazi villages thus differed little from those already described for the Mogollon. In some areas, however, the Anasazi constructed masonry structures not as dwellings, but to use as storage rooms. They then attached wattle-and-daub (*jacal*) dwellings made in a manner similar to those of the Hohokam, but not in or around a shallow pit. In addition, smaller subterranean structures sometimes served as specialized mealing rooms where multiple sets of manos and metates were used

61 to grind corn and other seeds. A typical Anasazi village thus consisted of a few masonry habitation or storage rooms, sometimes with attached *jacal* or masonry dwellings on the west or northwest side of the settlement, a centrally located kiva, and a trash area or midden to the east or southeast.

Groups of about 10–25 people lived in each village, on average for about 10–20 years. Like the Mogollon, the Anasazi were farmers who planted their fields in or along drainages where floodwaters would spread after heavy rains, but they also collected and hunted a range of wild plants and animals. They buried their dead in shallow graves, in a flexed position with the knees drawn up against the chest.

62,63 Anasazi pottery shares many characteristics with Mogollon ceramics, with white or red serving and storage vessels embellished with geometric designs in black (and more rarely white) paint. The Anasazi produced their

paints, however, by boiling plants, most likely Rocky Mountain beeweed (*Cleome* sp.), an annual common to the area, whereas Mogollon potters generally produced their paints from minerals. Cooking vessels were similar in shape and form to Mogollon vessels, but were gray rather than brown.

The expansion of Southwestern peoples into virtually every available niche is perhaps best exemplified by the Anasazi of the Grand Canyon. During the last half of the 11th century, the population here exploded and communities were established in scores of locations deep within the canyon. When Douglas Schwartz began work at one such community at Unkar Delta in May 1967, using a helicopter to bring in people and supplies because access was so difficult, he remembers that 'the first two days we were tested severely by the 120-degree heat and high winds that stung us with sand and knocked down every tent.'[4] Yet this was a setting where ten Anasazi families had constructed a masonry pueblo with 23 rooms and two kivas.

Similarities and differences

The Hohokam, Mogollon, and Anasazi thus share many aspects of their way of life, including similar economies, a focus on ritual, formal conventions for treatment of the dead, and artifact assemblages dominated by stone tools and ceramic containers. The differences are equally obvious and suggest the presence of some type of social or political divisions that almost certainly included linguistic distinctions along with variation in how each group conceived of their world and those deities who oversaw it. The Hohokam, in particular, organized their communities, worshipped their deities, buried their dead, and even made pottery in a manner that clearly separates them from the Mogollon and the Anasazi. To this uncomplicated conception of the ancient Southwest we must now add some of the variation that makes the prehistoric era so intriguing.

We can best explore the period from AD 700 to 1130 by examining the archaeological evidence from a handful of areas.

Hohokam communities in the Phoenix Basin

Between the end of the 7th century and the beginning of the 12th century many changes took place in the Hohokam region. We find evidence for significantly greater numbers of settlements and people coupled with the development of irrigation networks along the Gila and Salt Rivers. Growth rates were not constant, insofar as we can tell given the incomplete chronology for the Hohokam region. Like areas to the north, there appears to have been a particularly rapid population increase from the late 10th century into the first few decades of the 11th century. The first Hohokam ballcourts were constructed sometime during the 8th century, with a handful of well-dated courts by the mid-9th century and then over two dozen by approximately AD 1000.[5] In addition to the building of ballcourts and platform mounds, mortuary ceremonialism developed into a major focus, associated with the

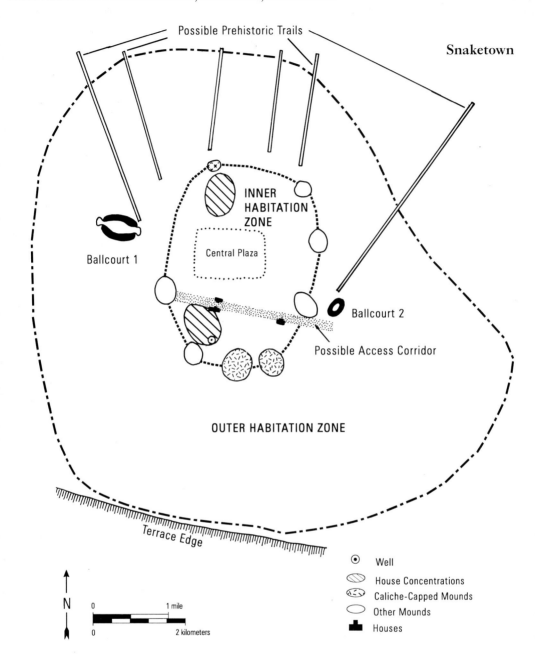

64, 65, 66 ABOVE Mounds, ballcourts, and large houses encircled a central plaza at Snaketown, with possible prehistoric trails leading to the north. Smaller houses characterized residential areas in the outer habitation zone. ABOVE RIGHT Excavations in one area of Snaketown uncovered more than 60 house floors (not all contemporaneous). One of the larger square houses is visible in the lower left corner. RIGHT The excavated west half of Ballcourt I at Snaketown. Ballcourts have been found as far south as the Maya region and were the locus of a game that had important ritual associations.

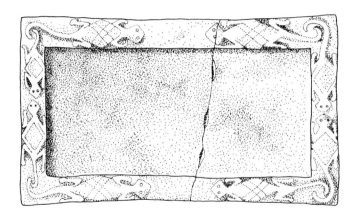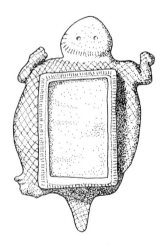

67 Hohokam stone palettes (above) have been found primarily in cremation contexts, while human figurines (far right) also appear to have had a ritual function. Etched shell ornaments (right) may have been status markers.

67 introduction of ritual paraphernalia such as stone palettes and censers and the construction of special crematory areas that may have been the location of village death rites. Cremation only became common after AD 700, although the Hohokam had cremated some of their dead in earlier periods.[6]

These innovations reveal significant transformations in the nature of Hohokam ritual and cosmology. Many of the changes may be related to the emergence of social hierarchies, both within and between communities.[7] Cemeteries became smaller, more frequent, and widely distributed spatially within settlements, supporting the inference of social change. Large Hohokam work crews of 25–100 people must have been required to excavate the extensive irrigation channels along the Gila and Salt Rivers, with main canals extending as much as 10–15 miles away from the river. Clearly such cooperative effort required an organizational structure. Several settlements shared each of the canal networks and differences in village size and types of ritual architecture suggest a settlement hierarchy, with some villages more important than others.[8]

Our knowledge of these settlements in the Hohokam region is greatest for the area around the confluence of the Gila and Salt Rivers, near the modern city of Phoenix, where we find the site of Snaketown, studied by archaeologists in 1934–35, and then again in 1964–65. At the top of the regional settlement hierarchy, Snaketown was occupied at its peak by 300–600 people, more populous than any other contemporary community.[9] Its residents created two ballcourts (one the largest ever built in the Hohokam region) and a central plaza flanked on the east and west by smaller plazas and on the north and south by platform mounds. Excavations have revealed some individual cremation pits, and one set of eight pits near a platform mound, suggesting a possible association between mounds and death rituals. The excavator of Snaketown, Emil Haury, highlighted the discovery of caches of

64–66

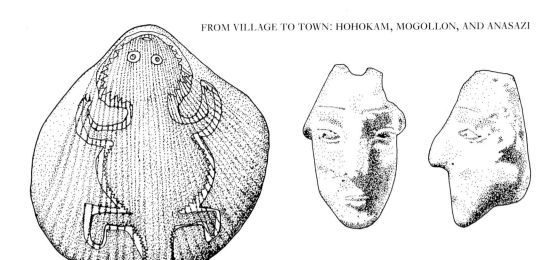

cultural goods which had been destroyed by fire and he suggested that fire was 'a revered and sacred agent, essential in death, in making sacrifices, and in ritual.'[10] Associated as offerings with cremations, but also present in other contexts, were elegant stone palettes and vessels, clay effigies with animal and human symbolism, and carved and incised shell with similar motifs.

Those living in the center of Snaketown built larger houses and cemeteries than those in the outer residential zone. The more central dwellings may have housed high-ranking individuals, members of an evolving elite. Archaeologists found 60 ceramic vessels and 28 copper bells in one of these houses, possibly a group storeroom. Two other unusually large houses were associated with this storeroom and may have served as council chambers. There are hints of a dual division in the organization of Snaketown, including two central residential zones, the two large council chambers, and the distribution of the eight mounds. Similar patterns have been discovered at several other Hohokam settlements.[11]

Ballcourts occur most commonly within a 60-mile radius of Snaketown and help define the extent of a regional network perhaps analogous to the Anasazi pattern of outlying Chacoan Great Houses and Great Kivas (see below).[12] Archaeologists have divided this network into a core region along the Gila, Salt, and Verde Rivers where ballcourts are most abundant, and more peripheral zones with fewer ballcourts and, in the most distant regions, dissimilarities in other cultural characteristics. Thus a shared cosmology and ritual pattern linked distinct social groups distributed over a broad area. But, in contrast to the northern Southwest where kivas were a regular feature of most villages, many Hohokam sites did not have ballcourts or platform mounds; Hohokam villages number in the thousands, but they constructed only about 225 ballcourts, 40 percent in the Phoenix Basin. This implies that different communities gathered together for ballcourt rituals.[13]

68

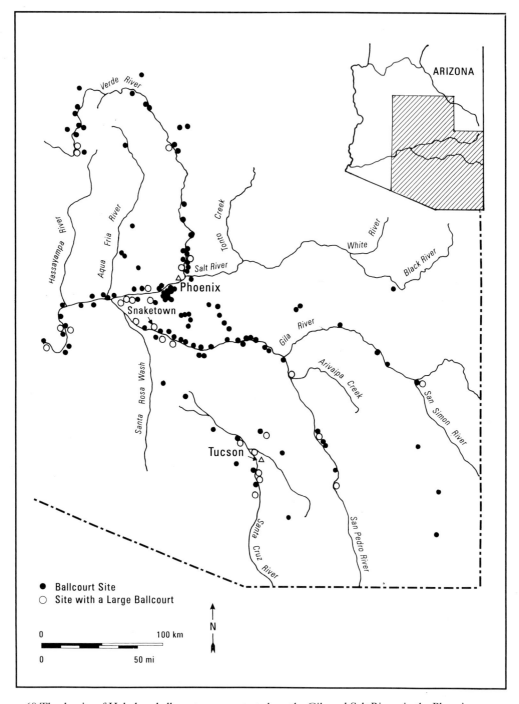

68 The density of Hohokam ballcourts was greatest along the Gila and Salt Rivers in the Phoenix Basin, but their distribution extends north along the Verde River and south and southeast along the Santa Cruz and San Pedro Rivers. Not all settlements had ballcourts, suggesting that the ballgame brought together multiple villages.

David Wilcox has proposed that the variation in the size of the ballcourts and the alignment of their long axes – large courts tend to alternate between a north–south and east–west orientation in adjoining settlements – suggests that the nearby courts were complementary, each a part of the yearly cycle of calendrical rituals which perpetuated the Hohokam universe.[14] Wilcox believes that the ballcourt may have served as a sacred context for settling feuds, creating social alliances, and promoting trade among the growing number of Hohokam communities. The New World lacked beasts of burden, like the horse, so transporting goods rapidly over long distances was a difficult task. One way to move goods was to establish ceremonial exchange systems which involved many different settlements throughout a region, thus supplementing the exchanges based on kinship ties.[15] Supporting this argument for village interdependency is evidence for specialization in the production of ceramics, ground stone, projectile points, knives for processing agave and shell, and, more specifically, in one village an association between a ballcourt and indications of ground stone production.[16]

In addition to such intra-regional exchange, trade with peoples outside the Hohokam region was common. Along with the Mesoamerican items (macaws, copper bells and shell, for example) known from Hohokam sites, pottery from the northern Southwest and from the Mogollon Mimbres regions has been recovered, indicating that the Hohokam network was in no way isolated from neighboring peoples.

These Hohokam ballcourt networks collapsed in the late 11th–early 12th century during a period of radical change, when many areas colonized during earlier decades were abandoned. In the Phoenix Basin, people left Snaketown and some other large sites for good. Where occupation continued, there are signs of reorganization as some villages expanded substantially while others decreased in size. By the beginning of the next period, the Phoenix Basin was dominated by three discrete clusters of settlements (see Chapter 6).[17]

Art and aesthetics: the Mimbres of southwestern New Mexico

The Mogollon area saw a highly varied pattern of development during the period after the first establishment of villages. Settlements remained small in some locales, with masonry pueblos of less than ten rooms. In others, moderate growth occurred in both village size and local population density. In a few of the most intensively studied areas, such as the Pine Lawn Valley of west-central New Mexico or the Hay Hollow Valley of east-central Arizona, population growth continued not only during the 12th century, but throughout most of the 13th century as well. In general, stability and continuity seem to be more characteristic of the Mogollon region.

One important exception to this story of continuity is the Mimbres area of southwestern New Mexico, famous for its beautiful black-on-white ceramics. Archaeological work has focused on one particular section, the Rio

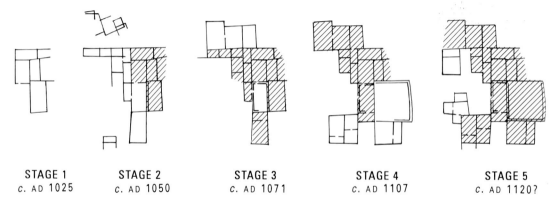

STAGE 1	STAGE 2	STAGE 3	STAGE 4	STAGE 5
c. AD 1025	c. AD 1050	c. AD 1071	c. AD 1107	c. AD 1120?

69 Unlike the Chacoan Great Houses, where large blocks of rooms were added in planned construction episodes, Mimbres pueblos such as NAN Ranch Ruin grew more gradually as families added small clusters of rooms.

Mimbres and several smaller, secondary drainages where prehistoric settlement was most dense. The only perennially flowing river in the region, the Rio Mimbres drains the mountainous area to the north where precipitation is relatively high for the Southwest. Within the area most intensively studied, the river lies in a broad valley with good agricultural soils and is flanked by low hills and lofty mountains covered with a piñon–juniper woodland. Low annual precipitation and the short growing season make agriculture a risky proposition in most years.

The early prehistory of the Mimbres people correlates well with the village pattern described earlier. As villages evolved and the Mimbreños increased in number, they moved from subsurface pithouses to surface pueblos and devoted more time to group rituals. But the Mimbres also departed from the pattern of exclusively small settlements typical of so many regions in the 11th and 12th centuries. From approximately AD 1000 to 1130, some of them lived in a dozen or so larger villages with several clusters of single-story dwellings with between 50 and 200 rooms. The room clusters in the larger Mimbres pueblos were not planned units built at the same time, but expanded as families grew, or as individuals married and established their own residences adjacent to their kin. Rooms were repaired, reused, and razed as villages gradually increased in size.[18]

These pueblos were unspectacular architecturally, with walls of rounded cobbles – not the most stable building material – and adobe generally only a single stone thick. Within each room cluster lived several families, each occupying a living room connected to at least one smaller storage room.[19] The standard living room had an adobe floor, a slab-lined hearth with an adjacent slab-lined ash bin, and an opening in the roof that served as both an entrance and a vent for smoke from the fire. Excavations have revealed that the Mimbres carried out many of their daily activities, ranging from grinding corn to cooking food, in adjacent plaza areas or on rooftops.[20] As

69

Mimbres villages grew, aspects of rituals shifted to open plazas from the large subterranean communal structures typical of earlier periods. Other rituals, perhaps for groups of limited size, were conducted in small rectangular kivas or larger-than-average rooms that were part of the individual clusters of masonry rooms. Most clusters had only one ritual structure.[21]

70 Classic Mimbres potters painted their black-on-white pottery in an exquisite representational style that depicted animals such as rabbits, deer, and birds, as well as mythical figures with both human and animal characteristics. Some of these scenes portray human decapitation, as shown in the vessel to the lower left.

The period beginning at approximately AD 1000 is noteworthy because of the fascinating developments in Mimbres ceramics, which are truly unique and elegant. Decorative styles changed so radically in the early 11th century – perhaps within a generation – and were so varied that it has been characterized as an artistic explosion.[22] Particularly intriguing is the evolution of a   70
representational style with depictions of birds, deer, fish, rabbits, lizards, and people that has no parallel anywhere in the Mogollon or Anasazi regions. Some of these designs occur more frequently at particular villages, raising the possibility that the designs were emblems for these communities or for lineages within the village.[23] Although the designs frequently illustrate commonplace animals and activities, the depiction of mythical figures with both human and animal characteristics, scenes of human sacrifice or beheading (perhaps involving supernaturals), and figures that resemble the   71–73

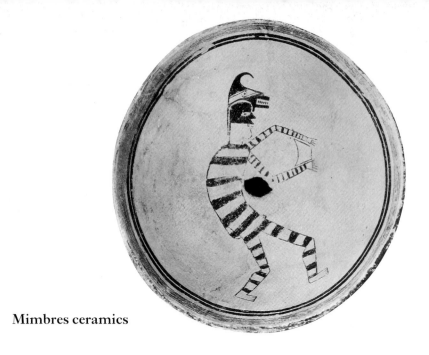

Mimbres ceramics

71–73 ABOVE A Mimbres black on white bowl depicting a human with a mask, perhaps another version of the horned serpent costume (see ill. 70 lower left). The horned or feathered serpent is important in both Mesoamerican and Southwestern cosmology. BELOW A Mimbres black-on-white vessel showing two human figures (detail RIGHT). The 'kill' hole in the center of the bowl is typical of Mimbres vessels and appears to have been part of burial rituals.

kachinas of contemporary Pueblo religion indicate that many of the objects or scenes had ritual significance.[24, 25] Supporting this assertion is the disproportionate number of these vessels found in graves as mortuary goods. The Mimbres burials in general are distinctive. The Mimbreños interred their dead in open areas adjacent to the room clusters or underneath the floors of rooms. They wrapped the corpse in a finely woven textile, laid it in a flexed or semi-flexed position in a pit parallel to the wall of the room, and covered the individual's head with an inverted Mimbres bowl with a hole punched in the bottom.[26]

Since most of the bowls are worn from previous use, they were not manufactured exclusively for these mortuary rituals.[27] Unfortunately, little is known about how these vessels were produced. One grave from the NAN Ranch Ruin that predates the development of the unique Mimbres pottery held a female with an assortment of pottery-making tools and three unfired jars.[28] Such discoveries are rare, but the few similar graves from other regions of the northern Southwest are invariably females as well, demonstrating continuity with the historic practice of vessel production and decoration by women. Some of the motifs that appear on different vessels are similar enough to suggest a single artist's hand, one tantalizing hint of specialized production by a handful of potters.[29] Sadly, these vessels have become so valued by collectors that almost all Mimbres sites have been looted by pothunters, seriously diminishing prospects for future excavations to help answer more questions about these fascinating ceramics.

The number of Mimbres people peaked in the early 12th century and the number of settlements then dropped rapidly in a manner comparable with some of the Anasazi areas to the north. The Mimbreños ceased to make their distinctive ceramics and there are no subsequent signs of the cultural tradition that had flourished earlier. Vessels recovered from some of the latest burials are so exceptionally worn that their production must have ceased before many of the villages were abandoned, perhaps an early indication of the deterioration of the basic fabric of Mimbres society.[30] The Mimbres people did not suddenly abandon their villages or leave *en masse*, but departed in an orderly manner, taking most of their belongings.[31] However, some occupation of the Mimbres region may have continued through the 12th century and there was renewed construction of some settlements during later periods.

Associated with the end of the Mimbres period is intriguing evidence regarding the impact that these people had on their local environment.[32] Analysis of wood charcoal reveals that as population levels increased, trees along the Rio Mimbres were progressively removed for construction and fuel, and possibly to open up new areas for farming. Analysis of plant pollens shows increases in weedy species that tend to colonize disturbed soils, and consequent reductions in naturally available foods that could be gathered during periods of poor harvests. The Mimbreños were now hunting more rabbits, birds, and other small animals and eating fewer deer, an overall reduction in meat and protein intake given the vast size differences between these animals.[33] Finally, settlement distributions demonstrate that more villages were established away from floodplains in areas where harvests were less likely to be successful, especially during years when climatic conditions were even slightly below normal. Between AD 200 and 1150, the population of the Mimbres region increased 16-fold, with a particularly large increase after AD 1000.[34] The Mimbreños were pushing the system to the limit and perhaps pushed too hard.

The burgeoning Anasazi of northern Black Mesa

The rolling uplands of northern Black Mesa in the extreme northeastern corner of Arizona, with piñon-juniper-covered hilltops and sage-covered valleys, typify many parts of the Anasazi region. Here elevations range from 6,300 to 7,000 ft (1,900–2,150 m), precipitation (rain and snowfall) amounts to little more than 10–15 in (25–38 cm) in most years, and the growing season is barely long enough for agriculture. Wild resources – including cactus fruits, piñon nuts and juniper berries, deer, rabbits, and a variety of other small animals – are present but not plentiful.

Intensive archaeological study of the northern Black Mesa region between 1967 and 1983 demonstrated that prehistoric people spent some time in the region as early as 7000 BC. Sporadic occupation characterized the next several millennia, including the critical period of village development. By AD 850–875, the Black Mesa Anasazi inhabited only a few small villages. During the period from AD 850 to 950, for example, no more than about 10–15 villages have been identified within a 46-square-mile area surveyed intensively by archaeologists, indicating a density of fewer than 1.5 people per square mile. Anasazi occupation of the region fluctuated considerably over the next 150 years, with some brief periods of rapid population growth followed by intervals of decline. Reductions in numbers during the 25-year period from AD 975 to 1000 may have left few, if any, inhabited villages at the dawn of the 11th century.

The 11th century, however, was one of rapid change. With the exception of a brief interval from about AD 1030 to 1050, population increased at rates without precedent, with particularly large jumps during the two to three decades following AD 1050. Maps of settlement distributions in AD 950–1049 and 1050–1150 illustrate the wholesale transformation in Anasazi occupation of the area. By AD 1080, the density of people had increased at least tenfold over numbers during the initial establishment of villages. Rates of increase were so great, in fact, that indigenous population growth alone cannot account for it; significant numbers of people must have moved into the northern Black Mesa area, most likely from the surrounding countryside. No migrations over long distances, however, are suggested by any of the archaeological evidence.

Despite the abrupt changes in population density, individual settlements

74

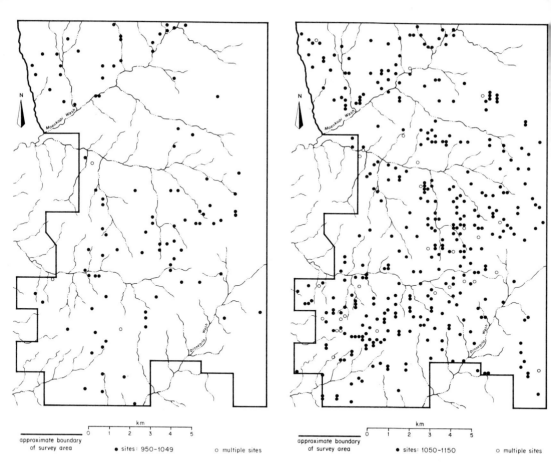

74 Between the periods of AD 950–1049 (left) and 1050–1150 (right), large numbers of new villages were constructed on northern Black Mesa as population levels increased several fold.

maintained remarkably constant characteristics. The basic configuration throughout comprised a small number of *jacal* dwellings and masonry storage rooms occupied by 10–25 people, with a single central kiva. Even the very largest villages probably had no more than 50 inhabitants.

75   There are few areas in the Southwest where crops receive sufficient moisture solely from rainfall alone. Historic Navajo and Hopi groups, who now occupy northern and southern Black Mesa, typically plant most fields on the banks of rivers or actually in drainage areas where floods or run-off will occur during heavy rains. As the prehistoric population grew and people settled and planted fields along smaller, secondary drainages, the risk that fields might receive insufficient moisture increased. And, as neighboring groups became more numerous, the territory over which each group could gather wild plants and hunt was reduced, hindering a group's ability to counter inadequate agricultural harvests. Whatever problems the Black Mesa people faced as their numbers declined at the beginning of the 12th century, agricultural intensification was apparently not the answer. No evi-

dence of irrigation canals, extensive terrace systems, or any other features designed to manipulate the distribution of water or to conserve soil moisture has been discovered.

As remarkable as we find the burst in the establishment of new villages through most of the 11th century, even more dramatic was the subsequent plunge in the number of Black Mesa settlements. The remaining villagers initiated no new construction after the decade AD 1130–1140, and by AD 1150 everyone had departed, taking with them all of their possessions, even their manos and metates, as was the case with the Mimbres people. No Anasazi people ever occupied the area again. This complete depopulation in a period of 40–50 years was duplicated in many other parts of the Anasazi region in the first half of the 12th century. Attempts to explain the phenomenon have produced a number of hypotheses, and we will scrutinize some of them later in the chapter.

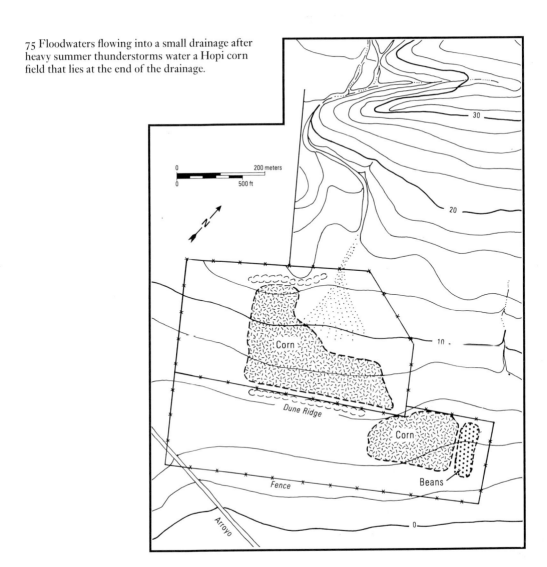

75 Floodwaters flowing into a small drainage after heavy summer thunderstorms water a Hopi corn field that lies at the end of the drainage.

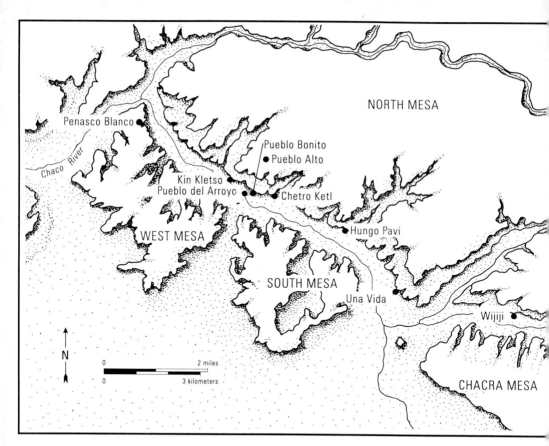

76 Great Houses in Chaco Canyon lie primarily along the north side of Chaco Wash, at the foot of steep sandstone cliffs.

The Great Houses of Chaco Canyon

The residents of Chaco Canyon in New Mexico's San Juan Basin also participated in the Anasazi world, but their lives were so unlike their counterparts on northern Black Mesa that few would mention both areas in the same breath. Whereas the Black Mesa evidence is interesting, but neither spectacular nor monumental, the archaeology of Chaco Canyon mesmerizes everyone who sets foot there. Visitors are initially conscious of the seemingly inhospitable environmental setting. As one descends into Chaco Canyon today the isolated buttes or mesas and the few trees along the ephemeral Chaco Wash do little to break the stark vistas. Vegetation is minimal as annual rainfall averages only about 9 in (22 cm). The growing season is highly variable and barely adequate for successful agriculture. Yet Chaco Canyon was the setting for arguably the most breathtaking suite of buildings of the entire prehistoric epoch in the Southwest. In association with these magnificent structures we find evidence that the Chacoans constructed extensive road networks and were skilled astronomers (see box p. 100).

76,77

85

77 Pueblo Bonito is the largest Chacoan Great House, covering almost 2 acres and incorporating 650 rooms that stood 4 stories high in parts of the village. The core-and-veneer architecture and multi-story construction employed at Pueblo Bonito produced massive masonry structures with walls as much as 3 ft (1 m) thick.

Pueblo Bonito

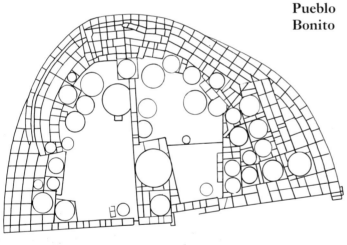

78–81 ABOVE and LEFT Pueblo Bonito is divided into two sections by a wall running north–south through the plaza. The single Great Kiva on either side of the wall creates a symmetrical pattern that typical of many Great Houses. BELOW An artist's reconstruction illustrates the terraced nature of the main roomblocks, with a single sto next to the plaza and higher levels one moves toward the exterior wal RIGHT Pueblo Bonito exemplifies multi-storey construction using thick core-and-veneer walls. Becau of the arid nature of the canyon, original construction beams commonly protrude from standing walls throughout the pueblo.

Pueblo astronomers

My great-great-uncle Muuete ... was the Special Officer of the Sun Clan, and was called Tawamongwi (Sun Chief). He would sit at a certain place and watch the sun in order to know when it reached its summer home. It was the work of the Chief of the Flute society to guide the sun on its way. When the sun had arrived at its summer home, my uncle would say to the Sun Clan people, 'Well, our great-uncle, the Sun God, has reached his summer home and now we must butcher a sheep and make prayer offerings for the sun, moon, and stars.' [35]

Many Native Americans schedule their ceremonies, predict the change of seasons, and determine when to plant their crops by observing movements of the sun and the moon. They also possess extensive knowledge of the stars and constellations. Archaeological discoveries show that the prehistoric Southwestern peoples had similar acumen. One of the most fascinating demonstrations of their ability is found on Fajada Butte in Chaco Canyon. Three sandstone slabs, each about 6.5 ft (2 m) high, that fell from the vertical walls of the mesa landed in such a way that they deflect light against the wall at certain times of the day. The Chacoans noticed this pattern and pecked one large and one small spiral on the wall behind the slabs so that the intersection of the daggers of light and the stone spirals mark important points in the movement of the sun. At the summer solstice on 21 June a single dagger of light cuts across the large spiral; at the winter solstice on 21 December two vertical stripes of light bracket each

side of the large spiral. The spring and autumn equinoxes are also marked. As one band of light cuts across the middle of the small spiral, a larger band falls to the right of center of the large spiral on 21 March. A similar pattern unfolds on 21 September, except that the dagger of light falls to the left of center on the large spiral. [36]

We also find tantalizing evidence that the Southwestern peoples noted and recorded the exceptional as well as the constant. In July AD 1054 a supernova appeared in the sky two degrees below a waning crescent moon. While no European accounts of this phenomenon are known, the Chinese report that the supernova was visible for 23 days. Tantalizing evidence suggests that both the Mimbres and Chacoans recorded this event. On a canyon wall near the Great House of Peñasco Blanco, a Chacoan painted a crescent moon with a star below it. Although these rock paintings cannot be dated, the correspondence between the date of the supernova and the concentration of building activity in Chaco Canyon between AD 1030 and 1130 is extremely suggestive. Equally beguiling is a Mimbres bowl showing a star-like object with 23 rays near the back feet of a rabbit. Astronomers Robert Robbins and Russell Westmoreland argue that the rabbit is a common symbol for the moon in Native American art and suggest that the bowl from a village occupied for several centuries, including the peak of the Mimbres occupation in the late 11th century, illustrates the supernova. [37]

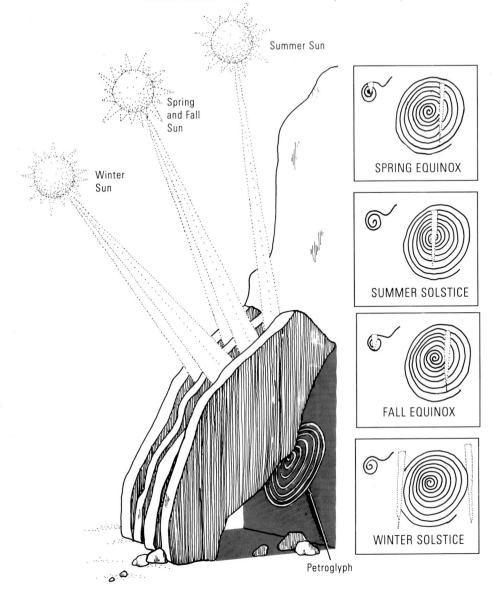

SPRING EQUINOX

SUMMER SOLSTICE

FALL EQUINOX

WINTER SOLSTICE

Summer Sun

Spring and Fall Sun

Winter Sun

Petroglyph

82 ABOVE Light deflected by three sandstone slabs intersects a large and small spiral pecked into the cliff-face of Fajada Butte, in Chaco Canyon, in such a way that the light patterns can be used to distinguish the spring and fall equinoxes and the summer and winter solstices.

83 LEFT A crescent moon and star painted on a sandstone cliff near Peñasco Blanco, Chaco Canyon, may have recorded the sighting of a supernova in July AD 1054.

The construction of the monumental and exquisite Chacoan architecture in such an inhospitable setting is a paradox that for decades has caused Southwestern archaeologists to scratch their heads. Whereas the people of Black Mesa and Mimbres appear to have invested a minimal number of days in building their dwellings, storage rooms, and kivas, the Chacoan people devoted an extraordinary amount of time – to be measured not in days, but in months and years – and labor to such efforts. Along a 9-mile stretch of the canyon floor lie at least a dozen Great Houses that range in size from Pueblo Bonito, the largest with over 650 rooms, to Wijiji with just over 100 rooms. Most were multi-story buildings with massive and beautifully coursed sand-stone walls up to 3 ft (1 m) thick at their base. Recent studies suggest that the construction of a single room required the builders to cut as much as 44 tons of sandstone from nearby cliffs. They also felled over 200,000 trees to create floors and roofs for all the Great House rooms. The species of trees used for

78
86

The Chacoan network

84 Only a stone's throw from Pueblo Bonito, Chetro Ketl has a roughly similar D-shape, but with between 450 and 550 rooms and a single Great Kiva it is slightly smaller. Construction of the Great Kiva would have required 29,135 person-hours, the equivalent of 30 people working 10 hours a day for 100 days.

85 Jackson staircase, named for explorer and photographer W.H. Jackson, carved into the sandstone mesa behind Chetro Ketl and was part of the Chacoan road system.

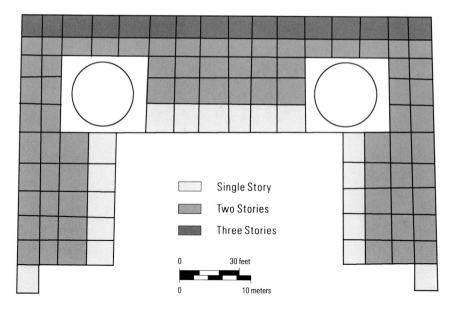

Single Story

Two Stories

Three Stories

0   30 feet

0   10 meters

86 One of the smallest Chaco Canyon Great Houses with just over 100 rooms, Wijiji exemplifies the more compact village plan that characterized Great House construction after *c*. AD 1100–1110.

87 Stages in the construction of Peñasco Blanco: Stage I, AD 900–915; Stage II, AD 1050–1065; Stage III, AD 1085–1090; Stages IV and V, AD 1090–1125.

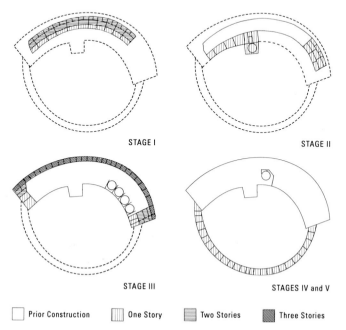

STAGE I

STAGE II

STAGE III

STAGES IV and V

Prior Construction   One Story   Two Stories   Three Stories

much of the construction did not grow in the Chacoans' backyard. Recent studies have demonstrated that they were harvested as much as 50 miles away, with most coming from the Chuska Mountains to the west.

In contrast to the gradual and somewhat haphazard growth of Mimbres villages, the Chacoans carefully planned the construction of most components of a Great House and built that section as a single unit. Some additions were single-story, whereas others were as high as three or four stories. They erected some, like Wijiji, in a single, swift construction effort between AD 1100 and 1115. In other cases, such as Peñasco Blanco, the Chacoans typically began by building a single rectangular roomblock. They completed this core roomblock at Peñasco Blanco between AD 900 and 915 and then, after a   87 lapse of more than a century, expanded the Great House in four additional building stages of AD 1050–1065, 1085–1090, 1090–1120, and 1120–1125.[38] The thin arc of rooms that enclosed the plaza at Peñasco Blanco and other Great Houses was usually the last part to be built.

Other features demonstrate that Great Houses were much more than a typical village grown large. These include a high frequency of subterranean kivas, including Great Kivas. Both types of kivas were striking in their own way. The Chacoans constructed corbeled or cribbed roofs over some of the smaller kivas, an extravagant use of wood given the distances these timbers   88 had to be toted. The creation of Great Kivas also demanded unusual effort. These structures typically range from 34 to 63 ft (10 to 19 m) in diameter[39]   89 and were excavated at least 6 ft (2 m) below the ground surface and enclosed by masonry walls. Stephen Lekson estimates that construction of the initial

88 The fallen roof beams of the cribbed roof of Kiva L at Pueblo Bonito, shown during excavations at the site.

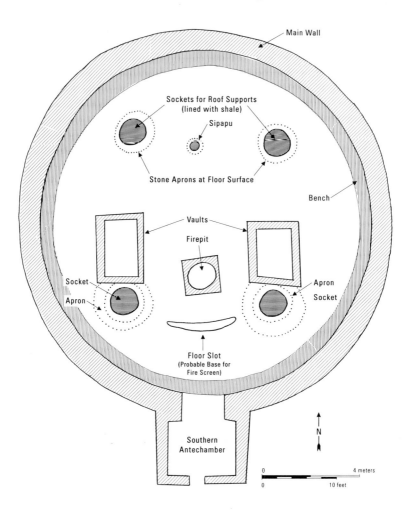

Main Wall

Sockets for Roof Supports
(lined with shale)

Sipapu

Stone Aprons at Floor Surface

Bench

Vaults

Firepit

Socket

Apron

Apron

Socket

Floor Slot
(Probable Base for
Fire Screen)

Southern
Antechamber

N

0   4 meters
0   10 feet

89 The floor plans of Chacoan Great Kivas, such as this example from Pueblo Bonito, typically included a central fire pit, a *sipapu*, 4 large sockets or seating pits for the large timbers that supported the roof, a fire screen or deflector, and two vaults that may have been covered with wood and used as foot drums.

90 Cylinder vessels are found almost exclusively at Chaco Canyon Great Houses. Large caches of these vessels within Pueblo Bonito suggest restricted production and control, perhaps by higher status individuals.

Great Kiva at Chetro Ketl required 29,135 person-hours, the equivalent of a   84
crew of 30 people working ten hours a day for 100 days.[40]

In association with the Chacoan Great Houses are hundreds of smaller
villages scattered throughout the canyon. Built on a more modest scale,
many of these villages nevertheless have more rooms than even the largest
Anasazi settlements in regions such as Black Mesa, though they did not
approach the size of the larger Mimbres villages. Great Kivas occur as isolated, detached structures between these clusters of smaller villages.

R. Gwinn Vivian, who began his studies of Chaco as a child when he
accompanied his archaeologist father to the canyon, believes that one answer
to the question of why Chaco is so unusual is that the Chacoans capitalized
on the water run-off from the many large expanses of bedrock along the
north rim of the canyon. Significant run-off from those areas is typical
during heavy summer thunderstorms, and Vivian found that the canyon
residents collected the water by building diversion dams and canals with   91
multiple headgates that channeled it into bordered gardens. Also significantly early in the occupation of the canyon may have been a small lake
formed by the creation of a sand dam at the west end, where Chaco wash

91 Chacoans captured the
rain from intense summer
thunderstorms that fell on the
bedrock mesas of the canyon
and cascaded into the arroyos
below. They built small dams
that diverted the water from
the arroyos into canals and
then into bordered gardens
constructed on the canyon
floodplains.

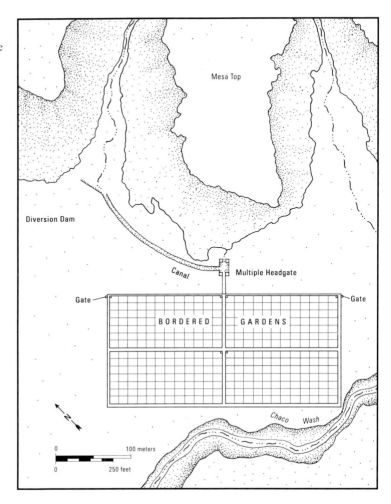

intersects with the Escavada. The dam initially formed through natural processes, but then may have been buttressed and repaired by the Chacoans.[41]

The extent of these fields, along with new analyses suggesting some corn may have been brought into the canyon from surrounding areas,[42] offers more than adequate testimony to a large resident population in the canyon. Estimates of the actual numbers vary widely, however, and have been the subject of considerable debate, a controversy that is central to an understanding of the development of Chaco. It is clear that the smaller Chacoan villages were residential, but what about the Great Houses? The abundance of kivas, the monumental architecture, and the recovery of ritual paraphernalia demonstrate that they were important loci for Chacoan rituals, but many archaeologists also believe that the Great Houses had considerable resident populations. Population estimates for Pueblo Bonito, for example, range from a few hundred to a few thousand people.

Symmetry and asymmetry in Chacoan society
Other clues to the conceptual – and possibly sociopolitical – organization of the Chacoans' world lie in details of their buildings and settlements. John Fritz notes that the eastern and western halves of most Great Houses and Great Kivas are roughly symmetrical.[43] The plaza at Pueblo Bonito is divided by a north–south running wall with Great Kivas on either side; two

78–81 Great Kivas are common at other Great Houses as well. Similarly, the east–west distribution of features within such Great Kivas as Casa Rinconada is also symmetrical. A roughly north–south line connection between the two Great Houses, Pueblo Alto and Tsin Kletsin, located at a distance north and south from the canyon rim, also bisects the population of canyon Great Houses.[44] The east–west balance contrasts with differences between north and south. Great Houses lie almost exclusively on the north

76 side of Chaco Wash, with primarily small pueblos on the south. Within Great Houses we find masonry rooms on the north side, with plazas and Great Kivas to the south. Within the Great Kivas, the numbers and types of features in the northern and southern halves do not match.

Fritz believes that the layout of the Great Houses was a metaphor for Chacoan concepts of order.[45] More specifically, he suggests that the east–west symmetry communicates social equivalence, possibly between groups comparable to the moieties that are so central to the modern Pueblo communities in the Rio Grande region of New Mexico. The two burial crypts at Pueblo Bonito, each the final resting place of scores of individuals, provide further support for a moiety division.[46]

Conversely, the north–south contrasts symbolize the sacred and profane. Fritz suggests, for example, that 'the northern half of the kiva was a stage on which those impersonating elements of the sacred could perform and from which they could move symbolically into the light and the world of the everyday.'[47] In Pueblo oral tradition, the Pueblo people emerged from the underworld at a location to the north and then traveled south to their current locations. His interpretation thus reinforces the idea that Great Houses, even if in part residential, were also important ritual centers.

Aspects of Fritz's interpretation also intersect with two of the most debated questions regarding Chaco. First, were Great Houses primarily ritual in function, serving as the setting for large public ceremonies attended by pilgrims from surrounding areas? Second, was Chacoan society headed by an elite class, with sociopolitical power and the ability to organize large projects such as the construction of the massive Great Houses?

The possibility that Great Houses served principally as settings for large public ceremonies arose largely from what some perceived to be a surprising paucity of burials and domestic hearths in conjunction with an equally unexpected density of ceramics in refuse mounds at the largest Chacoan buildings. The resulting conjecture explained these contradictions by positing that Great Houses had only small resident populations that periodically were joined by large numbers of people from surrounding villages and regions on the occasion of important rituals. The perceived contradictions, however, proved to be based on either insufficient analysis of available data or inadequate data. As in most historic pueblos, the occupants of Pueblo Bonito undoubtedly lived primarily in upper floor residences rather than in the dark, unventilated ground floor rooms. Although most of the ground floor rooms of Great Houses are well preserved, most upper floors collapsed long before the initiation of archaeological excavations, thus eliminating the likelihood of discovering most of the existing domestic hearths. Hearths are present in the floors of some of the surviving upper level rooms, however, and in other cases walls covered with soot demonstrate that firepits had once existed in the rooms. Moreover, new studies of refuse mounds have shown that the density of materials is proportionate to the estimated resident populations.[48] Thus, although Great Houses undoubtedly served as important ritual settings, most also had residential functions as well. We must always remember, however, that there is such variation in the size and internal characteristics of Great Houses that they must have differed in some functions.

Recent analysis of early records of historic excavations in the canyon has also suggested that the perceived lack of Great House burials is a product not of lower residential populations, but rather a result of a complex burial pattern in which higher status individuals were interred (or sometimes reinterred) in Pueblo Bonito in the two crypts mentioned above, with other residents likely buried in the smaller settlements where, not surprisingly, archaeologists have discovered hundreds of graves.[49] The characteristics of the Pueblo Bonito burial chambers are, like much in Chaco, unique in both the number of individuals and in the associated grave offerings.

The most intriguing room in the burial complex was number 33, excavated by George Pepper in 1896, where parts of at least 14 individuals were discovered. With at least two of these individuals, both buried beneath an unusual board floor, the Bonitans placed hundreds of turquoise or jet pendants and thousands of turquoise and shell beads which were once part of bracelets and necklaces. Above these two burials lay the other 12 burials (some articulated and complete, but some which were fragmentary and disarticulated) in association with numerous turquoise and shell beads and pendants, a few of the unique Chacoan cylinder vessels, several dozen shaped wooden rods that may have been prayer sticks, and seven large wooden flutes. Other individuals buried in nearby rooms were laid to rest on a mat of bulrushes and wrapped in feather-cloth robes and cotton fabrics.

The grave goods associated with these burials remind one of 16th-century Spanish descriptions of Native American 'rulers' in northern Mexico who wore 'a fine cotton cloak and a wristband of martin fur,' or 'who were well dressed in cotton and adorned with turquoise necklaces.'[50] Other evidence suggests that these individuals had greater power and rights than typical Chacoans. Analysis of the skeletal remains has revealed that the people in the Pueblo Bonito burial chambers were 2 in (4.6 cm) taller than the inhabitants of the small sites and they suffered from lower rates of anemia than was typical of most Southwestern groups,[51] probably because of their diet. Elites throughout much of the prehistoric New World ate better than their comrades, in particular consuming greater quantities of protein.[52]

Relations beyond Chaco Canyon
The final element in the riddle of Chaco Canyon is a network of prehistoric roads that has only begun to be documented since the 1970s. Largely invisible to a person standing on the ground, but detectable on aerial photographs as straight, dark lines, these roads not only join Great Houses within the canyon, but in some cases connect the canyon with areas as much as 62 miles distant. Settlements in the surrounding areas, sometimes in association with roads, are referred to as Chacoan outliers and have many of the unusual Great House features, such as core-and-veneer architecture and Great Kivas. Over 150 of these outliers and hundreds of miles of roads have been discovered, and the numbers increase every year.

92 When Chacoan roads traversed steep canyons, steps were often cut into the sandstone cliffs using little more than hard, rock hammers and a lot of sweat.

Chacoan roads rarely follow topographic contours or valleys, but are virtually straight paths, 13–30 ft (4–9 m) wide and cleared of large rocks and debris, across the landscape. Sections (primarily some of those closer to the canyon) were carefully engineered, with excavated road beds lined by earth berms, or masonry or adobe curbs. In areas of considerable relief or where cliff-faces had to be scaled, particularly near the Great Houses, the Chacoans cut stairways into the stone and constructed ramps and scaffolds. 85, 92 These features would have been difficult for the Anasazi to scale if they were carrying much of a load and they therefore suggest that the roads were not all constructed to ease the movement of goods into or out of the canyon. Other characteristics suggest that some of the roads served as important components in Chacoan ritual. In many cases the roads do not end at another settlement but rather simply extend a few miles from a Great House or outlier and suddenly stop. In other places the Chacoans laid out multiple roads.

The rise and fall of Chaco
How did Chaco come to be and what was the fate of its residents? It does not appear very different from other parts of the Southwest during the initial development of villages.[53] Although sites such as Shabik'eschee (see Chapter 4) were large for the time, counterparts did exist in some places. By AD 900, however, we find the embryonic stages of a few of the dozen Great Houses that formed the nucleus of the Chacoan world. Some population growth was characteristic of the 9th and 10th centuries, but a decline in construction activity and possibly population density also occurred during the late 10th and early 11th centuries. Then the Chacoans initiated an enormous construction program that began at approximately AD 1025, peaked between AD 1050 and 1100, and then declined sharply. Their fabrication and remodeling of the Great Houses probably ceased by AD 1130. The Chacoans' construction of the roads was also concentrated in the period AD 1030–1100. Many of the earliest roads lead to the south and west of the canyon, while others built late in the 11th century or early in the 12th century connect the canyon with regions to the north, particularly sites along the San Juan River. This shift in road construction coincided with the appearance in the canyon of greater numbers of vessels either similar to, or produced in, the San Juan region as well as the construction of large towns in that region. Chaco Canyon was not abandoned at that time, but the cessation of Great House construction and the paucity of other archaeological evidence indicate that the canyon was no longer central to the Anasazi world. Political leadership probably shifted away from Chaco to the San Juan region by at least AD 1130 and perhaps a few decades earlier.

Universal trends in the Southwest

The contrasts between the various peoples of the Southwest in the period AD 700–1130 were many, ranging from differences in village size to religious practices and types of pottery. Yet there are remarkable similarities too.

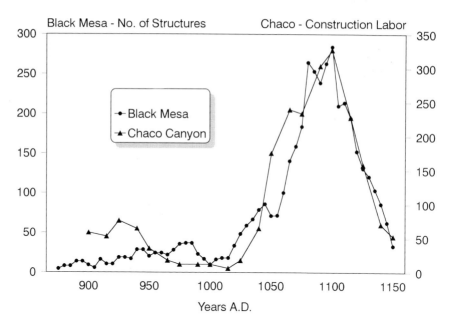

93 Population growth on northern Black Mesa, northeastern Arizona, in the 11th century and the subsequent decline that began around AD 1100 are strongly correlated with a rise and fall in the amount of effort expended in building Great Houses in Chaco Canyon. In addition to Black Mesa, population levels in many other sections of the Anasazi region follow the pattern of change in Chaco Canyon.

Perhaps the most salient trend was the growth in population. Skeletal studies show that increases in fertility, not decreases in mortality, produced the population rise.[54] The technological and social innovations described in the last chapter (pottery for boiling foods; sharing; storage), together with the more settled way of life and dependence on agriculture, raised potential fertility and provided incentives for families to have more children.[55] Since these changes coincided with a period of above-average rainfall favorable to agriculture, the result was a population explosion. Over several decades, numbers increased 10- to 20-fold and the Hohokam, Mogollon, and Anasazi filtered into almost every nook and cranny, from the bottom of the Grand Canyon to the top of isolated buttes. By approximately AD 1075–1100, people were more densely packed and widely distributed in the Southwest than ever before, a peak of population not reached again until historic times. The increase in numbers was not continuous through the period. Short periods of rapid growth could be followed by equally brief periods of slow or rapid decline, or periods of little change. But even here we find a remarkable degree of correspondence in the specific patterns of change, as shown by the graphs of population fluctuation on northern Black Mesa and of construction activity in Chaco Canyon. Correlations this strong are not the result of chance and demand consideration of contacts between areas.

93

The social landscape

As numbers reached their peak, Anasazi, Hohokam, and Mogollon groups must have increasingly been forced to settle in less desirable terrain where farming was less reliable. In the Mimbres Valley, on Black Mesa, and in the Phoenix Basin, we know that settlement expanded along secondary streams and rivers where not only were agricultural plots smaller, but the crucial seasonal floods and run-offs needed to irrigate crops were also reduced.[56] To counter the danger of inadequate harvests, people developed more localized networks of cooperation. They joined together for rituals, offered marriageable children to potential mates, exchanged pottery or shell, and shared agricultural surpluses. This can be seen in the growth of regional traditions in decorative styles on ceramic vessels. When archaeologists divide the region into smaller sections and refer to the Kayenta Anasazi or the Chaco Anasazi, they are in part alluding to sub-regional stylistic traditions that can be distinguished by the middle of the 11th century, if not earlier. Such differences contrast with decorative ceramic patterns in the 9th and 10th centuries when there were considerable similarities across broad areas of the Southwest.

A second indication of localized networks is the increased exchange of basic materials and tools. Stone for tool manufacture, such as chert and more rarely obsidian, was traded or exchanged primarily within sub-regions but occasionally over great distances. Hundreds, if not thousands, of ceramic vessels were also traded, including not only beautiful, decorated wares, but simple, undecorated containers used in cooking. The inclusion of such items demonstrates that this trade was not simply an effort to obtain goods or materials that were not available locally. In comparable agricultural societies today, a variety of goods are regularly traded as a means of establishing and maintaining social ties with other groups. Those social ties may then allow access to surplus food during periods of local shortages.

Exchange of scarcer and more precious goods may have been controlled by group leaders. Copper bells manufactured in northern or western Mexico, marine shell from the Gulf of California, and colorful scarlet macaws native to Mexico's Gulf Coast were all carried into the Southwest. In turn, turquoise from the northern Rio Grande has been discovered at Mexican sites. But long-distance travel was not an everyday occurrence.[57] David Doyel has calculated, for example, that only one trip every 8.5 months would have been necessary to supply the Hohokam with the *Glycymeris* shell found on their sites and that only three or four part-time specialists would have been needed to acquire the shell and manufacture it into bracelets, pendants, or beads.[58] The very scarcity of these items and the distances traversed to acquire them, however, may have enhanced their importance as markers of greater social status and significant religious paraphernalia.

The growth of a few major sites, such as Snaketown and Chaco Canyon, could be due in part to their suitable locations in relation to long-distance trade routes. Ethnohistoric and archaeological evidence from throughout the Southwest indicates that river valleys were important routes of travel. In

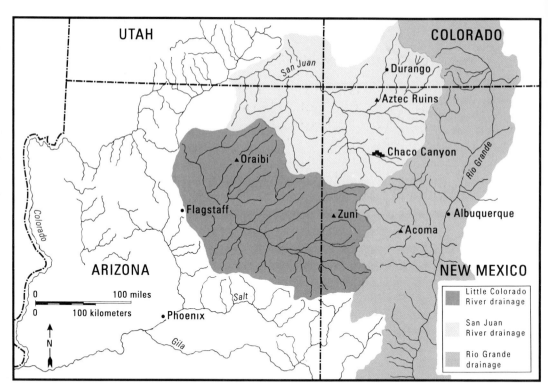

94 Chaco Canyon lies near the intersection of the three primary drainage basins – the San Juan, the Rio Grande, and the Little Colorado Rivers – suggesting that it played a major role in interregional movement, given that drainages were likely important routes of travel.

the absence of roads or detailed maps they were the easiest paths to follow, with few rapid changes in elevation or other obstacles to make travel difficult. Snaketown and Chaco are found at different points in their respective drainage networks, but there is one important similarity in their locations that has been overlooked. Snaketown lies near the terminus of the Salt River where it intersects with the Gila River, a placement that would have allowed access to groups along both rivers. Chaco sits in the upper reaches of the San Juan 94 drainage, within a small, unique area where the upper stretches of the Rio Grande, Little Colorado, and San Juan Rivers all converge, the intersection of three major pathways. These settings, in conjunction with the high frequency of trade goods in both locations, confirm that Snaketown and Chaco played a significant role in interregional movement within the northern Southwest. Interestingly, the earliest roads built in the Chaco region – running from the canyon to the south and southwest – lead toward areas of lower elevation that would have been the easiest routes for travelers to cross from tributaries of the San Juan into the Rio Grande and Little Colorado drainages.

The shrinking native world

The other common thread that tied together many areas of the Southwest during this period was the abandonment or reorganization of settlements and, in some cases, entire sub-regions in the late 11th and early 12th centuries, as people moved into neighboring valleys or settlements. In the Grand Canyon area of northern Arizona, in the Anasazi areas of southern Nevada, in sections of southern Utah and Colorado and northern New Mexico, the Black Mesa pattern of significant 11th-century population increase followed by depopulation or abandonment in the early 12th century has often been discovered by archaeologists. The pattern differed in detail in the Hohokam region, but a reduction in the size of the area inhabited still took place. Construction activity, and in many cases occupation, ceased at the largest settlements such as Snaketown; production of the characteristic ritual paraphernalia such as stone palettes, bowls, and effigies declined markedly; and few, if any, ballcourts were constructed.[59] Many of the unique aspects of the Chacoan network – cylinder vessels, lengthy roads, turquoise trade, and massive Great Houses – dwindled in number or disappeared altogether. As we will see in the next chapter, subsequent developments reveal that this was not simply a time of relocation, but one that gave rise to significantly different patterns of organization and ritual.

Southwestern archaeologists have tended to search for environmental causes to these departures and transformations, but there is little correlation between the abandonments and climatic fluctuations, since the periods of low rainfall documented for the 1130s occurred well after most people had departed or construction activity had dwindled. Furthermore, where we have information on the health of the Southwesterners, as on Black Mesa, there is little evidence that disease forced people to leave, nor do death rates suggest that groups were near extinction.[60] People suffered from nutritional and infectious diseases (see box p. 117), but that had been true for centuries prior to the abandonments. The scale of the population movements and the similarity in patterns across such a broad area suggest that other factors were more important.[61] Two factors that deserve particular attention are the impact that the ancient Southwesterners themselves had on their environment and the importance of the intra- and inter-community ties.

Environmental change: the human role

Despite the popular belief that it is only in the last few centuries that people have altered their environment dramatically, we now know that prehistoric peoples also often failed to live in ecological harmony. The virtually treeless landscape of Chaco Canyon today, for example, may be as much a product of the Chacoans' huge demands for fuel and construction wood as of natural environmental factors. Studies of packrat middens show decreasing frequencies of piñon and juniper trees through time, with particularly large reductions during the 10th and 11th centuries. Supporting a significant human role in this deforestation are the analyses of wood charcoal from Chaco sites that show increasing use of ponderosa pine and cottonwood, both of which are inferior fuel woods than the piñon and juniper. Research in the Mimbres Valley has also shown that, as the Mimbres people increased in number, they cleared most of the trees from the main floodplain, destroying the habitats of animals that were important sources of food. The Mimbres people needed to adjust to their increasing numbers, to the increased settlement of risky agricultural areas, and to changes in the availability of natural plant and animal foods, but were unable to do so without further modifying their environment or aggravating the problems caused by years of reduced rainfall and shorter growing seasons.[62]

These environmental impacts cannot be seen as the sole cause of the subsequent depopulation, because groups in other parts of the Southwest also modified their environments and yet still continued to increase in numbers. In addition, anthropological studies show that food shortages or environmental change rarely cause total depopulation. But the ways that the ancient Southwesterners altered their local environments undoubtedly accentuated any associated problems, and in those areas where overpopulation was greatest or where human modification of the environment had been most significant, adjustment to these changes may have been impossible.

Understanding the perspective of the ancient Southwesterners

The abandonments of many settlements and entire regions were not partial, but complete. This suggests that movement was an all or nothing proposition; the entire network of ties within and between communities was so indispensable to the survival of their world that it was inconceivable for some people to leave and others to stay.[63] These ties may have served a number of real and perceived purposes, ranging from the exchange of essential resource items, to providing a type of social glue, to contributing the materials and personnel for the proper conduct of ceremonies. For example, if groups depended upon one another for the performance of rituals thought to be necessary to maintain the world, such beliefs may have inhibited social fragmentation.[64] But once such cooperation broke down, society itself became irreparably damaged.

When archaeologists think about the prehistoric era, they tend to create dichotomies such as culture (e.g. trade ties) vs. nature (e.g. droughts) because from our own perspective these are separate phenomena. In our view the way we behave has no bearing on natural phenomena such as climate. Other peoples, however, do not share these same beliefs. Most native societies of the New World believe today, and almost certainly believed in the past, that there is no separation between culture and nature, and that the actions of their political or religious leaders can affect rainfall, agricultural yields, and virtually any other aspect of their lives. Anthropologist Peter Whiteley emphasizes that from a Hopi perspective, events such as droughts and epidemics are not random phenomena, but predictable 'and inextricable from the political administration of society.'[65]

Isolating the causes of culture change in the past is therefore not simply a matter of linking abandonments with climatic change and reduced

Life and death in the Southwest

A blunt reminder that the ancient Southwesterners' existence could be harsh and demanding comes from burial studies revealing age at death and evidence for disease and stress. The average Black Mesan, for example, lived only 25 years (males lived a few years longer on average than females), the people of Chaco Canyon for 27, and life expectancy may have been even lower in the Mimbres region. Only 5–15 percent of the population reached the age of 50. There is little evidence of severe malnutrition, but stress due to nutritional deficiencies and infectious disease contributed to the high mortality rates.[66]

The rate of infant and child mortality was particularly high. Prenatal stress occurred due to the mothers' poor health; infants suffered from problems such as anemia and chronic ear infections. Individuals who did survive to an older age show signs of arthritis and spinal degeneration from toting heavy loads. Skeletal indicators show that although males and females may have participated in different tasks, such tasks were equally strenuous.[67] The oldest individuals often had few teeth remaining because of the abrasive diet of fibrous plants and corn meal, which included grit from the stones used to grind the corn kernels. Some older females also suffered from osteoporosis, an affliction exacerbated by a deficiency of calcium and vitamin D.

The ancient Southwesterners, although lacking antibiotics and other 'wonder drugs,' exploited the substances available to them to treat the aged and infirm. A rare discovery in a burial from the NAN Ranch Ruin in the Mimbres area provides a particularly poignant insight into those practices.[68] A fossilized feces was preserved in the pelvic area of Burial 109, suggesting it had been in the descending colon at the time of the individual's death. Analysis of pollen extracted from the fecal sample revealed high frequencies of mustard, willow, and maize. Because grit from grinding stones was not found in the fecal sample and because willow and mustard are plants that Native Americans commonly use for medicinal purposes, the analysts believe that the individual drank a tea prepared with these ingredients. A type of pain killer, salicin, is present in willow bark. Burial 109 was a male, 5 ft 8 in (1.72 m) tall and between 35 and 40 years old, who died from unknown causes but was suffering from mild arthritis and an injured sacrum that may have caused him to limp. The tea may have reduced the pain from these afflictions.

agricultural yields. Rather, we must also allow for the impact of relationships within a community. In societies such as the Hopi, where leaders partly maintain authority by instilling fear of their supernatural powers into their subjects,[69] any events that lead people to question the power of their leaders is potentially highly disruptive. We must now turn to the next few centuries of Southwestern prehistory in order more fully to understand the disruptions and transformations that brought this era to a close.

6 · Cliff Dwellings, Cooperation, and Conflict AD 1130 to 1350

The prehistoric Southwest at about AD 1100 was densely settled by the largest number of ancient Southwesterners ever to have occupied the region. Walking across the landscape, one would have found it difficult to travel more than half an hour without encountering people going about their daily tasks. Forty years later the abandonments discussed in the previous chapter would have left some localities stark and devoid of human occupation, but other nearby areas still densely settled. By the first decade of the 14th century, however, archaeological evidence creates an image of a region where one could walk perhaps hundreds of miles and never see another person. People had emigrated from the mesa tops and canyons of the Mesa Verde and the many other homelands where their ancestors had lived for centuries. Ancient Southwesterners now resided in only a few parts of the region: the southern edge of Black Mesa, populated by the ancestors of the Hopi; west-central New Mexico, where the ancient Zuni ultimately constructed the fabled 'Seven Cities of Cibola'; sections of the Little Colorado River drainage and the Mogollon Rim country; the Salt and Gila River basins in southern Arizona; northern Mexico; the Rio Grande Valley; and a few other locations.

What happened to the ancient Southwesterners during those centuries? Many possible answers have been proposed, but before looking at them, let us first examine some general trends and investigate a few of the best-known regions. These trends and local histories have much to say about the broader issues.

Emigration and oral histories

Although fewer areas of the Southwest were occupied by the 14th century than two centuries earlier, it should not be assumed that large numbers of people died as areas were abandoned. Overall there was a drop in the total number of people, but it was not a sudden decline when we look at the region as a whole. Comparing developments in nearby localities, we often find that population seems to have risen in one area while declining in another. Long House Valley in northeastern Arizona, for example, witnessed considerable population growth as the area immediately to the south, Black Mesa, was

95 Kiet Siel, a well-preserved cliff dwelling in Navajo National Monument in northeastern Arizona, was first settled around AD 1240 and gradually increased in size until construction ceased in AD 1286.

being abandoned. Similarly, as the numbers of people in Chaco declined, regions within a three-day walk to the north along the Animas River, and to the southeast in the Rio Grande Valley, reveal sharp increases in the number of occupants.

This pattern has some significant implications. Among the most important is that local abandonments were not a product of large or sudden increases in mortality (a conclusion supported by the skeletal studies noted in the previous chapter), but simply reflect movement out of a particular area. Such mobility was probably always a characteristic of life in the Southwest, particularly in the Anasazi and Mogollon regions where the typical small village might be occupied for brief periods of only 10 to 20 years. During the 12th and 13th centuries, however, whole groups of people in a single area seem to have moved at the same time. And this happened in many parts of the Southwest, not just a few.

Different patterns of movement – the relocation of entire communities, or just individual families – are revealed by one of the most fascinating studies made of this period, an analysis of tree-ring dates from two cliff dwellings, Betatakin and Kiet Siel (Navajo National Monument), in the 95

Kayenta region of northeastern Arizona. Built within 6 miles of
in dry, protected alcoves under rock overhangs in the steep, san
faces of the Tsegi Canyon drainage system, both are sizeable
with wood suitable for tree-ring dating well preserved in the st
tecture. Each site forms an arc-shaped pueblo that follows the ...rving back
wall of the cave. Betatakin has 135 rooms and 2 kivas while Kiet Siel has at
least 155 rooms and 6 kivas. Much of the eastern half of Kiet Siel lies atop a
large artificial terrace created by dumping fill behind a substantial masonry
retaining wall 180 ft (55 m) long and in places more than 10 ft (3 m) high.
Although the slope and configuration of the cave floors creates an impression of three- or four-story ruins, no structures were actually more than two
stories in height. Springs at the eastern end of the alcoves at both Betatakin
and Kiet Siel provided a ready source of water for the inhabitants.

Jeffrey Dean of the Laboratory of Tree-Ring Research at the University
of Arizona painstakingly collected beams from as many rooms as possible at
each site, dated them through dendrochronology, and then examined the
processes of settlement growth.[1] He found that Kiet Siel initially grew in a
manner suggesting that the number of inhabitants had gradually risen here
through both natural population growth and the arrival of new groups. The
first parts of the village were constructed in the late 1240s or early 1250s. By
1271, 12 room clusters had been added and these were dispersed along the
back wall of the alcove. Each room cluster consisted of at least one living
room, one to six storage rooms, a courtyard, and sometimes a mealing room
where corn and other seeds were ground. Small families probably occupied
each room cluster. Dean believes that the community then experienced a
major influx of people between 1272 and 1275, as several new sets of rooms
were added, six were modified, the large retaining wall was built along the
front of the settlement, and three kivas were constructed. A change in the
types of ceramics used at the site was also notable. During the remaining
years of occupation, only a few room clusters were added. Construction and
remodeling ceased in 1286, and by 1300 the site was abandoned.

The founding of Betatakin illustrates a somewhat different pattern.
Initially, three clusters of rooms were constructed when the first settlers
moved in sometime during 1267, and a fourth was added in 1268. Ten more
sets of rooms, along with one or two kivas, were then built between 1275 and
1277. Additional clusters were added in a more gradual fashion in subsequent years. As happened at Kiet Siel, the occupants of Betatakin abandoned the pueblo sometime between 1286 and 1300.

The most interesting aspect of the growth of Betatakin is that the construction between 1275 and 1277 was accomplished with beams that had
been cut to standardized sizes and stockpiled, first in 1269 and again in 1272.
In addition, Betatakin is much more homogeneous architecturally than Kiet
Siel. Dean believes that Betatakin was established 'by a group of people who
already constituted a functioning community' somewhere else. He suggests

96 Two pueblo units, one at the base of the cliff and the other tucked into a hollow in the
canyon wall, define White House Ruin in Canyon de Chelly National Monument in the
Kayenta region of northeastern Arizona, to the southeast of Kiet Siel and Betatakin.

that the people who occupied the site in 1267 chose the location and settled it with the explicit purpose of preparing the cave for a larger group that would follow. Thus, while Kiet Siel appears to have grown through both natural increase and the sporadic addition of other, perhaps unrelated, social groups, the construction of Betatakin was a planned movement undertaken by a single group of people.

Evidence from other regions suggests that these movements were not atypical of the time. At Point of Pines in east-central Arizona, Emil Haury identified what appears to have been an enclave of people from the Kayenta region of the northern Southwest, over 200 miles distant, people who were still using Anasazi-style pottery that contrasted with local Mogollon vessels. The rooms occupied by the enclave had been burned, suggesting that the relationship may not have been a completely peaceful one.

Such movements by sizeable groups over long distances to join a pueblo occupied by a different group are strikingly similar to the oral histories maintained by the Hopi. These histories describe the growth of Hopi society through the addition of entire clans who immigrated to the Hopi country, sometimes after wandering over considerable areas, and were allowed to settle because they offered a particular set of skills or ceremonies. Don Talayesva, a Hopi Sun Chief, describes the growth of Oraibi after the village was established by Machito, the brother of the chief of Shongopavi:

> Other peoples began to arrive. Whenever a new clan came, a member of the party would go to the Chief and ask permission to settle in the village. The Chief usually inquired whether they were able to produce rain. If they had any means of doing this, they would say, 'Yes, this and this we have, and when we assemble for this ceremony or when we have this dance, it rains. With this we have been traveling and taking care of our children.' The Chief would then admit them to the village.[2]

The Hopi and many other Pueblo groups identify some Southwestern sites dating to the late 13th and 14th centuries as the ancestral homes of these migrating clans. Although these myths have undoubtedly been elaborated over the years, the similarity between the events they describe and the patterns of behavior visible archaeologically is striking.

Regional variation and localized polities

Given the increasingly patchy distribution of people and villages across the landscape, we should not be surprised to find increasing differences among localities. Regional ceramic traditions became increasingly distinct toward the end of the 13th century. Groups still traded over much of the Southwest and even beyond into the Plains and central Mexico. Nevertheless, economic activity tended now to be concentrated within localities rather than between them. These more localized polities can best be illustrated by looking at developments within one or two areas of the greater Southwest.

97 Mesa Verde is dissected by numerous steep-sided canyons. Canyon bottoms are so narrow that little farming was possible.

The Anasazi: Mesa Verde and the northern San Juan

The enthralling cliff dwellings of Mesa Verde National Park in southwest-   100
ern Colorado caught the attention of both archaeologists and the general
public in the late 19th century and early 1900s. Gustaf Nordenskiöld conducted the first scientific study of the ruins in 1891 and his description of the
largest of the Anasazi cliff dwellings, Cliff Palace, captures the sentiment of
many first-time visitors:

> Strange and indescribable is the impression on the traveler, when, after a
> long and tiring ride through the boundless, monotonous piñon forest, he
> suddenly halts on the brink of the precipice, and in the opposite cliff
> beholds the ruins of the Cliff Palace, framed in the massive vault of rock
> above and in a bed of sunlit cedar and piñon trees below. This ruin well
> deserves its name, for with its round towers and high walls rising out of
> the heaps of stones deep in the mysterious twilight of the cavern, and
> defying in their sheltered site the ravages of time, it resembles at a dis-
> tance an enchanted castle.[3]

Mesa Verde provided the setting not only for Nordenskiöld's pioneering   97
work, but also for many of the earliest studies of the prehistory of the
Southwest.

The Anasazi groups of the Mesa Verde were part of a broad network of
trade and interaction that encompassed the northern drainages of the San
Juan River, particularly the Mancos River and McElmo and Montezuma
Creeks. As elsewhere in the Southwest, there were striking shifts through

98 Balcony House in Mesa Verde National Park lies 600 ft (180 m) above the floor of Soda Canyon, just under the canyon rim, in such an inaccessible location that today visitors must climb a 32-ft (10-m) ladder to tour the pueblo. The 35–40 rooms of Balcony House were inhabited for 50 to 75 years at the end of the 13th century.

time in where and how people formed communities. In the late 11th century the typical village included 5–15 dwellings and storage rooms in association with a single kiva, the 'unit-pueblos' that are so characteristic of many parts of the northern Southwest. Somewhat more unusual was the tendency for several of these unit-pueblos to cluster within a small area.[4] The members of these communities would no doubt have been in contact with each other on a day-to-day basis and were often separated from other clusters by areas with little or no occupation. Single Great Kivas – the larger-than-average subter-ranean ritual structures – sometimes occurred with each cluster, suggesting collective rituals in which all members of the communities participated. Evidence for such inter-group ritual activity increases significantly in many areas of the northern Southwest during the 12th and 13th centuries. During the early 12th century, Chacoan outliers were also present, indicating that the people of the northern San Juan drainage region participated in the larger Chacoan network.

99 RIGHT Square Tower House, Mesa Verde National Park. The multi-story tower defines the right side of the cliff dwelling.

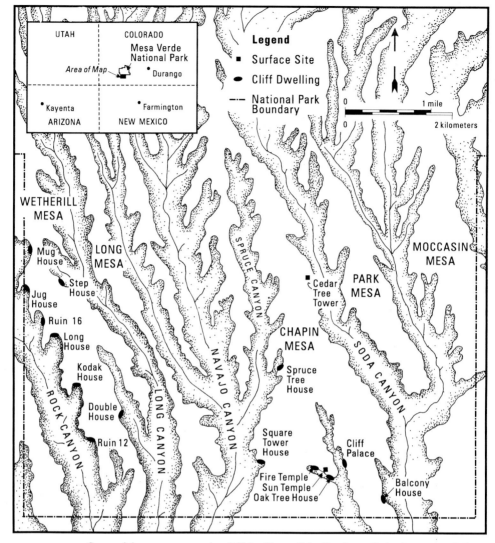

100 Some of the most spectacular cliff dwellings of the Southwest lie in the canyons below Chapin and Wetherill Mesa in the southwestern corner of Mesa Verde National Park.

The village clusters of the 11th and early 12th centuries foreshadow the formation of much larger individual villages in the late 12th and 13th centuries. Although many people still lived in smaller villages after 1150 (intensive surveys in the northern San Juan demonstrate that the typical village had fewer than 15 rooms[5]), the most salient characteristic of the period was the construction of large, multi-roomblock towns of several hundred masonry rooms and as many as 50–100 kivas. These large towns took disparate forms in different parts of the region.

98–104   Best known to the general public are the impressive Mesa Verde cliff dwellings, of which Cliff Palace is the largest and most spectacular. Built in

Living on the edge

101–103 LEFT The Anasazi people
constructed their cliff dwellings in alcoves
that had eroded in the canyon walls.
BELOW Even modest nooks and crannies
in the cliff-faces were blocked by masonry
walls to create small dwellings and storage
rooms such as this one in Canyon del
Muerto. BOTTOM Most cliff dwellings fell
far short of Cliff Palace in size, often
containing only 10–15 rooms. Oak Tree
House in Mesa Verde typifies these
smaller dwellings.

104 ABOVE Cliff Palace, with over 200 rooms and 20 kivas, is the largest and most spectacular cliff dwelling in the Southwest. Archaeologists have often highlighted the skill of the builders who in several places constructed terraces to provide a level foundation for the masonry rooms.

105 ABOVE RIGHT Many of the cliff dwellings were reached by scaling hand- and toeholds carved in the sandstone cliff-faces.

106 RIGHT The walls of kivas constructed prior to the 14th century were seldom decorated with murals such as those found at some later kivas. The rare designs that have been discovered in the earlier kivas often consist of simple geometric patterns such as this series of terraces on a kiva wall at Lowry Ruin in southwestern Colorado.

alcoves in the steep canyon walls, the cliff dwellings range from small storage structures and field houses, of only a few masonry rooms, to Cliff Palace's 220 masonry rooms and 23 kivas.[6] The dry conditions of the protected alcoves and the difficult access – many require lengthy climbs using hand- and toeholds pecked into the sandstone cliffs – shielded the villages from the elements and rival groups. Describing his excavations, Nordenskiöld both cursed and celebrated the dry nature of the deposits:

> Great inconvenience was caused ... by the fine dust, which rose in dense clouds at each blow of the spade. It was evident that not the least trace of moisture had been able to reach the rooms under the sheltering rock, and this explains how such things even as cotton cloth, wooden implements, string, pieces of hide, and the like were in a perfect state of preservation. The sun blazes with glowing heat during the greater part of the year, and the overhanging roof of rock affords an effectual shelter from the heavy showers of the short rainy season.[7]

Preservation of materials is so good that some dwellings still have roofs intact and paintings on the walls, fragile materials such as basketry and tex- tiles are found in excellent condition, and turkey droppings still lie in the pens where the birds were kept.

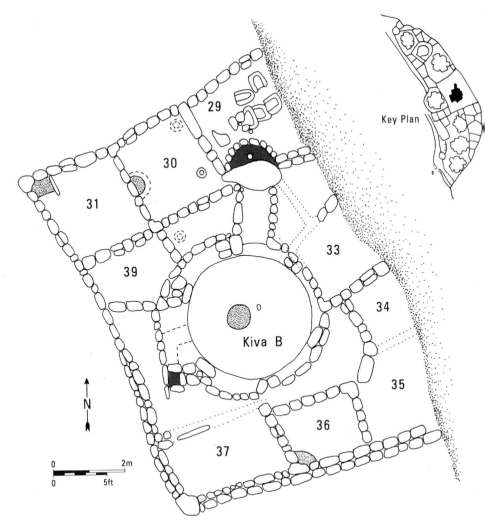

Key Plan

107 A courtyard cluster at Mug House, Mesa Verde National Park, with nine first-story rooms around a kiva. Between 10 and 13 second-story rooms (not shown) were also part of the cluster.

Mug House – named for a set of ceramic mugs found here – is one of the best known of the cliff dwellings thanks to studies by Art Rohn in the early 1960s.[8] Situated in a cave 200 ft (60 m) long and 40 ft (12 m) deep, Mug House is separated from the top of Wetherill Mesa above it by a shear 90-ft (25-m) sandstone cliff. Like many of the cliff dwellings, Mug House was used by the Anasazi for several centuries, but they began building the primary village of 94 rooms and eight kivas in the mid-13th century. The most fundamental architectural unit in the village is the room suite, defined by a small number of mutually accessible dwelling and storage rooms probably inhabited by a single household. A few of these suites share exterior space in a courtyard whose surface was often the roof of a subterranean kiva. These courtyard clusters are thus comparable in size to the unit-pueblos dis-

107

Clothing and fashion in the world of the cliff dwellers

The remote, inhospitable locations of the cliff dwellings often make visitors wonder about how ancient peoples coped with travel here or with the frigid winters, typical at elevations exceeding 7,000 ft (2,100 m), where snowfalls can exceed 65 in (165 cm) and temperatures can drop as low as -20°F (-30°C).[9] Fortunately the materials recovered from the dry caves and rockshelters of the region allow us to answer such questions in more detail than is possible for most regions of the Southwest (see pp. 54–55).

Sandals were fashioned from broad-leafed (*Yucca baccata*) and narrow-leafed (*Yucca harrmaniae*) yucca. Two types have been recovered, a twill-plaited sandal made of woven yucca strips and a finer model of twined yucca 'cloth.' These typically have toe loops and show significant amounts of wear. The cliff dwellers also made ankle-high socks by intertwining yucca cordage with feathers. One example recovered from Mug House reveals that it was worn with a sandal, because impressions from the sandal straps are still visible. Leather moccasins also have been recovered, but are rare.

Feather-cloth blankets helped the Mesa Verdeans protect themselves from the cold. They created one such blanket by wrapping strips of yucca cords with brown and white turkey-down feathers, laying several strips about 0.4 in (1 cm) apart, and then weaving the cordage together with individual strands to form a fabric. These blankets were also employed as burial shrouds. Some clothing was fashioned from deer and squirrel skins. Cotton cloth is less commonly recovered from the cliff dwellings and the fragments are too small to determine the type of clothing, but robes, sashes, kilts, and bags are all likely possibilities.[10]

cussed earlier. Multiple courtyard clusters occur in the larger cliff dwellings, however, an ensemble that has little precedent in earlier periods. Rohn estimates that as many as 80 to 100 people may have lived in Mug House during the peak occupation. Rohn also believes that the residents of the 33 Mesa Verde cliff dwellings shared farm land, a common water supply, a set of eight trails, and two communal ceremonial structures. Individual villages were thus part of a larger community that shared daily tasks and religious beliefs and ceremonies.

The cliff dwellings are justifiably renowned. Nowhere else in the Southwest can a visitor gain such a vivid impression of what life would have been like in the 13th century, from the smoke filtering out of kiva entryways, to the cries of infants resonating against rockshelter walls, to the appearance of the cliff dwellers themselves (see box p. 131). It is nevertheless important to recognize that the vast majority of Anasazi groups resided not in cliff dwellings, but in mesa top villages. In the McElmo and Montezuma Creek drainages northwest of Mesa Verde, we find large towns in mesa top settings that are two or three times the size of even the largest cliff dwellings.[11] Studies by the Crow Canyon Archaeological Center in the McElmo Creek area provide one of the most complete pictures of the development of Anasazi groups outside Mesa Verde. Surveys here have shown that small, unit-type pueblos typified this area prior to the late 13th century. As population density within the region rose from 13–30 people per square mile in the mid-10th century to 80–130 per square mile by the late 13th century, the average size of these smaller villages doubled from about six rooms to twelve rooms at the same time that their overall frequency declined. They also became increasingly clustered around two large Anasazi towns, Sand Canyon Pueblo and Goodman Point, constructed in the last half of the 13th century. By this time, over 50 percent of the population resided in these two towns.[12]

108

Two sites excavated by the Crow Canyon Archaeological Center exemplify the differences between the small villages and the much larger towns that evolved in the last half of the 13th century. The Green Lizard Site and Sand Canyon Pueblo are just over a half mile apart, both lying along the Sand Canyon. The Green Lizard Site is composed of two adjacent unit-pueblos, each with a kiva and associated masonry pueblos, that housed a few families. The village was inhabited in the middle to late 13th century, the similarities in pottery used here and at Sand Canyon Pueblo suggesting that they were occupied contemporaneously, an inference supported by two radiocarbon dates. The village occupants remained for a generation or more, long enough to remodel one of the kivas and create a deep trash deposit (over 5,000 potsherds were excavated from only a small part of the midden). A tunnel leading from one kiva into a nearby roomblock almost certainly served as a passage that ritualists could use in order to emerge magically, presumably from the underworld that is so important in Pueblo cosmology. Nothing else about the Green Lizard Site is exceptional or indicates any communal effort by its inhabitants.[13]

The Anasazi constructed Sand Canyon Pueblo surrounding a major spring, a characteristic common to most of the large towns of the region during this period.[14] Around 1250 the residents-to-be of Sand Canyon erected the site-enclosing wall, a massive structure built in a single construction episode that would have taken 30–40 people two months to complete. Over the next three decades, they added over 20 separate roomblocks incorporating at least 90 kivas and about 420 rooms that may have housed as many as 725 people at its peak. The basic residential group continued to be the household, each occupying a cluster of structures – minimally a residence, storage room, mealing room, and kiva – equivalent to the earlier unit-pueblos.[15]

Besides its size, Sand Canyon differs from the Green Lizard Site and from the earlier unit-pueblos in three more subtle, yet significant ways. The first is that household suites at Sand Canyon are more regimented with characteris-

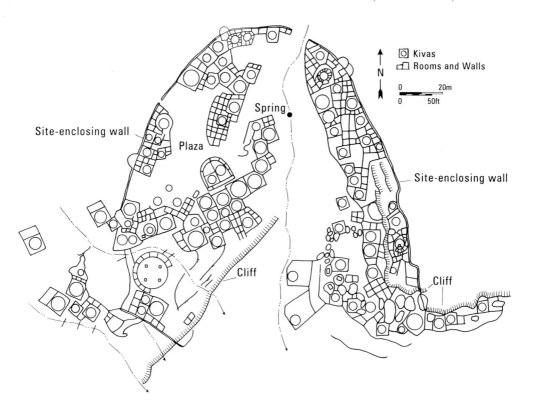

108 Sand Canyon Pueblo in southwestern Colorado was one of the largest pueblos constructed by the Anasazi in the 13th century. Like Cliff Palace, it has an unusually large number of kivas.

tics such as pecked surfaces on masonry blocks. These required greater construction time and suggest at least some differences in social status between the inhabitants of the two villages.[16] Second, the roomblocks, like the courtyard groups of the Mesa Verde cliff dwellings, encompass multiple households within a single architectural complex. This suggests a strengthening of the social glue that bonded together different households. The third, probably related, development is the association of new types of ceremonial structures or spaces with the growth of these large towns. These structures include Great Kivas, roofed plazas, towers, and bi- and tri-wall buildings that are rare outside the San Juan region. The towers, two or more stories high, are often associated with kivas, if not connected to them via tunnels,[17] and they also share some architectural similarities. At Mug House, although the two towers are in defensive positions, other characteristics suggest a ceremonial or ritualistic role.[18] The bi- and tri-wall structures are formed by concentric walls that encircle an above-ground kiva.[19] The Great Kivas of the northern San Juan are comparable in size to the structures built by many groups for their rituals and the Great Kivas show greater uniformity in their internal features and less evidence of use for secular activities.[20] Distinctive

99

133

characteristics such as caches of unusual materials, floor vaults, and multiple *sipapus* also differentiate the Great Kivas from their smaller counterparts.[21] To what extent the rituals conducted in these structures differed is unclear, but it is likely that they were associated with the need to promote cooperation among different households that had once lived further away from one another.[22] This issue will be addressed more fully below.

Despite the cohesion that Great Kivas and other public architecture helped to provide, the inhabitants of the Green Lizard Site, Sand Canyon Pueblo, and the cliff dwellings of the Mesa Verde abandoned their villages in the late 13th century. Tree-ring dates from the cliff dwellings demonstrate that building activity declined rapidly in the late 1270s (the last date for Mug House is 1277) and construction seems to have ceased altogether by the 1290s. Similarly, the dating of Sand Canyon Pueblo reveals remodeling of existing structures at least into the 1270s, but little evidence of occupation after 1280. Some sections of the pueblo show accumulations of trash implying that the village unraveled over a period of years with the successive departure of small groups, but the large numbers of ceramic vessels and stone tools left behind on the floors and roofs of other Sand Canyon rooms suggests that the last groups to leave did so very rapidly, or planned to travel such long distances that they left behind non-valuable utilitarian items.[23] By 1290, the thousands of people who had once resided in the northern San Juan had abandoned their villages and found new homes elsewhere.

The Hohokam of the Phoenix Basin

The traveler on the road west from Florence will frequently have his attention drawn to … mounds which loom above the mesquite and sage bushes as gray elevations bare of vegetation and easily distinguished from natural hills by the fragments of pottery or worked stone upon their surfaces.
J. Walter Fewkes, 1907[24]

The principal Hohokam villages in the Phoenix Basin, dating from 1150 to 1400, were scattered along the major irrigation canals that distributed water from the Salt and Gila Rivers. The largest of the villages each lay about 3 miles from neighbors of comparable size. Such settlements, typically located at the ends of canal networks, served as the primary administrative and ritual centers, coordinating canal use and resolving conflicts over water allocation.[25] The major villages may have housed as many as 300 to 1,000 people.[26]

109   An excellent example is the Lehi canal system, fed by the Salt River, near the modern city of Mesa, Arizona.[27] The main canal branches into three major distribution canals. Two irrigate land along the first floodplain terrace of the Salt, while the third supplies land farther away along the second terrace. Study of the settlement data by Jerry Howard suggests a hierarchy of three types of site. The largest settlement, Mesa Grande, covers 3 square miles and lies about 1 mile from the southwestern end of the canal network.

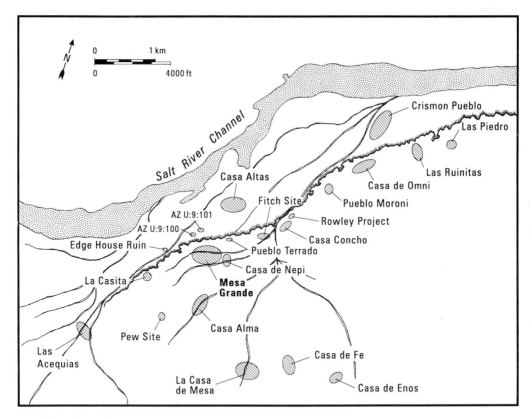

109 The Lehi canal system along the Salt River in the Phoenix Basin exemplifies the extensive irrigation networks that had evolved by the 13th century. A hierarchy of settlements occurred along these networks, with the largest settlements like Mesa Grande populated by as many as 300 to 1,000 people.

The presence here of the largest platform mound (by volume) anywhere in the Hohokam region – together with an enclosing compound, a ballcourt, a smaller platform mound, and numerous residential compounds and trash mounds – clearly differentiates Mesa Grande from other settlements that share the canal system. The pre-eminence of Mesa Grande is reinforced by evidence indicating craft specialization and greater access to imported ceramics and turquoise. Three-quarter grooved axes, obsidian tools, and shell jewelry were found in the vicinity of the large platform mound.

The second level of the settlement hierarchy includes several sites approximately 0.25 square miles in area, each with either a small platform mound or a ballcourt; these villages may have served as secondary administrative centers. One of the sites, Crismon Pueblo, is the only sizeable settlement on the first terrace and Howard notes that it 'occupies a strategic location adjacent to the three-way canal branch, and undoubtedly had actual control over water allocation for the Lehi canal system.'[28]

The third and final level of the hierarchy incorporates smaller, purely agricultural settlements characterized by only one or two residential compounds and few ceramic tradewares, axes, and objects of turquoise. The range of village types around Mesa Grande was considerably greater than elsewhere in the northern Southwest.

As in the Pueblo areas to the north, the 12th century was a time of significant change in the Hohokam world. Populations continued to rise in many parts of the region, but became concentrated in a more limited number of locales. Towns such as Snaketown were either abandoned or much reduced as new communities were established elsewhere.[29] The Phoenix Basin achieved a total population of between 30,000 and 60,000, one of the highest densities of people – living along the largest system of irrigation canals – anywhere in prehistoric North America.[30] Within that region there is evidence to suggest a shift in demographic dominance from the area of the Gila River north to the lower sections of the Salt River. The Lehi system is one of 14 such canal systems along the Lower Salt River.[31]

A variety of other aspects of Hohokam life changed about this time. The Hohokam now buried a greater proportion of their dead as inhumations rather than cremations, and those still cremated were often buried in vessels. More red-ware pottery was produced and less of the previously characteristic red-on-buff ceramics. Ornate ritual artifacts such as stone palettes, elaborate projectile points, and stone bowls and effigies virtually disappeared.[32]

Changes in public architecture further strengthen the idea of fundamental shifts in Hohokam society. Fewer ballcourts and more platform mounds were built, and, at those settlements inhabited through this period of transition, ceremonial precincts were often relocated.[33] Some of the platform mounds were much more substantial than earlier versions, approaching dimensions of 330 by 165 ft (100 by 50 m) and a volume of 1,235,000 cubic ft (35,000 cubic m) of earth fill in a few cases.[34] The Hohokam constructed these later mounds by first erecting a substantial rectangular retaining wall of coursed adobe and then filling the space defined by the wall with a combination of trash and soil. They capped the mound with a layer of plaster and surrounded it with a rectangular adobe wall.[35] In some instances the Hohokam built a platform mound in a single massive effort, while at other sites there were several construction stages, with the surrounding wall of the previous stage used as the retaining wall for the next episode. Jill Neitzel estimates that the labor costs of mound construction would have been considerable, requiring 36 people to work for a month to provide each 35,300 cubic ft (1,000 cubic m) of mound fill.

110   New types of domestic architecture also appeared. Wattle-and-daub structures built in shallow pits remain the norm at many settlements, but they are sometimes built inside rectangular- or square-shaped compounds defined by adobe walls. In addition, the Hohokam began to erect single- and multi-room adobe structures which became the standard dwellings at some settlements by the late 13th century.[36] The number of structures inside the compounds roughly equaled the number of pithouses in earlier clusters of houses, suggesting some stability in the size of basic social groups.[37]

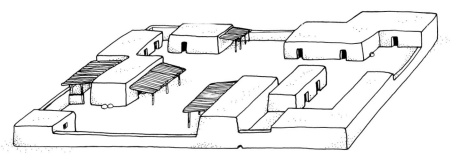

110 Residential compounds in the Hohokam region were enclosed by adobe walls and often included several adobe rooms, multiple courtyards, and ramadas that likely served as work areas. Compounds of this size may have housed between 2 and 5 families.

At the Salt River settlement of Pueblo Grande the compounds averaged 165 ft (50 m) in length and 65–100 ft (20–30 m) in width, with ten rooms inside the compound housing perhaps 15–20 individuals. That these individuals thought of themselves as a distinct social group is indicated by the fact that they maintained their own trash mound and cemetery, typically located to the north or east of the compound.[38]

At Pueblo Grande, those cremated were buried mainly in ceramic vessels within the cemeteries; those not cremated were sometimes buried in the cemeteries, but more commonly inside the walls of the compounds. The Phoenix Basin Hohokam often placed uncremated infants under house floors while older individuals were buried outside in the plazas. Mineral residues indicate that body painting may have been part of the burial ritual. Grave goods included ceramic vessels, beads, pendants, ears bobs, and bone hair pins; and prestige or ritual items such as shell, bird burials, and wooden staffs.[39]

At the biggest Hohokam settlements, a central precinct made up of large compounds, platform mounds, and ballcourts was surrounded by a zone of smaller compounds which in turn was encircled by scattered dwellings similar to those constructed during earlier periods.[40] Initially the Hohokam used the platform mounds almost exclusively for ritual dances, since virtually no residential structures appear on the mounds' summits before 1250.[41] Adobe walls built around the base of the platform mounds, however, indicate a desire to reduce the visibility of such rites. This suggests that public ceremonies conducted in the ballcourts were replaced or complemented by other rituals in which only a small part of the population participated. Then, perhaps as early as 1250, some Hohokam groups began to construct what seem to be residences on top of the platforms.[42] The elite occupants may have exercised increasing control based on their privileged access to ritual knowledge.

We have observed that there were distinct settlement hierarchies within individual canal networks in the Phoenix Basin. In addition, people of several different networks may have been politically and perhaps administratively allied by the end of the 13th century. The landscape was thus increasingly shaped by political forces, with alliances among some people and competition between others.

The Marana Hohokam

Although only about 100 miles southeast of the Phoenix Basin, the Tucson Basin illustrates the extent to which life could vary within the Hohokam region. Recent archaeological studies have focused on the nature of settlement from the valley bottoms along the Santa Cruz River to the flanks of the low mountain ranges that define the limits of the basin. The Santa Cruz carries water primarily after heavy summer rains; neither the volume nor the timing of the water flow is conducive to irrigation agriculture. In addition, elevation increases rapidly as one moves away from the river, producing narrower floodplains with less irrigable land. These deficiencies, however, are countered somewhat by the higher rainfall within the Tucson Basin itself (11 in (28 cm) annually at Tucson compared with 7.5 in (19 cm) at Phoenix), and by the greater diversity of vegetation within relatively short distances associated with the more varied topography.

Archaeological surveys around the major site of Marana in the northern Tucson Basin by Paul and Suzanne Fish have revealed that Hohokam peoples exploited both lowlands and uplands after the development of villages.[43] Early settlements in each zone tended to be sizeable, with similar artifact assemblages, suggesting a similar range of economic activities. The parallels extend to other dimensions of village life: ballcourts and trash mounds occur at the largest site in each zone.

Then from the late 11th century – as happened in the Phoenix Basin – the Hohokam began to transform their lives. They constructed more and more platform mounds with encircling compound walls, but few ballcourts. They established more settlements in a wider range of environments. The number of villages in the northern Tucson Basin rose considerably, resulting in a dense and continuous distribution from the valley bottoms to mountain slopes both northeast and southwest of the Santa Cruz River. Overall, the total area occupied increased threefold.

As these processes developed, some groups constructed a new platform mound and compounds at the site of Marana, midway between two earlier villages with ballcourts. Those members of the Marana community who lived closer to the Santa Cruz River appear to have farmed using both irrigation and floodwater methods. In the upland zones the largest settlements approached a half square mile in area and included compounds with house mounds, dry-laid masonry structures, and possibly pithouses. The residents of these upland villages, however, farmed in a very different manner from their lowland counterparts, using check dams, huge roasting pits, cobble terraces, and rock-pile fields. Terraces reduce the slope of the land and thus reduce soil erosion and increase the absorption of moisture. Rock piles help create a mulch, promoting absorption and reducing evaporation, and also protecting plants from rodents. Even today densities of plants are higher in the rock piles than in surrounding soils. It has been calculated that it took 14 person-years to form an estimated 42,000 rock piles and 36 person-years to build the check dams and 75 miles of terraces. Experiments show that construction of a rock pile takes about 40 minutes, while the cobble terraces can be formed at the rate of 5 ft 4 in (1.65 m) per hour.[44]

The Hohokam cultivated and processed a type of cactus, agave, in these upland field areas and associated roasting pits. Agave is a plant native to the Southwest, but does not grow naturally in the Marana area today and thus probably did not in the past. The plant is adapted to more arid environments and can endure droughts and sporadic rainfall. It is therefore particularly suitable for uplands where water is less abundant and predictable. Agave matures approximately every ten years at which point the hearts are harvested as a source of food and the leaves as a source of fiber. The rock-pile fields would thus have provided food and a raw material for craft production or trade.[45]

Paul and Suzanne Fish suggest that the relatively uninterrupted scatter of sites in the northern Tucson Basin after 1100, from the floodplain to mountain flanks, indicates a more integrated economy than in earlier periods, one that may have required stronger organizational ties.[46] They propose a three-tiered settlement hierarchy, with the Marana mound settlement at the top playing a leading role in the organization of economic activities. The mound is centrally located relative to the other villages, but it is not in a productive farming area, suggesting that it achieved dominance instead through the exchange of various types of foods from the different zones. And, like the dominant communities in the settlement clusters in the Phoenix Basin, Marana is at the end of a 16-mile-long irrigation canal.

Elsewhere in the northern Tucson Basin other contemporaneous groups developed distinct identities and different trading partners during the 12th and 13th centuries, judging by patterns of ceramic variation. Substantial variation in relative frequencies of ceramic types in various sections of the basin suggest that each group participated in different patterns of intercommunity contact and trade. The presence of several hilltop sites in defensive positions and the location of four platform mounds on high mesas overlooking the Santa Cruz River raise the possibility of growing competition and conflict among the various communities.

Although the agricultural basis of life in the Tucson Basin differed from that in the Phoenix area, similar trends characterized the late prehistory of both regions. Settlement hierarchies developed, ballcourts were replaced by the construction of mounds inside compound walls, and settlement clusters evolved. These trends suggest that the range of status differences increased as connections among settlements became more complex. The clustering together of settlements and the occurrence of defensive sites imply that not all these relationships were peaceful.

Common threads but different fabrics

There are striking parallels in the Hohokam, Mogollon, and Anasazi regions during this period, including cooperative methods such as irrigation to improve agricultural production, the growth of large settlements and social hierarchies, and clear signs of tension and conflict. Let us examine each of these three phenomena in turn.

Watering the crops

The precipitation which fell directly onto the fields was insufficient by itself to grow crops throughout the region under normal conditions, but farmers could increase the amounts of moisture available to crops with minimal effort simply by planting in areas with natural mulches (e.g. sand dunes) where evaporation is reduced, or in areas where run-off from storms was concentrated. Despite the limited area that could be cultivated, there is little evidence prior to AD 1150 for agricultural intensification outside the Hohokam region. After this time, however, we find growing evidence for new and cooperative efforts to increase the fertility of the land. The Hohokam greatly expanded the scale of their irrigation networks. More typical in the northern reaches of the Southwest, however, during the late 12th and 13th centuries were less labor-intensive practices. Anasazi and Mogollon farmers constructed stone walls across drainages or perpendicular to hill slopes to retard run-off and erosion and thus increase the absorption of moisture. In some cases they also created reservoirs to trap run-off, by excavating shallow depressions or by blocking drainages with more substantial stone walls.

111,113

One of the most complex water control projects is on Chapin Mesa in Mesa Verde National Park.[47] The key feature is Mummy Lake, a natural depression *c*. 90 ft (27 m) in diameter where water collected after the Mesa Verdeans formed an earth bank in the 11th century on the south and east

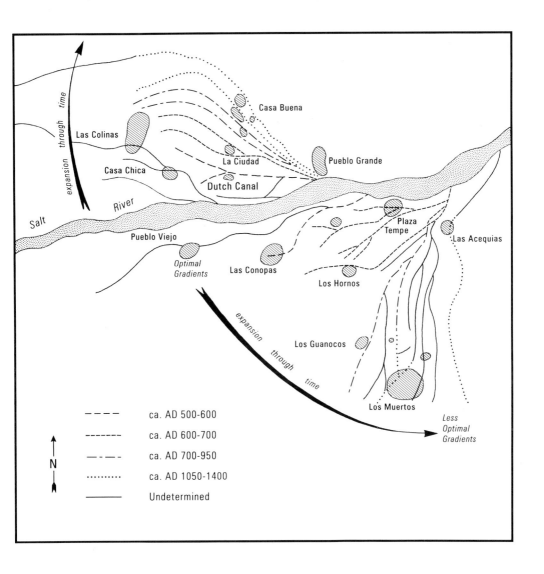

Casa Buena

Las Colinas

Casa Chica

La Ciudad

Dutch Canal

Pueblo Grande

River

Salt

Pueblo Viejo

Optimal Gradients

Las Conopas

Plaza Tempe

Las Acequias

Los Hornos

expansion through time

Los Guanocos

Los Muertos

Less Optimal Gradients

– – – – –	ca. AD 500-600
– – – – –	ca. AD 600-700
– · – · –	ca. AD 700-950
· · · · · ·	ca. AD 1050-1400
————	Undetermined

N

111 LEFT A series of masonry check dams blocks a small drainage on the Mesa Verde, forming small plots of farmable land.

112 ABOVE Through time the Hohokam canal networks became increasingly complex. Primary canals grew in length, more secondary canals were excavated, and areas farther and farther away from the rivers were farmed.

113 RIGHT Stone terraces near the pueblo of Nuvaqueotaka (Chavez Pass), a large 13th/14th-century pueblo in east-central Arizona.

sides supported by a wall. They also channeled water into the lake via a half-mile-long main feeder ditch. A second channel allowed the water to be diverted into another ditch leading to a series of farming terraces in a nearby ravine. In the 12th century the Mesa Verdeans added a third option, allowing water to be carried in a 30-ft-wide (9-m) canal, now named the Far View Ditch, over 4 miles down the main ridge of Chapin Mesa. The canal was primarily used for domestic water for nearby villages.

Most other water control features were not so extensive that they required so much time and labor, but the increasing frequency of such efforts by the people of the northern Southwest indicates a heightened concern with the possibility of unsuccessful harvests and the limits of agricultural land. The greater size of individual villages exacerbated matters: more people in a single location meant that the inhabitants had either to produce more food on nearby land or cultivate fields at increasing distances from the village.

The Hohokam of the Phoenix Basin invested even more labor and time than the Anasazi and Mogollon to improve fertility, a trend that began much earlier here, as noted in the previous chapter. One of the largest expanses of arable land in the Hohokam region, and in the Southwest in general, lies along the Gila and Salt Rivers near the modern city of Phoenix. Given the low rainfall in the area, contrasted with the high and reliable volumes of water in the rivers, it is not surprising that the Hohokam developed irrigation agriculture well before any other part of the Southwest.

The irrigation networks are best known along the Lower Salt River. Archaeologists have mapped the distribution and evolution of segments of the irrigation networks either by following depressions left by the canals or, more typically, by examining aerial photographs on which altered vegetation patterns on the disturbed soil are visible. Irrigation potential along the Salt River is greater than along the Gila because the latter carried much less water and more silt which clogged up the canals.

Although the Hohokam's initial irrigation efforts date to about the same era as the emergence of villages, early irrigation networks were simple discrete canal systems with only a few main branch canals that were constructed and maintained by one or two settlements. By the 12th and 13th centuries the systems had become complex, integrated networks with multiple branch canals, each associated with handfuls of Hohokam villages. The irrigation system may have reached its physical limits (covering a few hundred square miles along the lower Salt with as many as 190 miles of contemporaneous main canals) during the 13th and early 14th centuries and it has been estimated that 3,000,000 cubic ft (900,000 cubic m) of earth were moved in the excavation of these canals. What does that mean in human terms? To dig the main canals required 3,500 person-years; thus, if 100 people worked one month a year, they would have labored for 420 years just to dig the main canals. And that was only one part of the overall effort. We also estimate that 23 person-years were required to construct the irrigation features for one 20-acre field.[48] Sporadic floods would have demanded repair

112

work and people would have had to periodically clear the canals of silt. Hence to build and maintain the canal network was an enormous and unending undertaking carried out by generation after generation of Hohokam farmers.

During periods of inadequate river flow, it may have been impossible to distribute water to all areas, particularly those near the end of the canal network. Allocation conflicts between villages near the origins and ends of the canal systems would thus have become more likely. Such conflicts, along with the increased coordination required to keep the networks operating smoothly, could have encouraged more centralized management of the networks, placing greater power in the hands of fewer individuals and thus promoting social differentiation within the region. Did such centralization develop and, if so, is there evidence of similar patterns in the northern Southwest?

The growth of large villages
The northern San Juan, the Tucson Basin, and the Phoenix Basin all illustrate another general characteristic of this era, a trend toward increasing village size. Although there was still a considerable range of variation, the average number of rooms and people at settlements in many regions increased markedly beginning in the mid-11th century. Whereas a village of 50–100 was exceptional before AD 1150, such settlements were commonplace after that time. The largest pre-1150 town, Pueblo Bonito with approximately 650 rooms, was approached, if not matched, in size by many settlements in the northern and central Southwest by the late 13th century/early 14th century. At least three settlements in the El Morro Valley of west-central New Mexico were constructed soon after AD 1275–1280 and each included 500 to 1,000 rooms. Evidence from two of these pueblos suggests that construction was rapid and planned, indicating growth in a manner comparable to Betatakin, although on a much larger scale. In the Tucson Basin in southern Arizona, villages may never have approached this size, but settlements with up to 500 rooms are known and large areas are covered by almost continuous distributions of artifacts and other remains of occupation.

Archaeologists refer to this phenomenon as aggregation, the increasing clustering or association of social groups in one location. These expanding communities had to address basic questions such as how to organize cooperative tasks, resolve disputes, and reach community-wide decisions generally. Some kind of social hierarchy was the result. These group hierarchies took on different characteristics depending on the extent to which decision-making authority rotated from group to group – as in the Rio Grande Pueblos where control alternates between the winter and summer moieties – or became embedded within a particular social group such as an elite family or lineage. In both instances there is usually a small group of individuals who hold positions of authority and thus are responsible for the ultimate decisions. But an organizational structure in which authority rotates from one group to another inhibits, but does not prevent, the development of considerable status differences within a community, whereas a permanent structure reinforces and promotes such differences. The archaeological evidence suggests that the Hohokam followed a somewhat different organizational path from the Mogollon and Anasazi as the size of their villages increased.

Lineage, clan, and moiety among the Anasazi and Mogollon. In the Tsegi Canyon region where the Anasazi constructed Betatakin and Kiet Siel, in Mogollon regions such as the Hay Hollow Valley, and elsewhere in eastern and northeastern Arizona, the period from the late 12th century to the 13th century may have witnessed the evolution of the clan, a social unit that bound together previously isolated lineages (groups of people descended from a common ancestor).[49] Among modern western Pueblo peoples of the northern Southwest, descent is typically traced through the female line – grandmother, mother, and daughter. The more inclusive clans comprise several of these lineages and the original or common 'ancestor' is often a totemic plant or animal rather than a person. Thus, among the modern Hopi we find, for example, the Spider clan and the Bear clan.

The ratio of masonry storage rooms and dwellings to kivas is consistent with the hypothesis that clans may have evolved in parts of the Anasazi area by the 12th or 13th centuries. The anthropologist Julian Steward suggested over 50 years ago that a ratio of five or six masonry rooms to one kiva characterized pueblos occupied before about AD 1100, approximately the ratio that one would expect if each lineage typically constructed a kiva and conducted their own ceremonies.[50] During the late 12th and 13th centuries, however, room to kiva ratios increased, with ratios from 15:1 to 25:1 suggesting the possibility that two to four lineages had consolidated into clan units and were participating in group rituals. Although subsequent research has revealed more variation in room to kiva ratios than Steward found, particularly when development in several areas is compared, there nevertheless appears to be a general trend of the type Steward proposed through much of eastern and northeastern Arizona.[51]

In some of the northern and eastern parts of the Pueblo region, the development of moieties rather than clans has been proposed. The division of a society into two halves, or moieties, based on kinship ties, such as the winter and summer separation in Rio Grande Pueblos, is a common organizational structure in communities similar in size to those that developed during this period. Rohn's analysis of architectural patterns at Mug House in Mesa Verde supports the possibility of a dual division within the community. His proposal is based on architectural characteristics of the masonry rooms, including their arrangement and sequence of construction, as well as passageways within the cliff dwelling, similarities and differences between northern and southern sets of kivas, and the two towers at the northern and southern edges of the cliff dwelling.[52] A type of dual division has also been suggested for even earlier Southwestern communities where aggregations of a similar size were characteristic. In Chaco Canyon a wall dividing the plaza of Pueblo Bonito in half and the presence of a Great Kiva on either side of that wall, in addition to the indications of duality in Chacoan cosmology, are possible architectural signs of a moiety organization.[53]

It is significant that villages in the northern San Juan region with evidence of moiety organization are much larger than contemporary villages of the Kayenta or Hay Hollow regions, such as Betatakin and Kiet Siel.[54] The ratio of rooms to kivas also did not increase in the northern San Juan region during the 13th century. Both these characteristics suggest a different, and more inclusive, form of organization in the northern San Juan, where the problems of maintaining cohesion within such large villages would have been more severe.

In contrast to the 13th-century Kayenta and Hay Hollow settlements, villages in the San Juan and Chaco region possessed Great Kivas, and larger towns were surrounded by smaller satellite communities.[55] The larger and more standardized Great Kivas suggest that rituals in the San Juan communities were becoming more inclusive and formalized.[56] Anthropologist Roy Rappaport believes that public ritual performances are important because they 'establish conventional understandings, rules, and norms in accordance with which everyday behavior is supposed to proceed.' Participation conveys the message that the performer is accepting the principles on which the rituals are based. The Great Kivas may thus indicate a greater emphasis on public rituals that establish conventions for proper behavior. Such an emphasis is not surprising given the concurrent evolution of larger villages where increased tensions and conflicts were likely and where cooperation was needed for the village to survive. Also noteworthy is the lack of evidence for any significant degree of social differentiation,[57] indicative of consensual decision making and the fact that ritual knowledge was not associated with any particular social group.

These prehistoric social and ritual patterns match those in modern Pueblo society. Moieties are more typical of eastern Pueblos in the Rio Grande Valley region, while clans are more characteristic of western Pueblo groups like the Hopi. The prehistoric groups of both the Mesa Verde and Chaco Canyon regions have been regarded as more closely tied with subsequent developments in the Rio Grande region, with some scholars hypothesizing that it was to the latter region that Mesa Verde and Chaco groups moved when their homelands were abandoned. In contrast, the Kayenta region appears to have been more closely associated with the later growth of Hopi villages. The evolution of social and ritual differences between Pueblo groups may thus be visible as far back in time as the 12th and 13th centuries.

Administrative hierarchy among the Hohokam. In contrast to the Pueblo region, the Hohokam appear to have solved their organizational problems through greater social differentiation, with some groups having more power and control. The separation of multi-household compounds within a settlement by encircling walls and the increasing physical distances between these compounds suggest more clearly defined and socially distant groups.[58] Suzanne and Paul Fish hypothesize that such distinctions could have developed as a means to allocate prime agricultural land given the limited amounts available and the greater densities of population. They also suggest that larger, multi-household groups would have provided a bigger labor force as the Hohokam struggled to maintain the canal networks.[59]

The high labor demands would have encouraged larger family sizes, and increased competition between individuals to recruit followers and expand the available workforce. These needs may have amplified health problems within the Hohokam population. Limited studies of burials indicate high infant mortality, chronic nutritional stress among the young, and such high rates of anemia among women that many died during childbirth.[60] Leaders who recruited more followers would have reaped better harvests, which could have been one important factor leading to greater social differences.

Changes in Hohokam public architecture reflected and reinforced the new concentration of power in the hands of a small number of people within each canal system.[61] The earlier transition from public ballcourts to platform mounds with restricted access indicates that participation in and control over ritual activities was now confined to a small elite.[62] Perhaps the clearest indication of differential status among Hohokam groups of the Phoenix Basin are the residential compounds on the summits of platform mounds. These compounds were probably inhabited by leaders, who, by controlling the sacred sphere, could enhance and justify their political power. The fact that the mounds needed more labor to construct than could have been provided by the inhabitants of the elevated compounds illustrates the extent of this power. Likewise the relatively high proportion of space allocated to storage within some of the compounds suggests that leaders here attempted to amass surpluses in order to recruit followers and build political alliances.[63] Economic clout may have been an important component of ritual and political power.

The signs of conflict

Despite cooperative building efforts and new types of social bonds, there is indisputable evidence that not everyone in the Southwest loved his or her neighbor. More and more villages became established in nearly inaccessible locations where defense seems to be the only logical explanation for site placement.[64] Although such sites are relatively few in number, they nevertheless represent a significant departure from the previous five or six centuries when ancient Southwesterners almost universally felt free to locate their homes in open, undefendable locations.

114   The *cerros de trincheras* (fortified hills) characteristic of parts of southern Arizona and northern Mexico perhaps best exemplify these new settlements.[65] Situated atop steep and isolated hills or mesas, that require consid-

erable time and effort to ascend, the sites are sometimes shielded by masonry walls and walled entrances with loopholes to provide views of the surrounding area. Terraces constructed on the northern side of hill slopes where there would be protection from the afternoon sun and better moisture conservation emphasize that these were settlements inhabited by regular farmers and not solely refuges during times of conflict. The elevated setting may have had ritual and symbolic importance.[66] Farming and ritual significance, however, do not exclude a defensive function as well, particularly given the absence of such sites during earlier periods.

Sites in similar types of locations and with perimeter walls are known, too, from central Arizona on the perimeter of the Phoenix Basin, and from the Anasazi and Mogollon regions to the north.[67] The frequency of such sites varies greatly from one locality to another, however, as do the characteristics of the individual settlements. In most of these areas, walls or alternative ways of restricting entry are typical. Some of the cliff dwellings characteristic of the northern Southwest, for example, were built in very inaccessible locations. In the case of Mug House, Mesa Verde, about the only important advantage of living in the rockshelter was the ease of defense. As Arthur Rohn has written, 'It would be far more comfortable and sanitary to live in a house on the mesa top near most of the fields. Temperatures in the caves are unpleasantly cool most of the year, and the ... relatively difficult access to the cliff site would ... be a daily inconvenience to the inhabitants.'[68]

Jonathan Haas and Winifred Creamer organized one of the few systematic efforts to study conflict and defense in a single locality.[69] Their research focused on Long House Valley in northeastern Arizona and on nearby localities, including the canyons where Kiet Siel and Betatakin are found. Haas and Creamer found that around AD 1250 the inhabitants of the broader valleys moved from exclusively valley floor settlements into discrete clusters of villages surrounding a central or 'focal' village. These were larger settlements of 75 to 400 rooms, typically with reservoirs, situated on easily defendable hilltops, knolls, or isolated cliffs that provided commanding views of all main access routes into the valley. One settlement, Organ Rock Ruin, sits atop an isolated, high sandstone ledge 600 ft (185 m) above the valley floor and overlooking the major access route into the valley from the north. To reach the site a steep talus slope had to be scaled 'followed by a vertical 15-m (49-ft) climb up steps and hand- and toeholds through a narrow crack in the cliff.'[70] Moreover, no arable land or regular source of water occurs on top of the cliff. Difficulty of access thus took precedence over proximity to water or arable land. There seems to be no rationale for the setting of the site other than defense. 116

Haas and Creamer also believe that the focal villages were located to provide a clear line of sight with other settlements so that the inhabitants could communicate. In the one instance where the sloping side of Black Mesa obstructed the view between two focal settlements, Tower House and Fireside, the Anasazi cut a deep notch in order to create a line of sight.[71] 115

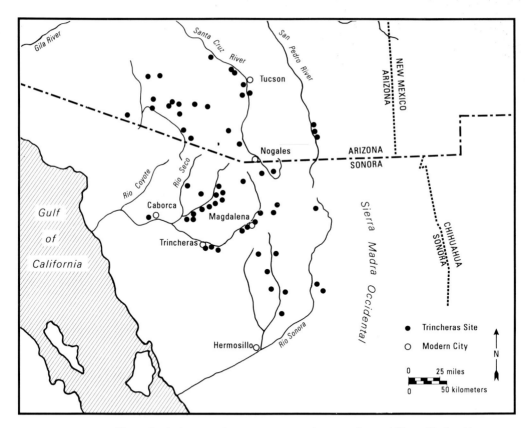

114 *Cerros de trincheras*, settlements constructed on top of steep hills and isolated buttes, have been found in parts of southern Arizona and northern Mexico. Evidence suggests that they were residential, but they may also have been important for defense and ritual.

The settlement changes within the narrower canyons differed from those in the valley, but still demonstrate a concern for defense. While the valley residents established their focal sites, the canyon inhabitants shifted from easily accessible residences on the canyon floor or in caves to other more isolated shelters with difficult approaches. The extreme of inaccessibility is exemplified by a site named Twoozis Kin, or Glass House. Haas and Creamer describe their effort to reach it, which involved calling on the assistance of a specialist rock-climber after their own unsuccessful attempts to find an access route:

> Following a technical climb up through the crack [in the canyon wall] and skirting around the open edge of the cliff face about two-thirds of the way up, he encountered the first hand- and toeholds. He was then able to follow these into the shelter, where he found not a single isolated storeroom but a hidden pueblo of 25 to 30 rooms. There were no signs in the site of anyone ever having visited it or recorded it in the 700 years since it was abandoned in AD 1300.[72]

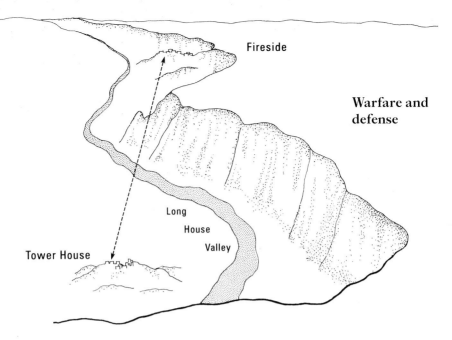

115 The Anasazi of the Long House Valley in northeast Arizona gouged a notch in the escarpment of Black Mesa to allow line-of-sight communication between the villages of Tower House and Fireside.

116 A defensive site in Clear Creek in east-central Arizona, located on an isolated mesa in the middle of the canyon in a manner comparable to sites such as Organ Rock Ruin in Long House Valley.

Conflict and cannibalism

They found the skeletons of a man and a woman, with a child twelve or fourteen years old. Their skulls had been crushed in – and the boys found that the blade of a large stone axe beside them just fitted the dents in the skulls. With the murdered three was a child only a few months old, with the bones of its skull scattered.[73]

This description of the explorations of the Wetherill brothers in the late 19th century illustrates the violence that sometimes characterized life in the ancient Southwest. Quite apart from the location of settlements in defendable settings, there is a wide variety of other evidence for conflict. This includes palisades of wood or stone encircling villages; burned settlements where the complete artifact assemblages and burned and unburied skeletons suggest that the occupants were surprised by the fire; mass graves that include the skeletal parts of several individuals or burned bone; evidence of scalping; kiva and rock art that illustrates combat; and, in a few instances, skeletons with embedded dart or arrow points.[74] Individually none of these discoveries demonstrate widespread warfare; collectively, however, the evidence points to the occurrence of endemic competition and conflict in at least some places, in some time periods.

Some startling recent studies have convincingly demonstrated the very rare occurrence of prehistoric cannibalism. Excavations from the site of 5MTUMR-2346, a small village in Mancos Canyon just south of Mesa Verde National Park, have recovered the remains of 33 individuals from nine deposits in several rooms in the pueblo. All the deposits include the remains of more than one individual, but these were not the typical burials discovered elsewhere in the village, but rather mixed collections of disarticulated and broken bones so fragmentary that reconstruction of any of the skulls was impossible.[75] Careful study by physical anthropologist Timothy White documented abundant evidence of burned bones, cutmarks, chopmarks, polished bones, and fractures and crushing using a hammerstone.[76] Based on such evidence, he argues that the individuals were 'partially or entirely skinned, segmented, roasted, and defleshed … the crania and postcranial skeletal elements were fractured, with a focus on the larger limb-bone shafts. This fracturing is inferred to result from efforts to recover brain and yellow marrow tissue.'[77] The polished bone may have resulted from cooking the bones in ceramic pots in order to extract the bone grease, and other patterns suggest that the spongy bone segments may have been crushed and eaten in bone cakes or incorporated in stews. In short, 'the Anasazi who lived at 5MTUMR-2346 may have killed and eaten their enemies. They themselves may have been killed and eaten by such enemies. Alternatively, the people of a starving pueblo may have slowly consumed friends, relatives, acquaintances, or strangers who had died of starvation.'[78]

Similar behavior has been discovered at least 19 other sites in the Southwest.[79] Alternative hypotheses that might account for these remains, such as ritual behavior or carnivore disturbance, have been examined and consistently found insufficient to explain all aspects of the skeletal remains.

Other evidence supports the idea of increasing conflict in the Southwest during this era (see box p. 150). We should be aware that signs of force or discord may be difficult to observe archaeologically. Aggressive encounters may have been rare or short-lived because, as ethnographers point out, the object of raids may be to acquire food, steal wives, or gain prestige rather than kill one's adversary. Few casualties or weapons would be left behind for the archaeologist to discover. At some of the Kayenta defensive sites the scarcity of nearby sources of water and the considerable distance from fields are consistent with the idea that, if protection was important, it was not needed for long periods of time. Nevertheless, the mere existence or threat of conflict is often a significant social force.[80]

The suggestion of greater conflict raises the obvious question of conflict with whom? For the Long House Valley, Haas believes that the threat was external because of the proximity of defensible settlements and the lines of sight between them.[81] Whether groups in nearby valleys were the primary threat or were themselves allied with Long House Valley against even more distant peoples is unclear. Ethnographic accounts, however, document the frequently shifting relationships of conflict and cooperation even among proximate groups; trading partners one day may be bitter enemies the next.

In nearly all parts of the Southwest, during the period AD 1250–1300, we find more evidence for warfare than in any preceding epoch.[82, 83] Some archaeologists regard the discord as a critical factor in the trend toward aggregation,[84] arguing that groups of people banded together for protection. Conversely, it could be suggested that the concentration of more people in fewer areas created acute shortages, which gave rise to conflict among groups. Whether aggregation is the cause or the effect of conflict, an association between the two is clear. It is worth recalling that earlier pithouse villages situated in inaccessible locations were also often larger than average.

Dénouement in the Four Corners region

No discussion of this period is complete without some consideration of the most debated issue in Southwestern prehistory: abandonments. The residents of Mug House, Cliff Palace, Sand Canyon Pueblo, and other parts of the northern San Juan drainage left their homes, never to return again. In the Kayenta region of northeastern Arizona, the villages in Long House Valley and the cliff dwellings such as Betatakin and Kiet Siel in Navajo National Monument and White House and Antelope House in Canyon de Chelly were deserted at the same time. No Pueblo peoples ever again built homes in southern Utah and Colorado, northeastern Arizona, or northwestern New Mexico.

96,117

Why did these abandonments happen? As with many of the earlier episodes of significant cultural change, fluctuations in rainfall have received considerable emphasis as causal forces during this period. In the northern Southwest, studies of tree-rings revealed a period of significantly below-

117 Antelope House in Canyon de Chelly National Monument was inhabited as early as AD 400–700, but the cliff dwelling was constructed between AD 1140 and 1270. It includes a southern roomblock with about 25 rooms and 4 kivas, and a northern roomblock with fewer rooms and 3 kivas.

average rainfall from AD 1276 to 1299 that is referred to by archaeologists as the 'Great Drought.' The rough association between the drought era and the abandonment of the northern San Juan and many other parts of the northern Southwest, along with the tendency for many of the large sites to be located near permanent sources of water, is often cited as evidence that it was a lack of rainfall that first caused people to aggregate around sources of water and ultimately to leave the area. In the south, it has likewise been suggested that both reduced rainfall in the late 13th century and floods in the early 14th century had a devastating impact on the Hohokam irrigation systems.

Most evidence, however, supports no simple cause-and-effect relationship between these different phenomena. The trend toward aggregation in the mid-13th century, for example, does not coincide with above- or below-average rainfall. Research by Carla Van West has also shown that even during the supposed 'Great Drought' there was enough productive agricultural land to support all of the people living in the northern San Juan.[85] Historic records certainly indicate that droughts could have a devastating impact, but we also know that ancient Southwesterners suffered through many droughts without wholesale abandonments. Although AD 1300 is often cited as the date for the start of abandonments, tree-ring dating consistently shows that construction activity diminished rapidly in the 1270s. The timing of the

'Great Drought' is such that it is more accurate to view it as the proverbial 'straw that broke the camel's back' rather than a calamity that initiated the abandonment process.

It is thus an oversimplification to see climatic change as the primary cause of the abandonments. Such views treat culture change as little more than an automatic human response to environmental stimuli, without recognizing that the people themselves are the central players. We must acknowledge that larger sites may be close to permanent sources of water simply because greater numbers of people living in a single location had greater demands for water. Human impacts on the environment may have also produced degradation that was more significant than normal climatic variation.

In order to better understand the cultural dynamics of the 12th and 13th centuries, we must consider the reasons why individual families would choose to join with others in large towns and why they might leave those towns. Important factors are the significant changes in the social landscape that occurred throughout the period. As local populations grew, access to productive land may have been reduced.[86] As more intensive agriculture was practiced, protecting access rights could have become even more important. These trends may have encouraged greater stability and cohesion among kin units. Residence in larger towns may also have attracted individual families because towns were more effective in protecting access rights, whether through the symbolic messages of impressive architecture or through the greater ability to mobilize large numbers of people should any threat arise.

Once large towns develop, however, mechanisms must exist to keep internal conflict and self-interested households from ripping the towns apart. Despite the development of public architecture and public ritual, these efforts were ultimately unsuccessful in most of the Southwest. As we examine in the following chapters the communities that somehow survived the turmoil of the late 13th century, we must ask whether there were new social mechanisms that allowed many of them to prosper into modern times. That information must then be blended together with a discussion of conflict, climate change, agricultural practice, and demographic change to create a picture that offers a more realistic portrait of the complex nature of human behavior. Occam's Razor – 'It is vain to do with more what can be done with less'[87] – is often invoked as a justification for choosing simple rather than complex explanations. When we study prehistoric human behavior, however, we must recognize that there are no simple answers to the question of why people behaved as they did.

7 · Towns, Mounds, and Kachinas

Abandonments at the end of the 13th century transformed the social landscape of the Southwest. The once vibrant cliff dwellings of the Kayenta and San Juan regions became vacant and mute. The more numerous surrounding settlements, both large and small, on mesa-tops and in other settings were also deserted. Not a single Mogollon or Anasazi inhabited vast areas once densely settled – including all of southern Utah and Colorado and much of northeastern Arizona and northwestern Mexico. Overall, the center of social gravity shifted decidedly to the south and east, with the Phoenix Basin continuing to be a key region and the Rio Grande Valley, the Zuni region of west-central New Mexico, and the Casas Grandes area of northern Mexico evolving into important centers. The Hopi area, once on the southern edges of the Anasazi territory, became isolated in the northwestern corner of the Pueblo world. This redistribution of people was simply one aspect of a complex process of metamorphosis that affected almost all the Southwest during the late 13th and 14th centuries.

Even in the southern and eastern areas where overall population grew, the number of inhabited villages actually dropped as the local people and any newcomers coalesced into large towns. Some of these towns were no larger than Cliff Palace or Sand Canyon Pueblo, but others approached a dimension that matched, and in many cases exceeded, the largest settlements of the preceding millennia. The greater number of people living in some locales meant more mouths to feed, more people to organize, more conflicts to resolve, or, from the point of view of aspiring leaders, more allies to recruit and more labor to exploit.

Community cycles: boom and bust in the Rio Grande Valley

When we examine a small region, such as the Rio Grande Valley, it becomes clear just how intermittent and episodic was the pattern of coalescence characteristic of the late 13th century and after. So far there has been little mention in this book of the prehistory of the Rio Grande, a neglect that must seem odd to anyone who has visited the numerous pueblos of that region. Despite the presence of one of the few large rivers in the Southwest that carries water throughout the year, the valley was thinly populated before about AD 1000. Human numbers grew during the next two centuries, but Anasazi villages remained scattered in comparison with neighboring Anasazi and Mogollon areas. That pattern changed, however, in the late 12th and early 13th centuries as people moved into the area from the west and northwest and their numbers were augmented by indigenous population growth. The somewhat later pattern of development in the Rio Grande Valley is also shown by the late rise of pueblo architecture. By the end of the 13th century, pueblos with 10–50 rooms were unexceptional and a few had 100–200 rooms or more. Sometime during the 14th century, many areas of the Rio Grande Valley witnessed an even greater increase in population, but the exact timing of this growth varies throughout the Rio Grande region.

Yet between these phases of expansion and coalescence there were puzzling episodes of abandonment. Take Pot Creek Pueblo, near Taos in northern New Mexico, eventually a 250–300-room settlement loosely arranged around a central plaza with a large kiva.[1] Anasazi settlers built a few rooms in the 1260s, many more in the 1270s, scarcely any during the 1280s, and none at all in the 1290s. They then renewed their building activity in the 1300s, an effort that continued into the next decade at a rate suggesting that new groups moved into the pueblo. By the 1320s Pot Creek had been abandoned, less than 70 years after it had first been settled.

Two similar cycles of expansion and decline characterized the occupation of Arroyo Hondo, an even larger pueblo located about 4.3 miles south of modern-day Santa Fe, along a tributary canyon of the Rio Grande. Analysis of the tree-ring dates shows that the initial settlers built at least a single roomblock by AD 1315 and then over the next 15 years quickly erected one of the largest pueblos anywhere in the Southwest, ultimately 1,200 two-story rooms distributed among 24 roomblocks arranged to define 13 plazas of roughly similar size.[2] This precipitous growth was followed by an even more rapid decline. By the mid-1330s the pueblo was almost, if not completely, deserted. A second cycle of growth and decline commenced during the 1370s and 1380s when a group of new residents initiated a second but much smaller pueblo of 200 single-story rooms. They stayed until at least AD 1410, when a devastating fire destroyed much of the pueblo, incinerating racks of stored corn cobs.[3]

These relatively short-lived occupations by large numbers of people, along with the rapid nature of both growth and decline and evidence that groups cooperated in the construction of several roomblocks, show how fluid the social landscape was in the 14th and early 15th centuries. People moved together, *en masse*, in a manner similar to some of the earlier population shifts in the middle of the 12th century. Groups who once formed communities of smaller, discrete villages, joined others to form new, larger pueblos for short periods of time. The somewhat different dates for the growth and decline of Pot Creek Pueblo and Arroyo Hondo suggest that this social fluidity lasted for a century or more. Many groups must have traveled considerable distances. For example, over 125 miles separates the Mesa

118

Verde of southwestern Colorado from the nearest areas in northeastern Arizona or northwestern New Mexico where Anasazi settlement continued at the beginning of the 14th century. Such unprecedented journeys would not have been made without preparation, provisions, and prayer offerings.

Farming, food, and famine?

Why did people abandon sites like Arroyo Hondo, leaving behind the hundreds of rooms they had labored for years to construct? One reason is that inhabitants of these larger settlements faced greater difficulties in accumulating sufficient food.

Despite the presence of a large, perennial river, agriculture in the Rio Grande Valley is not without its risks. Average annual rainfall is below the minimum required for maize at all but the highest elevations, and growing seasons at those upper elevations are shorter than the 120 days maize needs. To minimize the risk of crop failure, Anasazi settlers adopted a diverse range of agricultural practices. Irrigated fields along the Rio Grande were complemented by fields in upland regions in which a variety of water and soil conservation methods – check dams, terraces, gridded fields with stone borders between individual plots, and stone walls to direct run-off to the plots – were employed to maximize soil moisture. Yet we know that these techniques were not always sufficient, as studies of the food remains and burials at Arroyo Hondo show.

Even the best agricultural land around Arroyo Hondo was not very productive. Probably no more than 400–600 people could have been fed during the average year, and it would have been difficult to accumulate adequate reserves in good years to allow everyone to survive when harvests fell short in consecutive bad years. The recovery by archaeologists of starvation foods such as cattails, cholla cactus, and grass seeds indicates that the residents of Arroyo Hondo did in fact face periods of hunger.[4] These famines caused many residents to suffer from growth problems or afflictions such as iron deficiency (anemia), infections, and fractures. About 15 percent of the people had bowed long bones, a product of periodic or endemic malnutrition. Infant and child mortality was very high – 26 percent died before reaching their first birthday and 45 percent before the age of five. Average life expectancy for all inhabitants of Arroyo Hondo was only 16.6 years, the shortest period discovered for any group of prehistoric Southwestern people.[5] Life expectancy was so low and infant mortality so high that it undoubtedly hindered the functioning of the community.[6]

The abrupt florescence and decline of large settlements such as Arroyo Hondo and Pot Creek Pueblo also typified many other areas of the northern Southwest during the 14th and early 15th centuries. In some cases, growth of towns was associated with a rise in the number of people, as in the Rio Grande Valley, but elsewhere population often declined overall. In the Cibola region of west-central New Mexico the ancestors of the Zuni reached

118 Arroyo Hondo in northern New Mexico is a large 1200-room pueblo with 24 roomblocks arranged around 13 plazas. Located just south of Santa Fe, the first cycle of construction began in AD 1315, but occupation may have ended by the 1330s. A second construction episode was initiated in the 1370s and 1380s and ended about AD 1410.

a peak population of *c.* 9300 in 17 pueblo towns near the end of the 13th century. Yet only 6,500 people remained in 10–11 towns in the mid-14th century, possibly followed by an even more rapid drop to 900 people in the last half of the 14th century, and then a subsequent recovery.[7] The growth of large towns was thus not necessarily a product of rising population levels.

Nor were all large towns short-lived. The Hopi region of northeastern Arizona witnessed a striking rise in the size of individual settlements in the late 13th century as groups from surrounding areas moved into the region. Some of the larger towns such as Awatovi and Oraibi housed as many as 500 to 1,000 people and, more importantly, some of them remained major settlements for several hundred years. Awatovi was a thriving community when the Spanish entered the Southwest in the 16th century and remained so until the first few years of the 18th century. The Hopi still inhabit Oraibi today, the longest continuously occupied settlement in the United States.

Why did some communities endure while others collapsed? Although successes and failures at harvest time are part of the answer, conflict between settlements must have played its part as well.

Warfare and defense

Ethnographers have noted there is considerable evidence that conflict was once a much more important component of Pueblo life. For example, in oral traditions village defense is often given as the reason for admitting new groups to Hopi settlements:

> The Kokop people are said to have reached Oraibi after they had formerly lived in a home situated far to the northwest. At first Matcito refused to admit them to his pueblo, so they circled to the south of the mesa and made a temporary settlement there. From time to time their leaders beseeched Matcito to allow them to move into the village, offering to be his 'hands' (warriors), but the chief remained obdurate. In revenge, the head man of the Kokops secretly sent word to the Chimwava, huge men with gigantic feet, supposedly the worst enemies of the Hopi, inviting them to make a raid on Oraibi. Soon after, the people on the mesa were horrified to find a large host of the dreaded Chimwava marching upon

119 Contiguous roomblocks grouped around central courtyards such as Plaza G at Arroyo Hondo restricted access to the pueblo. Typical was an arrangement in which the builders left only a single narrow passage between two of the roomblocks.

120 Upper-story pueblo rooms could only be entered by climbing ladders like these at a historic Hopi village.

their town. Matcito gathered his men, but realizing that his forces were inadequate, he remembered the Kokops' promises and sent word that the clan would be allowed to reside in Oraibi if it would help beat off the invaders.[8]

Archaeological evidence supports the case for conflict in prehispanic times. In the late 13th and early 14th centuries village plans were increasingly designed in terms of defense. Roomblocks were built at right angles to each other to form open areas or plazas inside the pueblo. Such plazas occur at Arroyo Hondo and Pot Creek Pueblo, as well as hundreds of other pueblos throughout the northern Southwest. Narrow passages restricted access to the plazas.[9] Ground-floor rooms could be entered only using ladders placed in openings in the roof. An individual standing outside the pueblo was thus confronted with solid masonry walls several feet in height.[10] Even if one gained entry to the plaza, the ladders required for further access could be quickly raised from above, providing an additional barrier.

119

120

The Spanish found the plaza-oriented village plan an effective impediment during their battles with Pueblo groups. Coronado's exploration of the Southwest in 1540 almost ended during his attempt to storm the first pueblo he encountered, the town of Hawikuh in the Zuni area. The Hawikuhans initially resisted by retreating to the rooftops of their houses: 'The people who were on the top for defense were not hindered in the least from doing us whatever injury they were able. As for myself, they knocked me down to the ground twice with countless great stones which they threw down from above, and if I had not been protected by the very good headpiece which I wore, I think that the outcome would have been bad for me.'[11]

In earlier times the towns would have been protecting themselves against other Anasazi and Mogollon groups, rather than European intruders. Several other pieces of evidence support the case for internecine strife. A few of the large towns were in fact built in highly defensible locations. Best known of these is another pueblo of the Zuni region, Atsinna in El Morro National Monument, a pueblo with 750–1,000 rooms that sits atop Inscription Rock where Oñate and other explorers recorded their presence by carving names and dates in the face of the cliff. Other settlements had wells dug in the central plaza rather than in unprotected territory outside.[12] Skeletal remains show an increase in trauma and violent deaths during this period, including evidence of scalping.[13] Some sites, such as Arroyo Hondo and Casas Grandes in northern Mexico, were severely burnt.[14] And we also have signs that Anasazi and Mogollon settlements were clustered together for defense, with considerable gaps – of tens and sometimes hundreds of miles – left between each cluster. The Hopi, Little Colorado River, and Cibola regions are perhaps the clearest examples of this type of distribution, but there were similar clusters, separated by smaller distances, in the Rio Grande area as well.[15] Both village plans and intra- and inter-regional settlement distributions could thus be explained as efforts to increase protection from outsiders.

Ancestors, clouds, and kachina ritual

Plazas were not simply an architectural effort to restrict access to the pueblo. Some Anasazi and Mogollon people had always used plaza areas for a variety of domestic activities such as food preparation, but during this period we also see the first evidence that plazas became the setting for the public kachina dances that are so well known from historic times.

As discussed in Chapter 1, kachinas feature prominently in modern-day western Pueblo (Hopi, Zuni, and Acoma) beliefs and ritual. Kachinas are ancestral spirits that act as messengers between the people and their gods. They also bring rain, themselves forming clouds summoned annually to the villages.[16]

Kachinas are present on earth only half of the year, approximately from winter solstice to summer solstice, after which they return to the underworld through the *sipapu* in the San Francisco Peaks, the entrance through which humans first emerged from the underworld. Individuals dressed in costumes that include a mask impersonate the kachinas during their time on earth, performing a variety of group dances. The Hopi believe that when the impersonator wears the kachina masks, he (and it is always a male) becomes empowered with the characteristics of the spirit being represented and should therefore be regarded as sacred. There are a variety of different types of kachinas and kachina societies among the Hopi, and all individuals are initiated into one of these societies.

121 A male wearing an intricate feather headdress and a kilt and sash carries two prayer-sticks or *pahos* in his right hand, and a small pot in his left hand in this 15th-century kiva mural from Pottery Mound near Albuquerque. The feathers on *pahos* and other objects are common in Pueblo ritual and are significant in conveying prayers to Pueblo deities.

122 ABOVE Public kachina dances, such as this Niman ceremony by the Hemis kachinas at the Hopi pueblo of Shungopavi in 1901, are one of the most important and vibrant elements of Pueblo ritual.

123, 124 Hopi artisans carve wooden kachina dolls to educate their children about the many different kachinas that are important in Pueblo ritual. Kachinas are spirits who serve as emissaries between the people and their deities. From the winter solstice to the summer solstice they live in the upper world and then return to the underworld for the remainder of the year.

Kachina ritual as it is conducted today requires large, public spaces for 122–124,131 group dances, and plazas are the typical setting. Plazas, as we have seen, developed in the late 13th and early 14th centuries, and there are other changes at this time – particularly in ceramic decorative styles and the introduction of kiva murals – suggesting that modern Pueblo rituals had their origin during this period.

125 A Fourmile polychrome bowl from Homol'ovi I in east-central Arizona.

As regards ceramics, in the first half of the 13th century, the Rio Grande Valley, the Cibola and Little Colorado regions, the Hopi area, and the Mogollon Rim country all quickly came to share a similar style of vessel decoration despite the considerable distances between each area.[17] That style, a radical departure from those of earlier periods, was characterized by birds and human figures in addition to geometric designs, by asymmetric patterns, and by a change in the focus of decoration from the walls of bowls to the center. Vessel color ranged from yellow to orange to red, with designs painted in both black and red. 125–127

Patricia Crown studied the representational forms on such vessels and she concludes that most are symbols of the earth, sun, weather phenomena, or

126 Some polychrome pottery, such as these Jeddito black-on-yellow vessels, was made in the Hopi region and traded widely throughout the northern Southwest, but similar design styles can be found on pottery made in more distant areas.

fertility. The commonest icon is the snake or serpent, often depicted using elongated triangles with hooks (fangs) at the apex, an eye inside the triangle, and a curving horn or plume emanating from the back of the triangle.[18] Pueblo groups today believe that the horned serpent controls flooding and rain and both the icon and its interpretation are reminiscent of Quetzalcoatl, the plumed serpent of native Mesoamerican religions. Crown suggests that the serpent and other representational symbols express and reinforce concepts of the universe, afterlife, weather control and fertility that were central to the religious beliefs of the Southwestern societies.

The centrality of these concepts is supported by the occurrence of the symbols in a variety of contexts other than ceramic vessels. Archaeologists have discovered similar patterns of decoration painted on the walls of a few 14th- and early 15th-century kivas at half a dozen pueblos in the Little Colorado River Valley, the Hopi region, and the Rio Grande Valley.[19] Several layers of murals are sometimes present, a result of the annual or seasonal replastering of kiva walls typical of certain ceremonies, a practice recorded among some historic-period Pueblo groups. At Awatovi and Kawaika-a in the Hopi region, the archaeologist Watson Smith recovered fragments of more than 200 individual murals from approximately 20 kivas. Smith believes that the painted designs supplemented, and sometimes substituted for, the wooden altars characteristic of Hopi kiva rituals when they were last

121,128–130

127 Associated with the development of kachina ritual was the increasing appearance of polychrome vessels that were red, orange, or yellow in color with black, white, and red designs (see also ill. 126). Many of these vessels continued the tradition of symmetrical, geometric patterns, but asymmetric and representational designs became more common.

observed by outsiders in the early 20th century.[20] These murals not only contrast with the rare examples of earlier kiva decorations – dominated by simple geometric designs – but also illustrate a greater variety of subjects than those on contemporary ceramic vessels, including plants, animals, anthropomorphs, and altars. Perhaps the single most significant motifs are the anthropomorphs with features characteristic of the kachinas of historic Pueblo groups.

The kiva murals, the rapid appearance of the new decorative style on ceramics, the introduction of large plazas, and changes in burial practices all suggest that Pueblo ritual was transformed during the late 13th and 14th centuries in the northern Southwest. Among the most significant changes was the development or elaboration of kachina ritual. Some scholars believe that kachina ritual provided a sort of social glue, bonding together people within a pueblo because everyone must cooperate for the ceremonies to be conducted properly, and membership in kachina societies crosscuts the discrete and potentially divisive clans and lineages. Certainly the public nature of the kachina dances in the open plazas suggests an increased emphasis on public affirmation of conventions for proper behavior. Kachina rituals helped reinforce the norms of social behavior. Such an emphasis in these late prehispanic times would not be surprising given the concurrent evolution of larger and socially more diverse villages where increased tensions and con-

128 ABOVE Kiva mural painted in the Fourmile/Jeddito decorative style, from the prehistoric Hopi village of Awatovi.

129 BELOW Anthropomorphs were commonly illustrated in rock art from the 14th century through to the 16th century, such as these two figures from Petroglyph National Monument just outside Albuquerque. The figure to the left wears a *tableta*, a terraced board with painted designs common in many Pueblo rituals. The figure on the right stands on the back of an unidentifiable animal.

Kiva murals and rock art

130 BELOW Kiva mural from the prehistoric Hopi village of Kawaika-a, showing a confrontation between two individuals. To the left is a victim pierced by an arrow or spear and to the right is the victor carrying a white shield. These designs formed a continuous panel in the corner of a room as illustrated in the smaller drawing below.

Corner

flicts were likely and where cooperative behavior was needed for the village to survive.

Another noteworthy aspect of the archaeological evidence of kachinas, that contrasts somewhat with the historic focus of kachina ritual, is the depiction of shields and hostile encounters in a few of the kiva murals. Some of these simply illustrate two figures confronting each other, but in one mural from a kiva at Kawaika-a, 'the ultimate act of warfare is very realisti-   130 cally portrayed, for here the victorious champion, with shield borne before him, stands over the vanquished foe, who has fallen backward, pierced by an arrow or spear.'[21] The particular kachinas most likely depicted in early kachina murals and rock art are also associated with warfare in modern Pueblo ritual, often sanctifying warfare (in some oral traditions kachinas assist Pueblo groups during conflicts, for example) or commemorating important encounters.[22] Thus, kachinas initially may have had a dual role as warriors as well as rainmakers. To propose that both increased cooperation and increased conflict characterized the 14th and early 15th centuries in the northern Southwest may appear contradictory, but these patterns are not irreconcilable. A greater emphasis on ritual and cooperation within villages is often associated with social tensions between villages or regions; an emphasis on internal unity is a logical counterpart of the risk of threat from others.

Green stones for red feathers: trade and elites in the Southwest

Trade in a variety of goods demonstrates the strong and multifaceted relationships between regions, in combination with the ties suggested by similarities in ceramic decoration with kiva murals. Turquoise, parrot feathers, cotton and cotton cloth, shell, buffalo hides, obsidian, and pottery are a few of the many items exchanged by the ancient Southwesterners. Certain groups specialized in the production of particular goods. Inhabitants of settlements along the Little Colorado River near the modern town of Winslow, for example, may have specialized in cotton farming, trading either raw cotton or textiles for other commodities. The long, 172-day average growing season around Winslow would have provided an excellent environment for cotton cultivation as long as the Little Colorado River provided sufficient irrigation water. Plant remains from two of the pueblos, Homol'ovi II and III, demonstrate that cotton was a primary agricultural plant, close to maize in importance, and more abundant than in any other area of the Southwest.[23] Although cotton was grown elsewhere, including the gravel mulch fields of the Rio Grande Valley,[24] the residents of the Homol'ovis and the Hopi villages may have been the primary providers of raw cotton and finished textiles; we certainly know that the Hopi played that role when the Spanish arrived in the 16th century (see box p. 170).[25]

131 A 19th-century Hopi kachina doll.

132 Kiva mural from the prehistoric Hopi village of Kawaika-a, showing frogs, fish, and ceramic bowls. One bowl is filled with cotton bolls.

Cotton, clouds, and kachinas

Our knowledge of cotton cultivation in the Southwest in the late 19th and 20th centuries contrasts sharply with archaeological information and with early Spanish observations. By the time that in-depth anthropological studies of the Pueblos began in the late 19th century, European-introduced wools had largely displaced cotton, but earlier there is every indication that it was an integral part of the lives of the native peoples of the Southwest. The Spanish observed that most Southwesterners grew some cotton, with the exception of the Zuni, and found prolific trade in cotton textiles. These fabrics were valued enough and traded over distances large enough that a native inhabitant of Santa Barbara, California, told the Spanish in 1579 of a land to the north (probably the Hopi region) where the people raised cotton for clothing.[26] Southwestern textiles have been recovered from archaeological sites in California and in the Mississippi Valley.[27] When Antonio de Espejo journeyed from Awatovi to other Hopi villages to the west on 22 April 1582, one member of his group, Diego Pérez de Luxán, wrote that they traveled two leagues (roughly 6 miles), 'one of them through cotton fields,'[28] an observation that should not be surprising given the ubiquity of cotton seeds recovered from the two pueblos, Homol'ovi II and III, in the nearby Little Colorado River Valley. As Espejo and other Spanish explorers visited pueblos, particularly those in the west, they were given large quantities of cotton blankets:

> ... the chiefs ... of the province, seeing the good treatment and the gifts that I gave, assembled between them more than four thousand cotton *mantas*, some colored and some white, towels with tassels at the ends, blue and green ores, which they use to color the *mantas* and many other things.[29]

At the Hopi Pueblo of Walpi alone:

> More than one thousand souls came, laden with very fine earthen jars containing water, and with rabbits, cooked venison, tortillas, atole (corn flour gruel), and beans, cooked calabashes, and quantities of corn and pinole, so that, although our friends were many

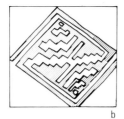

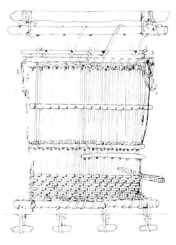

133 Tunic, kilt and textile designs from Awatovi and Kawaika-a kiva murals. The dot-in-square pattern is common in Mesoamerican textiles and was produced using a tie-dye technique.

and we insisted our friends should not bring so much, heaps of food were left over. Then they presented us with six hundred pieces of figured and white cloth and small pieces of their garments.[30]

These accounts, perhaps somewhat exaggerated, nevertheless show that the cultivation of cotton and the weaving of *mantas* must have consumed considerable time and effort and that such fabrics were integral to trade and other social relationships. In addition to symbolizing elite status, cotton also was central to ritual. The link between cotton and kachinas is a particularly strong one.[31] The development of the kachina cult and the beginning of extensive cultivation of cotton in the northern Southwest roughly coincide, both falling in the late 13th or early 14th century. The kiva murals from Awatovi and Kawaika-a depict bolls of cotton in ceramic bowls and intricate kilts and sashes almost certainly made from cotton. When the Hopi prepare a corpse for burial, a cotton mask in placed on their face to make the body light;[32] the cotton has been referred to as a cloud mask[33] which 'plainly identifies the dead with the Kachina.'[34] Cotton, clouds, and kachinas seem to be linked conceptually.

Ceiling Beam

Permanent Upper Bar

Tension Bar
Warp Bar
Warp Selvage

Shed Rod

String Loops
Heddle Rod   Heddle
Batten

Weft
Weft Selvage
Warp Selvage
Cloth Beam
Floor Level
Loom Anchor

134, 135 ABOVE A vertical loom of the type used in kivas. LEFT Spinner and weaver in a Hopi kiva, c. 1902.

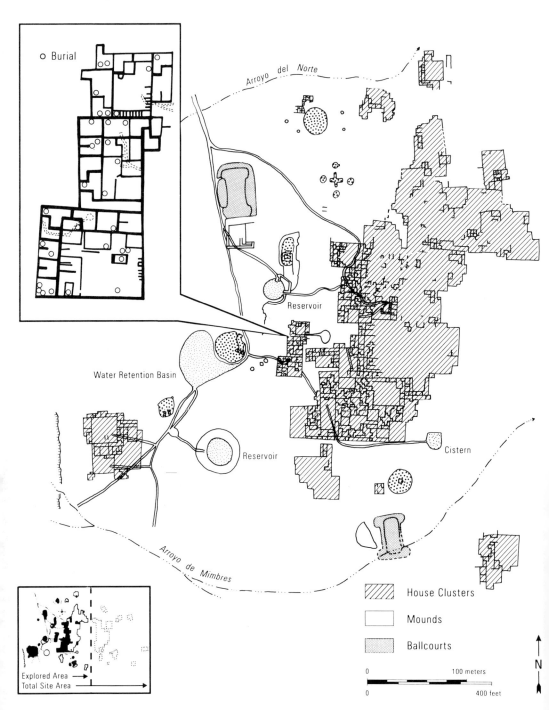

Burial

Arroyo del Norte

Reservoir

Water Retention Basin

Reservoir

Cistern

Arroyo de Mimbres

House Clusters

Mounds

Ballcourts

Explored Area
Total Site Area

0   100 meters

0   400 feet

N

136 Casas Grandes in northern Mexico was the largest prehistoric settlement in the Southwest with over 2,000 pueblo rooms. Although domestic architecture was more similar to the Pueblo region, the ritual architecture of mounds and ballcourts has stronger parallels to the Hohokam region and to Mesoamerica.

The Casas Grandes polity

The clearest picture of the range and amounts of goods being traded among Southwestern communities comes from northern Mexico. Roughly 150 miles south of the U.S.–Mexican border lies the spectacular pueblo of Casas Grandes (also known as Paquimé), once the nucleus of probably the most developed and centralized polity in the prehistoric Southwest. Prior to the growth of Casas Grandes, the people of this region had lived in small, agricultural villages. Here, in the early 13th century,[35] people began building a unique settlement that differs in many ways from most Southwestern pueblos. A contemporaneous population explosion also occurred in the surrounding hinterland.[36] The town, occupied for several centuries, reached its zenith between *c.* AD 1300 and 1400, with remodeling of residential areas and construction of most of the ceremonial mounds and public space.[37]

136,137

Casas Grandes is noteworthy in several ways. With over 2,000 pueblo rooms in several discrete roomblocks constructed of adobe, the settlement was the largest that ever existed in the prehistoric Southwest, its resident population numbering in the low thousands.[38] Public ritual architecture included at least 18 morphologically unique, earthen and stone mounds concentrated in the northwestern part of the village. These ranged from a roughly circular platform, 13 ft (4 m) high with a stone façade and staircase,

137 Casas Grandes was partially excavated between 1958 and 1961 by the Amerind Foundation. At its height between AD 1300 and 1400 the town was the center of a polity about 40 to 70 miles across. The abundance of shell, copper, turquoise, and macaws and elaborate burials suggest that control of trade by an elite social class was an important reason for the growth of Casas Grandes.

to irregular shapes that in at least one case the excavator, Charles Di Peso, suggests depicted a bird.[39] The Paquimans also constructed three ballcourts, all of which are I-shaped in a manner typical of ballcourts to the south and unlike those previously discussed in the Hohokam region of southern Arizona. The town's water supply system is unique in the New World. A canal network carried water from warm springs 2.2 miles to the northwest. The main canal fed into a reservoir with a settling tank from which small, stone-lined channels took water into the roomblocks; an outflowing sewer and ditch systems removed fluids from the rooms. All of these characteristics suggest a populous, well-planned, and integrated town.

It is the artifacts and animal remains, however, that above all distinguish Casas Grandes from its contemporaries and demonstrate its role as a trade center. Excavations uncovered a total of 322 scarlet macaws (*Ara macao*), an exquisitely colorful parrot native to the humid Gulf Coast region of Mexico, 81 green military macaws (*Ara militaris*) native to the forested regions of southern Sonora and Chihuahua, and 100 macaws that could not be identified as to species.[40] These are tremendous numbers given that fewer than 200 scarlet macaws are known from all other Southwestern sites, of all time periods combined, and that only a portion of Casas Grandes was excavated. Even more infrequent elsewhere, but abundant in several plazas at Casas Grandes, are breeding and nesting boxes – sets of contiguous adobe compartments that were covered with mats and had round, doughnut-shaped stone circles with plugs that served as front entrances to the pens. The pens, along with the presence of macaw eggs, nestlings, and birds of all ages confirm that Casas Grandes was one of the northernmost breeding locations currently known. The Paquimans also bred turkeys. Pens for those birds along with 344 skeletons were discovered during excavations.

138,139

138 Plaza 3–12 at Casas Grandes with two rows of macaw nesting boxes. Nesting boxes were made of adobe, with doughnut-shaped stone entrances and pestle-shaped stone plugs.

139 Macaw depicted in rock art, Petroglyph National Monument.

At Casas Grandes and at earlier settlements in the Mimbres region, the ancient Southwesterners sacrificed the macaws in the late winter or spring (the vast majority died between 10 and 13 months of age) and then interred the complete skeleton, probably after plucking the long tail feathers that would have been fully formed by spring time.[41] Padre Luis Velarde described a similar practice in 1716: '... at San Xavier del Bac [near Tucson] and neighboring rancherías, there are many macaws, which the Pimas raise because of the beautiful feathers of red and of other colors ... which they strip from these birds in the spring, for their adornment.'[42] The tail feathers would have been used for adornment, as noted by Velarde, or for ritual purposes; feathers have been described as 'the most basic and widely used class of objects in the entire field of Pueblo ritual.'[43] Pueblo people offer prayers by making *pahos*, sticks with feathers attached, and depositing these at shrines and other locations, and they also affix feathers to many ceremonial paraphernalia. (Mimbres bowls from the 11th and 12th centuries depict prayer sticks with attached feathers comparable to those that Pueblo peoples use today, providing a clear prehistoric analog to modern ritual practices.[44]) They place feathers on other objects – from peach trees to rock art[45] – to enhance fertility or to bring rain. Feathers were thus conduits through which petitions could be conveyed to the supernaturals. Colors also symbolize directions among the Pueblos, perhaps adding to the significance of macaw feathers.

121

Casas Grandes was undoubtedly a major link in a trading network for macaw and turkey feathers that encompassed much of northern Mexico and the Southwestern United States.[46] Trade in turquoise was also important: in 1536 Cabeza de Vaca reported that the peoples of northern Mexico traded parrot feathers to people who lived in large houses to the north in exchange for green stones.[47] These 'green stones' almost certainly were turquoise which occurs naturally in parts of Arizona and New Mexico. Turquoise was abundant at Casas Grandes, with 5,895 pieces weighing 4.6 lbs recovered during excavations,[48] but these amounts are not as unusual as are the high frequency of macaws.

Di Peso did find shell in extraordinary amounts at Casas Grandes, almost four million items (counting individual beads) weighing 1.5 tons, all produced from species native to the west coast of Mexico. Prior to the 13th century, the Paquimans buried much of the shell as grave offerings, but later we find almost all of it in three rooms, two in a single roomblock, together with a large concentration of copper artifacts. This suggests that there was some type of central control over the acquisition and distribution of shell and copper, and that a few individuals were able to accumulate significant wealth. The discovery of almost 700 copper artifacts throughout the site and the presence of copper ore indicate that some manufacturing occurred at Casas Grandes. As with the scarlet macaws, copper items are certainly known from more northerly sites, but occur in much lower frequencies and without any indication of manufacturing.

Casas Grandes was the center of a polity roughly 40–70 miles across in northern and northwestern Chihuahua. Evidence of macaw breeding, similar ballcourts, and a unique type of pottery, referred to as Ramos Polychrome, produced at Casas Grandes tie this region together. None of the villages in the hinterland approach the scale of Casas Grandes – all are smaller and none have any mounds[49] – indicating that Casas was at the apex of the political and religious organization.

There seems to have been an elite class at Casas Grandes which accumulated and traded these macaw, shell, and copper goods and was buried in the elaborate tombs. Copper, turquoise, and certain types of cotton cloth symbolized high status in parts of the New World when Europeans arrived, and it was often the more powerful elites who regulated access to these materials.[50] Coronado and de Niza's accounts from their travels in northern Mexico illustrate similar patterns.[51]

One mound, at Casas Grandes, seems to have functioned as an elaborate tomb for a few individuals, a significant contrast with normal burials at the site which were in simple pits beneath plaza or dwelling floors.[52] At the base of the ground lay the remains of two men and a woman held, except for their skulls, in unusually large Ramos Polychrome vessels and accompanied by a musical rasp made from a human long bone, a necklace of human phalanges, and other objects.[53] The burials were disarticulated, indicating that the bodies had been laid out elsewhere while their soft parts decomposed, again

140

140 A Ramos Polychrome vessel from the pueblo of Casas Grandes. Bold designs painted with red and black paint on a cream or yellow paste characterize these wares, the majority of which were produced at Casas Grandes (with some production at nearby settlements) and traded as far north as southern Arizona and New Mexico.

a departure from the typical mortuary practices at the settlement. Together these patterns evoke an image of a privileged social class who controlled long-distance trade, lived in distinctive residences, and were buried in special tombs.

Scholars commonly acknowledge the presence of such hierarchies in Mesoamerica, but in the Southwest most have argued that Pueblo people were highly egalitarian, with minimal differences in social and political status. They highlight the likelihood of considerable variation in harvests from year to year which they believe would have hindered individual accumulation of food or such items as turquoise and shell. They argue that minimal differences in the amounts of grave goods found with burials support this assertion.

Others have argued, however, that the magnitude of population movement during the late 13th and 14th centuries created opportunities for pioneer groups to control the most productive land, while late arriving groups may have been forced to cultivate less productive tracts. Those who controlled the best lands may have been able to harvest corn more consistently or grow crops such as cotton, providing an advantage in trade with other groups.[54] Hopi oral traditions describe such a process of land allocation as new groups were allowed to settle in existing villages; disparities still exist today in the quality of agricultural land controlled by different Hopi lineages and clans.[55] These disparities may have been enhanced by the inevitable rise in tensions and the need for cooperation whenever larger numbers of people live together. These needs may promote the development

141 The 'big house' at Casa Grande in 1890, Casa Grande National Monument. The best preserved of the Hohokam 'big houses,' this massive adobe structure was four stories high and was constructed in a single episode by a sizeable labor force. It served as a residence for the higher status groups and may also have been used as an astronomical observatory.

of formal offices held by individuals who have the authority to make and enforce decisions. Also, in many of these societies differential ritual education, such as knowledge of the proper ways to conduct various ceremonies, may have been significant in creating and reinforcing social and economic differences, particularly when people believed such knowledge could influence the weather and thus agricultural success. Social distinctions based on knowledge, rather than wealth, will be less likely to produce significant differences in grave goods, making them harder to detect with only archaeological evidence.

Hohokam big houses

Elsewhere the development of a more privileged class of people is most evident in the Phoenix Basin. It is true that for most Hohokam people the basic fabric of life remained much as before – built around irrigation canals, (a declining use of) ballcourts, and platform mounds, now with residential compounds built on their summits. Nevertheless, we also find evidence for the largest towns ever seen in the Phoenix Basin, far-flung trading contacts, specialized production of particular goods, and large public building projects. The town of Los Muertos, for example, was inhabited by as many as 1,000 people living in 30 different compounds. New polychrome and yellow-ware ceramics appear, similar to, and in some cases traded from, the north, including Jeddito black-on-yellow pottery produced in the Hopi region. Spindle whorls for spinning cotton and possibly yucca fiber commonly occur at platform mounds suggesting that the production of textiles may have been in the hands of specialists, possibly controlled by the elites who lived atop the mounds.

Perhaps of greatest significance is the construction of massive tower-like structures or 'big houses.' At least three of these adobe buildings are known to have existed in the Hohokam region, but the complete base of only one has survived at the site of Casa Grande near Phoenix. Originally this tower 141 had four stories and was constructed on top of an artificially filled first story (thus resembling a platform mound). The residents of Casa Grande erected the structure in a single episode, requiring the procurement of nearly 600 roof beams, each about 13 ft (4 m) long, from woodland areas over 60 miles away, and the excavation of over 1,440 cubic yd (1,100 cubic m) of soil to make the adobe walls. It would have taken at least 15–20 families working full-time for three months to erect the building.[56] In addition to serving as an elite residence, the tower may have functioned as an astronomical observatory. Holes in the walls were probably used to measure the movement of the sun in order to predict solstices and equinoxes and properly maintain the ritual calendar.[57] Once again we find that higher status individuals were central to group ritual.

Conclusions

Some trends in the Hohokam area parallel those in the north, but social differences here and in the Casas Grandes region appear greater than among the Mogollon and Anasazi during the 14th and early 15th centuries. This emergence of higher status individuals and elites characterizes all areas of the New World where civilizations developed, from the Valley of Mexico to the Inca empire of the Andes. It appears to be a significant and necessary transition that accompanies the evolution of more complex societies.

In both the Hohokam and Casas Grandes regions, however, population levels dropped in subsequent periods and simpler organizational patterns again prevailed. In the century following AD 1350, the large towns of the Phoenix and Tucson Basins were abandoned and Casas Grandes was burned. This episode of abandonments, now a recurrent theme of Southwestern prehistory, was duplicated in some, but not all, areas to the north as well. Mogollon and Anasazi groups once again deserted densely inhabited areas, including the pueblos along the Little Colorado River and its southern drainages and large settlements along the Mogollon Rim. Only the pueblos of the Cibola, Acoma, Hopi, and Rio Grande Valley regions endured. It was these settlements that were to witness an even more momentous epoch with the Spanish incursions of the 16th century. In the next chapter, we will turn to the last century and a half of the prehistoric period and the beginning of the historic period.

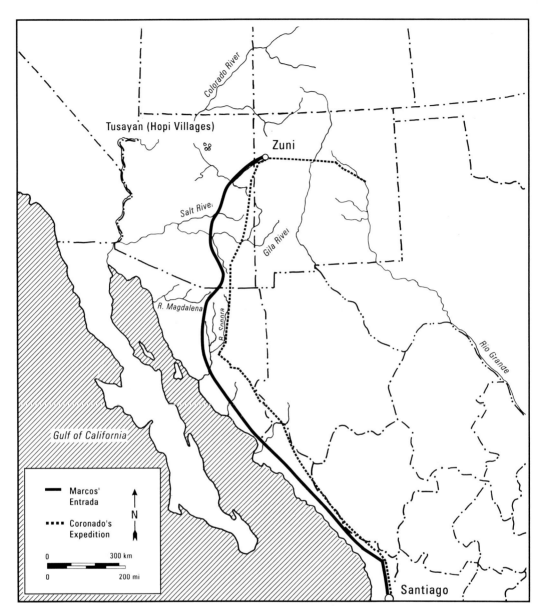

142 Possible routes traveled by Fray Marcos de Niza and Coronado from central Mexico to the Southwest.

8 · From Prehistory to History

'This pueblo has a fine appearance, the best I have seen in these regions. The houses are as they had been described to me by the Indians, all of stone, with terraces and flat roofs, as it seemed to me from a hill where I stood to view it.' *Fray Marcos de Niza*, 1539[1]

De Niza's description of the Cibolan pueblo of Hawikuh as seen on a summer's day in AD 1539 marks an abrupt transition from prehistory to history in the northern Southwest. Spanish authorities in Mexico City had sent de Niza to verify earlier reports by Cabeza de Vaca and three other Spaniards of fertile valleys, prosperous Indian settlements, and seductive hints of gold and other precious metals in the north. De Vaca and his companions had been members of a Spanish expedition that was shipwrecked on the Texas coast in about AD 1528. After swimming ashore and then living as the slave of an Indian group on the Texas coast for over a year, de Vaca escaped to the interior where he survived by serving as a trader and medicine man. Remarkably, some five years after the shipwreck he was fortuitously reunited with three other survivors of the same expedition. Together the group traversed western Texas and northern Mexico – the first Europeans to set foot in the Southwest – and, after several months of wandering, ultimately were reunited with their fellow countrymen in western and central Mexico.

Although the Spanish established no permanent settlements in the Southwest until the end of the 16th century, de Vaca's report prompted several investigations over the next few decades. De Niza's brief journey in 1539 was the first, initiated with instructions to observe the ways of life of the native peoples of the Southwest and to estimate their numbers, to describe the plants, animals, and topography, and to bring back samples of anything of interest.[2] De Niza's ensuing fanciful report of cities 'larger than Mexico City' and of gold 'that the natives make into vessels and jewels for the ears, and into little blades with which they wipe away their sweat'[3] prompted the subsequent exploration by Coronado between 1540 and 1542.   142 The lives of native peoples would never be the same again.

Not that change was a new phenomenon in the Southwest. As we have seen, the prehistoric era in the Southwest was hardly a stable one, and the last few centuries before the arrival of de Vaca, de Niza, and Coronado were no exception. In the Pueblo country of the northern Southwest the seemingly never-ending process of movement and abandonments persisted from the 1400s into the historic period. Pueblo groups left Chavez Pass, Grasshopper, and other sizeable towns north and south of the Mogollon Rim and they abandoned the Homol'ovi settlement cluster and other major towns such as Fourmile Ruin in the Little Colorado River Valley during the late 14th or early 15th centuries. Occupation continued in the Hopi region and the Rio Grande Valley, where there are some indications of population growth, and in the Cibola area of west-central New Mexico. Although the lifetimes of many Pueblo towns continued to be measured in a few decades, some of the pueblos discussed by the earliest Spanish explorers had been established during the last centuries before contact and continued to be important settlements well into the historic period; a few are still occupied today. There is thus no question that there is a strong, direct relationship between the late prehistoric peoples of the region and modern-day Pueblos.

Cultural continuity is not so easy to document in the southern reaches of the Southwest, where the Hohokam abandoned many, if not most, of their largest settlements and irrigation canals sometime between AD 1350 and 1400 or 1450. Indeed, so few sites have been securely dated to the post-AD 1400 period that a coherent Hohokam tradition is difficult to identify.[4] Many scholars therefore hypothesize a major transformation and collapse of Hohokam society, particularly in the Phoenix Basin. Some even question whether we can demonstrate cultural continuity between the prehistoric Hohokam and the Pima Indians that Spanish explorers encountered and who still live in the region today. These uncertainties must be kept in mind as we explore how first the Spanish and later the Americans rudely interjected themselves into the lives of the native peoples of the Southwest.

The transition to history in the Hohokam region

The Spanish recognized several different groups within the Pimería Alta – their phrase for the areas of southern Arizona and northern Mexico occupied by Piman-speaking groups. These included mobile hunters and plant gatherers in the arid west and semi-sedentary Tohono O'odham farmers in higher and wetter areas. But it is the fully sedentary Piman groups, more heavily dependent on agriculture, and residing in permanent villages along such major drainages as the Gila, Santa Cruz, and San Pedro Rivers, who are most relevant to questions about cultural continuity.

Father Eusebio Kino, a priest who founded several Jesuit missions in the Pimería Alta after 1687 and left the first detailed descriptions of the region, depicts a pattern of small, scattered native villages or *rancherías*, each consisting of dispersed houses themselves surrounded by individual agricultural fields. These *rancherías* thus differ significantly from the populous Hohokam villages of the 14th century with their closely spaced residences, often within compound walls, and distant irrigated fields. Spanish accounts make no mention of the hundreds of ballcourts, numerous platform mounds, or hundreds of miles of irrigation canals that once typified the Hohokam landscape.[5] Human numbers had declined dramatically too by the time of Father Kino's travels. In the Phoenix Basin alone, archaeologists estimate that the population fell from a peak of 50,000–80,000 in the 13th and 14th centuries to 3,000–5,000 in the late 17th century.[6] What brought about the demise of Hohokam culture?

The end of the prehistoric era: catastrophe and conflict?
Perhaps the most popular explanation for the Hohokam collapse focuses on the elaborate network of canals needed to irrigate their fields. Low river levels between AD 1322 and 1355 followed by a decade of catastrophic floods, it is argued, led the Hohokam to abandon the canal systems and relocate.[7] These inferences about river flows, however, are based on rainfall patterns inferred from tree-ring records for the northern Southwest and their relevance to southern Arizona is still unclear.[8] Moreover, Hohokam groups had undoubtedly survived a variable climate and damaging floods during preceding centuries without drastic reductions in population; indeed people who live in arid regions tend to expect climatic fluctuations and have developed ways to cope with them.[9]

A second possible cause of the collapse is conflict.[10] In addition to the evidence for tensions summarized in the last chapter, Piman oral tradition refers to general strife during this period. Ethnographer Frank Russell, for example, summarizes a victory over the chief of Casa Grande by Elder Brother, a figure who had led the Pima from the underworld and watched over them:

> Elder Brother's greatest enemies were the people living in the large pueblos, the ruins of which still remain scattered about the Gila and Salt River Valleys. He and his supporters approached one of the easternmost of these pueblos on the Gila, which is now known as Casa Grande.... They attacked and defeated the forces of Morning-Blue Si'van and then moved about 18 miles northwestward [towards another large pueblo].... The chief of this extensive pueblo was Kia-atak Si'van. His forces were defeated and his pueblo overrun by Elder Brother's warriors ...[11]

A third and final cause of the collapse may have been the declining health of most Southwestern people.[12] Farming difficulties and conflict could have contributed to that deterioration, but the growth in particular of densely packed settlements such as Casa Grande must have promoted the spread of diseases including gastroenteritis, tuberculosis and treponematoses and increased infections resulting from bacteria such as staphylococcus and streptococcus.[13] Food shortages, civil strife, and overcrowding could all have created an environment in which infectious diseases that had typically been mild in form instead became epidemic.[14]

Continuity amidst change: 'I came to a pueblo, in green irrigated land ...'
Whatever the cause of the Hohokam decline, one should not exaggerate the ubiquity or depth of the changes that brought this decline about. Some aspects of culture continued much as before, for instance styles of ceramics, diet, and burial ritual, including the use of both cremation and inhumation.[15] Discussion of the Hohokam also tends to overemphasize the Phoenix Basin with its towns and irrigation systems. It is in this region that the magnitude of change during the 15th century appears to have been greatest. More continuity is discernible in other parts of southern Arizona and northern Mexico.[16]

Likewise scholars have tended to emphasize Kino's observations from the late 17th century at the expense of explorers such as de Niza and Coronado 150 years earlier. For example, Kino saw little native settlement north of the Santa Cruz River and Rio Magdalena, but de Niza had reported substantial villages north of these drainages.[17] On his travels, de Niza saw much of the Pimería Alta and reported only two *desploblados* or unoccupied zones between the lower Rio Sonora and Zuni.[18] On his journey through this region, he observed an area 'thickly settled with people,' with settlements of 'good size,' irrigation canals, abundant supplies of food and cotton, and extensive trade with the Zuni. At the pueblo of Ojio, which perhaps lay near the confluence of the San Pedro and the Gila Rivers,[19] de Niza wrote:

> I came to a pueblo, in green irrigated land, where many people came to meet me, both men and women. They were clothed in cotton, some wearing skins of the cattle [buffalo], which in general they consider better material than cotton. In this pueblo they were all bedecked with turquoises, which hung from their noses and ears and which they call *cacona*.

Many people were evidently living in large villages rather than the scattered *rancherías* that Kino observed a century and a half later. No doubt some of de Niza's statements were exaggerations, designed to promote the search for souls to be baptized and rare metals to be mined. Yet historical and archaeological research increasingly supports him, lending weight to the idea that there was much cultural continuity between the prehistoric and earliest historic periods.[20]

The impact of European diseases
So what happened in the Pimería Alta, after de Niza's 1539 visit, to create such a radical decline by the time of Father Kino? The answer is simple but horrifying: frequent epidemics of smallpox, measles, and typhus. These diseases carried by European explorers appear to have had a far greater initial impact than the many physical assaults by the Spanish. Having lived for mil-

lennia in isolation from the Old World, Native Americans had no resistance to these hidden killers. When an epidemic struck – and the assault was intermittent – thousands of people died within a relatively short space of time. A smallpox pandemic that decimated the Aztec city of Tenochtitlan, for example, was a critical factor in Cortés' ability to conquer that great imperial capital.[21]

Two elements contributed to the temporal and geographical impact of these epidemic diseases, particularly in groups with no previous exposure. First, disease did not affect all age groups equally. Children suffered in particular.[22] Only a small percentage survived to reproductive age, thus depressing potential population growth and leading to subsequent population collapses.[23] Second, the diseases could be transmitted over long distances in short periods of time without direct contact between infected individuals and previously unexposed individuals. Smallpox is extremely contagious. It can be passed from mothers to infants still in the womb, and transmitted through respiratory discharges or from contact with the clothing or other possessions of victims. Even more ghastly, studies have discovered 'that scabs from a single smallpox case, when stored in raw cotton at room temperature for 530 days, still remain a viable virus.'[24] Measles can also be transmitted by clothing or other material infected by the virus. It is therefore possible that death and destruction were transmitted through trade relationships that often included the exchange of materials such as cotton. As a result of the ease of transmission, we find that the smallpox pandemic that helped devastate the Aztecs spread in only a few years to Lima, Peru, over 2,600 miles away where the Incas also suffered an enormous loss of life.[25]

Dating the first epidemics

Given that the Southwest is closer than Lima to central Mexico, several scholars have hypothesized that the native peoples of the Southwest suffered from the torment of European diseases in the 1520s, well before they actually saw a Spanish explorer.[26] However, a recent review of a large body of historical data from northern Mexico and the Southwest discovered no indications of epidemics prior to or during the expeditions of de Niza and Coronado, perhaps in part because northward transmission of the disease was inhibited by the paucity of settlements in northern Mexico.[27] The earliest epidemics in the Southwest were probably delayed until sometime between AD 1593 and 1630. A smallpox epidemic that raged from 1623 to 1625 in parts of northern Mexico could have been one of the first to decimate the inhabitants of northern Sonora and southern Arizona.[28]

The loss of life from the initial epidemics must have been catastrophic. The lack of census data inhibits precise estimates for the Pimería Alta, but in many parts of the New World native population levels were reduced by 90 percent by the end of the 18th century, with the largest losses typically occurring just before and after sustained contact with the Spanish. The total number of deaths was often further increased by periods of famine because of the reduction in the numbers of those fit enough to tend fields or harvest crops.[29]

Such an enormous loss of life caused communities to fall apart. Moreover since the diseases spread most easily where people lived closely together in large groups, the epidemics encouraged movement from densely settled villages and towns to the less concentrated *rancherías*.[30] Once the missions were established at the end of the 17th century, the Jesuits 'assumed many rights and responsibilities formerly held by the principal chiefs, supervising the distribution of lands, the production and redistribution of surpluses, the conduct of long-distance exchange, and mediating disputes,' thus making native organization alone, as described in documentary sources, appear less complex, with minimal social differentiation.[31] From this perspective, the discontinuity between the prehistoric and historic periods in the Pimería Alta was a two-stage process. At the beginning of the 15th century there was a marked decline in Hohokam culture, but perhaps the most severe changes came in the decades after the 1590s with the massive loss of life caused by European diseases.

The Spanish missions and early Spanish settlement

It was not until Father Kino's missionizing efforts after 1687 that the Spanish initiated steady contact with the inhabitants of the old Hohokam region, establishing the mission of Nuestra Señora de los Delores in northern Sonora and subsequently aiding in the founding of others in northern Mexico and southern Arizona. Kino has been characterized as an 'irrepressible expansionist' who offered the natives 'Christianity at a distance, Christianity on their terms' as he traveled through his domain once or twice a year carrying gifts for the Pima and introducing them to Catholicism, but not demanding everyday allegiance to the Church.[32]

For two decades after Kino's death in 1711, Spanish efforts rarely extended beyond northern Sonora, but the Jesuits renewed their efforts in the 1730s, pushing the frontier northward into southern Arizona once again. Native groups to the north along the Gila River or to the west were generally outside the Spanish colonial or mission system throughout the entire period of Spanish control.

Occasional revolts by the Pima pushed the mission frontier back to the south, with the most notable uprising in 1751 when Pima forces led by Luis Oacpicagigua ransacked the missions and killed two padres and at least a hundred colonists and natives, forcing a retreat into northern Sonora. Native hostilities increased in subsequent decades as they encountered increased Jesuit demands for Pima labor and compliance with Catholic tenets; Christianity became much less distant and more intrusive. Moreover, once the Church extended the frontier in various sections of the Southwest, Spanish colonists typically followed soon after, appropriating the prime agricultural lands and further restricting native groups.[33]

The greatest threat to the Spanish settlers increasingly became not the Pima, but the Apache who had filtered into much of the Southwest in the 16th century and who sheltered in the mountains to the north and east. Indeed, to the Spanish the Pima served as a buffer against the increasing Apache attacks; Pima warriors joined Spanish soldiers in periodic campaigns against their mutual enemy.

Efforts by the Jesuits and later the Franciscans to encourage the more mobile Pima groups to settle permanently at the missions undoubtedly contributed to the impact of disease during this period, as epidemics spread along the river drainages and flourished in the mission communities. Spanish contact also modified the Pima economy. The introduction of horses and cattle was significant throughout the Southwest,[34] but in the Pimería Alta the arrival of European wheat was equally important. Wheat could be planted in the fall and harvested in the spring when indigenous maize could not be grown, and thus it doubled agricultural harvests.[35] An expanding market for surplus wheat developed and the Pima became an important component in the Spanish economy. These agricultural changes, together with the Apache raids, promoted denser, more compact settlements and greater integration and cooperation among the Pima.[36]

The transition in the Pueblo region

Disease epidemics had an equally severe impact in the Pueblo region where we have better 17th-century records because of a longer and more substantial Spanish presence. In the Rio Grande Valley, as many as half the villages may have been abandoned in the first part of the century, a process largely attributable to disease, although population fluctuations and settlement shifts had been characteristic of Pueblo life for several millennia.

Massive loss of life also characterized those pueblos that remained inhabited through the period. One of the best known is Pecos. Sitting atop a small mesa on the eastern edge of the Pueblo world, the town played a significant 'middleman' role in Pueblo trade with Native American groups to the east. Beginning with Coronado, the Spanish used the pueblo as a point of departure for exploration of the Plains region. Fray Andrés Juárez, in charge of the Pecos mission from 1622 to 1635, estimated a native population of about 2,000 people when he began his tenure. Scarcely 20 years later, in 1641, another observer tallied a 40 percent reduction to 1,189 inhabitants, and by 1694 the numbers had dropped almost 40 percent again to 736. John Kessell, the modern author of an engaging chronicle of the history of Pecos, writes that 'in human terms, where three Pecos had lived in 1622, only two lived in 1641, and only one in 1694.'[37]

A general, but less accurately documented, decline for the Pueblo world as a whole can be discerned. The total Native American population for the region may have exceeded 100,000 by the late 16th century.[38] By 1680, only 17,000 survived in Arizona and New Mexico combined, a loss of over 80

The Navajo and Apache: 'newcomers' to the Southwest

The Navajo and Apache speak dialects that belong to a general language family referred to by linguists as Athapaskan. The distribution of other Athapaskan-speaking peoples in North America combined with historical and archaeological evidence suggest that these Southwestern groups moved into the region from an earlier homeland in west-central Canada where other Athapaskan-speaking groups still reside today. The degree of linguistic similarities and differences among Athapaskan groups implies that the Navajo and Apache – at that time one group rather than the two ethnic groups we recognize today – separated from their Canadian relatives within the last 1,000 years. Archaeological and historical evidence places the entry of these people into the Southwest more recently, with substantial numbers not present until the first half of the 16th century.[41]

These Athapaskans probably moved into the Southwest from the Plains where 16th-century Spanish accounts identified them as 'dog nomads,' mobile groups who hunted bison, lived in tents, and used dogs to pull travois loaded with their possessions. During his travels to the plains east of the Pueblo region in April 1541, Francisco Coronado wrote:

> After seventeen days of travel, I came upon a ranchería of the Indians who follow these cattle [bison]. These natives are called Querechos. They do not cultivate the land, but eat raw meat and drink the blood of the cattle they kill. They dress in the skins of the cattle, with which all the people in this land clothe themselves, and they have very well-constructed tents, made with tanned and greased cowhides, in which they live and which they take along as they follow the cattle. They have dogs which they load to carry their tents, poles, and belongings.[42]

percent in less than a century. Disease was undoubtedly the primary factor in this decline, but more direct Spanish impacts must also be remembered. During Coronado's exploration, his men were ordered to attack two pueblos and burn the survivors at the stake when the inhabitants protested after the Spanish had made demands for food and clothing and molested some of the women. Such tensions and conflict only increased when Spanish forces remained permanently in the area after the late 16th century. The Spanish Crown had established a policy of both salvation and exploitation in its treatment of native societies of the New World, 'based on the naive supposition that you could save a man's soul while you were breaking his back.'[39] Large numbers of Southwesterners were forcibly drafted for building projects, to farm fields for the friars, to labor on Spanish *haciendas*, or to produce various crafts. Moreover, the frequent conflicts between the church and civil authorities over who had jurisdiction over the Pueblo land and labor ultimately forced the Pueblo people to try and serve not one master, but two. The

143

The Plains dogs were slightly smaller than Eskimo dogs and were described by the Spanish as very white, with black spots and 'not much larger than water spaniels.'[43] Recent experiments have shown that these dogs may have pulled loads as heavy as 50lb on long trips at rates as high as two or three miles an hour.[44]

Although some scholars have suggested entry dates into the Southwest as early as the 13th and 14th centuries AD, most believe they arrived only a few decades prior to the Spanish. Finding a clear answer to this puzzle is complicated by the way of life of these peoples. Because of their hunting and gathering lifestyle, they constructed less-substantial dwellings than most other Southwestern groups and used a more austere set of material goods. It is thus more difficult for us to locate the sites where the early Athapaskan groups lived or even demonstrate that the remains were left by Athapaskans rather than another group.

Trade between the Athapaskans and the Pueblos had become important to both groups by the mid-16th century, with the Pueblos receiving bison meat, hides, and material for fashioning stone tools in exchange for maize and cotton, and Coronado observed the Plains people wintering near the Pueblos. It was not until the late 16th and early 17th centuries, however, that the Apaches moved into other parts of the Southwest.[45] Thus, Coronado rode through the modern Western Apache area in 1540, but reported it to be uninhabited. In the 1580s, the Spanish first mention Apache living west of the Rio Grande, and the Athapaskans continued to expand their range through the 17th century, occupying much of the area that the Pueblos had abandoned during the prior centuries.[46] The Spanish first mention the Navaho in the 1620s, referring to the 'Apachu de Nabaju' in the Chama region east of the San Juan River, and by the 1640s they commonly used the term to refer to the Athapaskan people of the northern Southwest, from the Chama on the east to the San Juan on the west.[47]

European intruders also relentlessly attempted to suppress native religion and enforce conversion to Catholicism, burning kivas, confiscating kachina masks, and prohibiting native ceremonies. Pueblo resistance to these efforts was often countered by harsh actions.

Further catalysts for conflicts were the relationships with the Apache and Navajo, who had moved into the area by the early 16th century (see box p. 188). At that time contacts were generally peaceful, but Spanish raids to capture Apache and Navajo for sale as slaves in northern Mexico shattered the relationship. The Apache and Navajo fought back, making effective use of a growing supply of horses, frequently stolen from the Spanish. It was the Pueblo peoples who suffered most, however, since many of their settlements were unprotected on the frontier. During an Apache attack on the Zuni Pueblo of Hawikuh in 1673, 200 people were killed, 1,000 were taken captive, and the village was burned.[40] Several factors thus contributed to the precipitous drop in the Pueblo population.

143 This painting by Jan Mostaert is thought to show the attack on the Zuni pueblo of Hawikuh by Coronado in 1540. The conquistador's exploration of the Southwest almost ended during this encounter when the Zuni knocked him off his horse by dropping rocks from above and pierced his foot with an arrow.

The Pueblo revolt

These attacks were only one reason among many why the Pueblo groups joined forces in 1680 to drive the Spanish from the Southwest. Tewa and Tiwa leaders from the Rio Grande Valley initially guided the revolt, plotting to act just before the Spanish supplies of weapons, horses, and ammunition were replenished by a caravan sent every three years from Mexico. As the time for action neared early in the month of August, two messengers were dispatched to the allied pueblos to coordinate the uprisings, but the Spanish received word of the messengers and arrested them. News of the arrest then spread among the Pueblo villages and the uprising began the next morning on 10 August. Of the 33 Franciscan priests assigned to Pueblo villages, 21 refused to leave and were killed along with several hundred Spanish colonists. Although the Spanish authorities initially attempted to remain in their capital at Santa Fe and resist, Pueblo warriors surrounded the town and impeded supplies of food and water from the outside. On 21 August, Spanish Governor Otermín was allowed to lead a long caravan of wagons to the southernmost mission at El Paso. Here, despite immediate efforts to recolonize the Rio Grande Valley, they remained until 1692, 12 years after the uprising. Some Pueblo peoples did not support the revolt and so accompanied the Spanish and established new settlements in the El Paso area. This was one of the first significant episodes of intra–Pueblo factionalism after European contact.

The 12 years of freedom from Spanish oppression were not stable ones for the Pueblo people. The alliance that had made the revolt a success deteriorated, although it was powerful enough that a Spanish attempt at reconquest during the winter of 1681–82 was rebuffed. Many pueblo dwellers in the Rio Grande Valley relocated, some back to areas they had occupied before Spanish interference, others to the west in fear of Spanish retribution. The Hopi village of Hano is still occupied today by descendants of a Tewa-speaking group from the northern Rio Grande who resettled in northeastern Arizona in the years after the revolt.

In addition to emigration as a means of protection, some pueblos moved their entire village short distances to more defensible locations on top of 144 mesas. Protection against fellow Native Americans as well as the Spanish was the aim. It was during this brief period of Spanish withdrawal that the several Zuni pueblos coalesced into one settlement because of Apache attacks from the southeast.

144 The Hopi pueblo of Walpi and nearby sheep corrals, *c.* 1875. Soon after the Spanish entry into the Southwest, many Pueblo groups moved their towns to more defensible locations on top of isolated mesas.

145 One of the first steps taken by Spanish priests as they were assigned to pueblos in the 17th century was to force native laborers to build missions such as San Estevan del Rey, constructed at Acoma beginning about AD 1630.

The return of Spanish domination

Only in 1692 did the Spanish under Don Diego de Vargas regain control of the Pueblo region. From then on it would remain under the domination of outside cultures. But Hopi villages to the west, and, to a lesser extent, the residents of Zuni and Acoma, succeeded in maintaining a certain independence, even if at a cost.

145

The dilemmas for the Pueblo people in continued resistance are well exemplified by the fate of the Hopi village of Awatovi. Located on Antelope Mesa, 9 miles east of the Hopi towns still occupied today, Awatovi was founded in the late 13th century. By the 17th century it was one of the largest Hopi pueblos and perhaps the most important village east of Oraibi. Franciscans established a permanent mission here in 1629, naming the town San Bernardo de Aguatubi. During the Pueblo revolt in 1680, the inhabitants killed the resident priest, Fray José de Figueroa. Archaeological excavations indicate that they also destroyed the church and converted the friary into native residences.

On regaining control of the Pueblo region, the Spanish reconsecrated the remains of the church, but only sent priests in May 1700. Prevented by other Hopis from visiting nearby towns, the priests departed later that year. Men from the neighboring settlements now acted to deter future Spanish interference at Awatovi. According to Hopi oral tradition, it was the village chief himself who requested that the chiefs of Walpi and Oraibi assist him in destroying his own pueblo.

> The Awatovi chief said, 'You are my friends. I need your help. My people are out of control. The Castilla missionaries have returned and they are preparing to stay forever. The village is in chaos. The young insult the old, women are raped, the shrines are desecrated. The ceremonies are ridiculed, contempt is shown for the kachinas, and the *kwitamuh* run wild. Thus the evil that followed us from the Lower World has torn us into pieces. Awatovi must be destroyed. Its people must be scattered and its houses razed to the ground.[48]

During the last few days of 1700 or the first days of 1701, men from other Hopi pueblos attacked Awatovi, killed many of the male inhabitants, took the women and children to their own pueblos, and burned the town. Excavations in 1892 confirmed aspects of native history, as J. Walter Fewkes found that 'in almost every room which was excavated evidences of fire or a great conflagration were brought to light.' No other incident better symbolizes the dilemmas and internal turmoil created by the Spanish intrusion and by their attempts to impose their own way of life and beliefs on the native peoples of the Southwest. Unfortunately such problems continued into the modern era, for once the Spaniards left, Americans with similar goals and intentions replaced them as foreign invaders.

Epilogue

The Spanish never again established a consistent presence among the Hopi. Exposure to European maladies was thus reduced, allowing small population increases and a period of relative cultural stability at a time when native groups in the Rio Grande Valley were still declining in numbers. In the latter area, a major epidemic struck during almost every decade between the Spanish return in 1692 and 1828, with over 5,000 perishing from one small-pox epidemic in 1780–81 that originated in Mexico City and spread northward.[1] By 1789, the once teeming village of Pecos had been reduced to only 138 people.

Although the impact of disease continued to be severe, Spanish policies toward Pueblo groups improved in the Rio Grande Valley area after the reconquest. Fewer new missions were built and Spanish settlers were no longer allowed to collect tribute. Efforts to suppress native ceremonies and destroy ritual paraphernalia were largely abandoned. Instead the missionaries devoted their energies to a growing non-Pueblo population while the civil authorities focused on attacks by Utes, Comanches, Navajos, and Apaches. Pueblo warriors in fact served as important allies in campaigns to control the threat from marauding enemies. Pueblo families also moved to join new Hispanic settlements. Thus, while the total Pueblo population of New Mexico remained fairly constant through much of the 18th century, the size of non-Pueblo communities quadrupled.

Stored wheat in Piman villages proved attractive targets for Apache raids, as did the increasing numbers of ranchers and miners who moved northward into the Pimería Alta in the early years following the Mexican victory over Spain in 1821. For the next several decades, Piman groups served as the primary military deterrent against the Apaches as first the Mexican and later the American government (after the Gadsden purchase of 1853 added the northern Pimería Alta to the United States) relied upon Piman forces to reinforce minimal numbers of government troops.

Changing protagonists: the American intrusion

The trend toward less interference in Pueblo life continued in the first half of the 19th century, aided by the declining power of Spain in the New World

146 The arrival of large numbers of Americans after the conclusion of the Civil War forever transformed the lives of the native Southwesterners. Competition over land and water ultimately led to the creation of reservations that restricted freedom and forced significant changes in the native peoples' way of life.

and the Mexican Revolution. The attention of first the Spanish and then the Mexicans became fixed on attacks by Apaches and other raiders, and on the possibility of a foray into the region by American settlers as they pushed westward. Spanish and Mexican contact with the western Pueblos all but ceased with Mexican independence and the formidable presence of the Apache and Navajo diminished contact between the eastern and western halves of the Pueblo world. In the Pimería Alta, the number of Franciscans living with native peoples declined in the first half of the century and the practice of Catholicism among these groups was largely left to the secular or lay clergy who were few in number.

The world of the native peoples of the Southwest received new shocks in the latter half of the 19th century. The end of the American Civil War 146 shifted attention to the West, leading to the increasing presence of Americans as railroads were built through the region. Competition for land became a major issue both in the Rio Grande Valley region and in the Piman area as Americans and Hispanics encroached upon native territory. Growing American settlement upstream from the Pima reservation (which was established just prior to the Civil War) diverted water from the Gila River without regard for the devastating impact on native irrigation systems and agricultural fields. This usurpation of a critical resource transformed the Pima from independent farmers to wage laborers and even welfare recipients. The Pima refer to the subsequent decades as the 'years of famine.'[2]

Missionaries, primarily members of Protestant sects, returned in large numbers by the end of the 19th century in an attempt peacefully to persuade Pueblos to abandon their native religion. Disease also continued to afflict Pueblo communities, although total population levels at the beginning and end of the century were roughly similar after a mid-century decline. Individual villages continued to fall into ruin, however. The once flourishing pueblo of Pecos, at Spanish contact one of the largest towns in the Southwest, was abandoned in 1838 by the less than two dozen surviving inhabitants. When Alfred Kidder began his trailblazing excavations of the pueblo in 1915, he described the deterioration:

147
148

> The town itself, which was doubtless in ruinous condition when it was abandoned, fell quickly into decay, a process aided by the fact that the Mexicans who lived in the vicinity habitually robbed it of beams and timbers for use as firewood.... The roof beams of the church were removed about 1860, to be used as corral posts, and its adobe walls, unprotected from the rain, have gradually disintegrated. The pueblo went to pieces even faster, the upper walls fell, the timbers below rotted away or were pulled out, and not until a sheltering mound had formed itself over the lower stories was the process of ruin arrested.[3]

In the early 1900s, descendants were still visiting the pueblo and making pilgrimages to nearby ritual sites.

147 The Spanish mission and the foundations of the associated convent where the priests resided and conducted church business and activities. The residents of Pecos constructed the first mission in 1625 and subsequently destroyed it during the Pueblo revolt of 1680. The walls visible in this photograph are from the second church built in 1717.

148 In a successful effort to identify the changing sequence of pottery used during the centuries that Pecos was inhabited, A. V. Kidder, using the then new technique of stratigraphic excavation, focused much of his effort from 1915 to 1929 on the deep trash that had accumulated on the eastern edge of the Pueblo. The pottery sequence was to be the key to establishing a regional chronology for the northern Rio Grande.

The late 19th and 20th centuries in the Southwest

The last half of the 19th century also witnessed American campaigns against the Apache and Navajo, resulting in a tremendous loss of life because of a military policy of extermination rather than a more compassionate attempt to control raids and hostilities. These campaigns were the beginning of a significant and constant role by the American government in Native American affairs. By 1890, reservations for all native Southwesterners had been established and agents were appointed to oversee them. New attempts were made to suppress indigenous customs and beliefs. Certain rituals were prohibited and boarding schools established away from reservations where the use of native languages and customs was forbidden. Children were encouraged to accept Christianity and American culture. Not surprisingly, these efforts provoked hostility. Don Talayesva, a Hopi born in 1890, tells us that 'I grew up believing that Whites are wicked, deceitful people. It seemed that most of them were soldiers, government agents, or missionaries … I was taught to mistrust them and to give warning whenever I saw one coming.'[4] Government policies were countered by native efforts to preserve their ritual practices, efforts that sometimes promoted disagreements within villages between those most and least receptive to the outsiders.

The 20th century has in many ways seen a reversal in the decline in Native American fortunes. Indigenous populations have grown substantially thanks to better medical treatment, particularly smallpox vaccines that finally curtailed the largest killer of native peoples during the previous three centuries. Since the 1930s there has also generally been a more enlightened government policy of religious freedom and native autonomy over their own affairs. Greater opportunities for work in towns, on railroads, or in coal mines have lessened the dependence on agriculture. Native crafts have flourished too, with greater recognition and appreciation for the distinctive skills required and the beauty of Southwestern pottery, jewelry, baskets, and weaving. Finally, land issues have become increasingly significant, with numerous court cases in the 1980s and 1990s involving issues of land allocation among native groups or efforts to retroactively gain compensation for the appropriation of native territories by outsiders.

During the millennia since their ancestors first settled the mountains, plateaus, and deserts of the Southwest, the native peoples have thus survived a multitude of hardships ranging from encounters with Pleistocene mammoths to periods of conflict among themselves to the forceful intrusion of alien people who brought with them a very different view of the world, a destructive set of weapons, and an invisible and horrifying forces in the form of smallpox and measles. Such events have transformed their ways of life in a manner that could neither be anticipated nor averted, yet these resilient people have not only endured, but have done so in a way that is both inspiring and enlightening. In the absence of writing, their story went unrecorded, but through the course of their lives they left behind a different type of testimony in the form of broken fragments of pottery, kiva murals, and the remnants of their dwellings and public buildings. These buried clues form a text that the archaeologist must translate, a text that is timeless in a way that other evidence is not – for 'one generation passeth away, and another generation cometh: but the earth abideth forever.'[5]

Map of the Southwest

Guide to the Southwest

Notes to the Text

Further Reading

Sources of Illustrations

Index

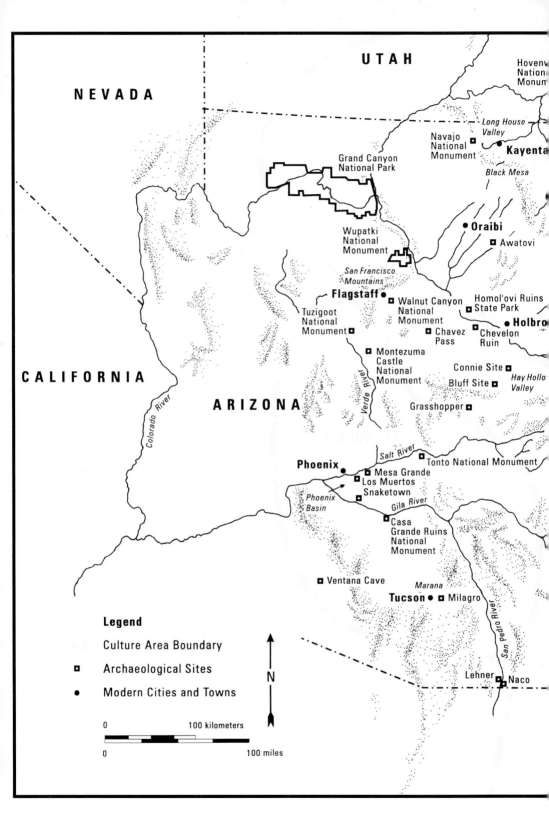

NEVADA

UTAH

Hoven
Nation
Monum

Long House
Valley

Navajo
National
Monument

Kayenta

Black Mesa

Grand Canyon
National Park

Oraibi

Awatovi

Wupatki
National
Monument

San Francisco
Mountains

Flagstaff

Homol'ovi Ruins
State Park

Holbro

Walnut Canyon
National
Monument

Tuzigoot
National
Monument

Chavez
Pass

Chevelon
Ruin

Montezuma
Castle
National
Monument

Connie Site

CALIFORNIA

Bluff Site

Hay Hollo
Valley

Colorado River

ARIZONA

Verde River

Grasshopper

Salt River

Tonto National Monument

Phoenix

Mesa Grande
Los Muertos
Snaketown

Phoenix
Basin

Gila River

Casa
Grande Ruins
National
Monument

Ventana Cave

Marana

Tucson ● Milagro

San Pedro River

Lehner Naco

Legend

Culture Area Boundary

□ Archaeological Sites

● Modern Cities and Towns

N

0   100 kilometers

0   100 miles

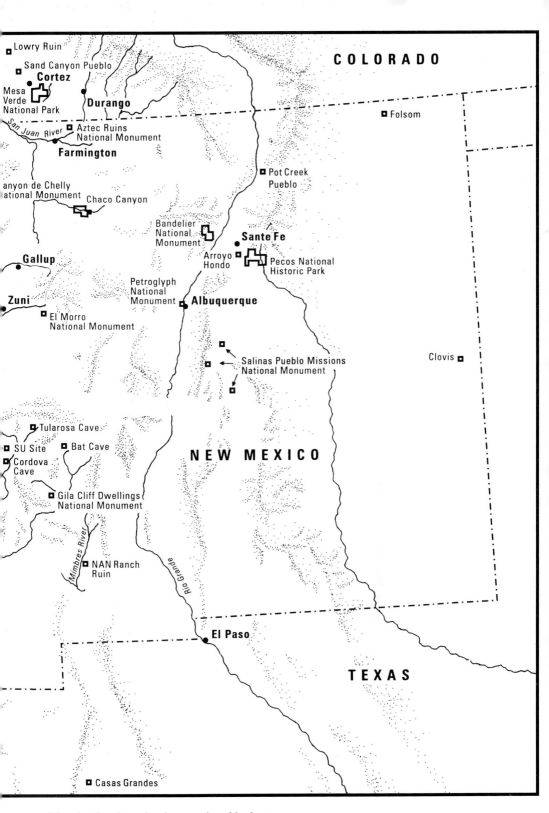

149 Map showing the major sites mentioned in the text.

Guide to the Southwest

Why do so many people with an interest in ancient cultures visit the Southwest each year? There is probably no other region in the world where one can study the prehistory of an area and at the same time connect that past so clearly to a living group of people as in the Pueblo region. Here the relics of the past – cliff dwellings, pottery, ballcourts, and kivas – are tangible and touchable.

With so much to see, any visitor should come well prepared and with a clear plan in mind. The national parks and monuments are open all year round, but winters in the Southwest (particularly the northern half) are often colder (and more windy) than newcomers to the area expect, and are not ideal for that reason. Most choose to visit in the late spring, summer, and early fall. At the beginning and end of that period one should be prepared for the chilly evenings that are typical; a coat or warm sweater are definitely advised. During the warmer months, particularly July and August, visitors should expect some very hot days. Hats, sunglasses, sunscreen, and light-colored clothing are recommended. Even short trails can be demanding in the late afternoon, so it is wise to carry a water bottle. Those who normally live at low elevations should also allow themselves a few days to adjust to the higher altitudes as they will tire more quickly than usual.

First-time visitors should have the five-star attractions – Chaco Canyon and Mesa Verde – at the top of their list of places to visit. A tour connecting those two areas with Albuquerque, Santa Fe, and Taos will provide the opportunity to see modern pueblos in the Rio Grande Valley; to visit the Pueblo Indian Culture Center and several museums; to go to other parks and monuments such as Bandelier, Aztec and Salmon Ruins, Pecos and Petroglyph monument; and to spend more money on native crafts than you ever planned. In northern Arizona, Flagstaff is a convenient starting place, beginning with the Museum of Northern Arizona, Wupatki National Monument, Homol'ovi Ruins State Park, and the Hopi Cultural Centre Museum and nearby villages. Although a bit more off the beaten track, Canyon de Chelly and Navajo National Monuments in northeastern Arizona are two of my favorite places because of the combination of spectacular scenery and intriguing archaeology. There are many options and no bad choices.

Arizona

In the heartland of the Anasazi area in northeastern Arizona are **Navajo National Monument** and **Canyon de Chelly National Monument**. Betatakin and Kiet Siel, two of the best-known Anasazi cliff dwellings, can be visited in Navajo National Monument. Betatakin is the more accessible pueblo, but requires a 1-mile round-trip hike down into Tsegi Canyon. A tour of Kiet Siel requires a permit and a strenuous 16-mile round-trip hike or a horseback ride with a Navajo guide. Canyon de Chelly National Monument is known for its lovely canyon landscapes, numerous small cliff dwellings, including White House Ruin, and caves with evidence of earlier occupations. Access to White House Ruin requires a 2.5-mile climb from canyon rim to canyon bottom (and, even worse, back up). Half-day and whole-day tours in World War II vintage 'trucks' are also offered, along with private tours with Navajo guides. Visitors to the Four Corners region should also consider a stop at the **Hopi Cultural Center Museum** on Second Mesa on the Hopi Reservation.

Within an hour's drive from Flagstaff in the north-central part of the state are several national monuments or state parks. To the north is the largest, **Wupatki National Monument**. Eruption of a nearby volcano (**Sunset Crater Volcano National Monument**) in AD 1064 deposited a layer of ash and cinders that provided a natural mulch and enhanced the farming potential of the area. A rapid population increase resulted. Several pueblos – including the Citadel, Lomaki, Wukoki, and Wupatki – dating primarily to the 11th through to the 13th centuries can be visited within the monument. East of Flagstaff is **Walnut Canyon National Monument** with a multitude of small cliff dwellings constructed mostly in the 12th and 13th centuries. Several villages on top of isolated promontories lie nearby. **Montezuma Castle** and **Tuzigoot National Monuments** are south of Flagstaff. Montezuma Castle is one of the best-preserved cliff dwellings and is associated with nearby Montezuma's Well, a limestone sinkhole fed by a natural spring. Small surface pueblos, pithouses, and remnants of an irrigation system are also present, including a Hohokam pithouse built during the northward spread of Hohokam culture and people. Nearby Tuzigoot is a two-story masonry pueblo with just over 100 rooms. Finally, although most people visit **Grand Canyon National Park**, northwest of Flagstaff, because of the spectacular landscapes, the prehistoric occupation of the canyon is also of interest. Tusayan Ruin, a small 12th-century pueblo, and the nearby Tusayan Museum are worthwhile stops.

The **Museum of Northern Arizona** in Flagstaff has focused on the native peoples of the Southwest since its inception. Attractive exhibits illustrate native lifeways during the prehistoric and historic periods.

To the east of Flagstaff along Interstate 40 are **Homol'ovi Ruins State Park** and **Petrified Forest National Park**. The state park incorporates a set of medium to large pueblo ruins dating to the 14th and early 15th cen-

ous smaller ruins, and rock art. The Petrified Forest in east-
ona is renowned for the largest collection of petrified logs in the
. the prehistory of the park is also of interest. On the border
.he Mogollon and Anasazi regions, the park had a unique and long
.ry and was inhabited longer than most areas to the north.

sa **Grande Ruins National Monument** and **Tonto National**
.ument in the southern part of the state, east of Phoenix, exemplify
u. erent types of settlements. Most notable at Casa Grande in the Sonoran
desert is the Hohokam 'big house,' still preserved to a height of several
stories. Tonto sits amidst a saguaro forest in an upland, mountainous setting
and incorporates two small cliff dwellings. The **Pueblo Grande Museum**
in Phoenix, the **Arizona State Museum** at the University of Arizona in
Tucson, and the **Amerind Foundation Museum** in Dragoon all offer
engaging exhibits about Native American life in the Southwest.

Chihuahua, Mexico

The **Casas Grandes** (or **Paquimé**) **Ruins** lie just southwest of the
modern city of Nuevo Casas Grandes. Parts of the extraordinary
prehistoric town have been excavated, as well as mounds, ballcourts, and
macaw pens. A small collection of artifacts from the ruins are exhibited in
The Museum of Ancient Indians in the Motel Piñon in Nuevo Casas
Grandes.

Colorado

The most spectacular cliff dwellings in the Anasazi region can be found in
Mesa Verde National Park between Cortez and Durango in southwestern Colorado. Most accessible are Spruce Tree House, Cliff Palace,
Balcony House, Square Tower House, Oak Tree House, and New Fire
House on Chapin Mesa. Visitors can take a walking tour of Spruce Tree
House and also see the nearby museum where there are several worthwhile
exhibits of artifacts recovered from the park. The other cliff dwellings that
are open to the public lie along two short drives. For tours of Cliff Palace
and Balcony House visitors must obtain tickets at the Visitor Center. A
second area of the park, Wetherill Mesa, is also open during the summer.
The cliff dwellings of Long House (for which a ticket is also necessary),
Step House, Kodak House, and Nordenskiöld No. 16, along with mesa-top
pueblos and pithouses can be seen or visited on Wetherill Mesa. The dis-
plays at **Anasazi Heritage Museum** in nearby Dolores focus on the prehistory of the Anasazi region, and two archaeologists can be visited in the
grounds of the museum.

Hovenweep National Monument includes six different groups of
ruins in Utah and Colorado accessible only via gravel or dirt roads. The
larger pueblos date primarily to the 12th and 13th centuries and are unusual

for the high frequencies of multi-story masonry towers within or near the villages.

New Mexico

The densest and most exceptional concentration of large pueblos anywhere in the American Southwest occurs within **Chaco Culture National Historical Park** in northwestern New Mexico, between Albuquerque and Farmington. These include the well-known ruins of Pueblo Bonito, Casa Chiquita, Chetro Ketl, Hungo Pavi, Kin Kletso, Peñasco Blanco, Pueblo Alto, Pueblo del Arroyo, Una Vida, Wijiji, and the Great Kiva, Casa Rinconada. Many of these Chacoan Great Houses lie near the road through the park, but a few require long hikes. Also accessible are some smaller pueblos on the south side of Chaco Wash.

Aztec Ruins National Monument northwest of Farmington is an example of a large Chacoan outlier with comparable architecture to the Great Houses in Chaco Canyon. The early-12th-century pueblo includes a Great Kiva, now reconstructed and well worth a visit. Parts of the pueblo post-date the decline of Chaco and appear more closely tied to events in the Mesa Verde region of southwestern Colorado. A second Chacoan outlier can be seen at nearby **Salmon Ruins**, in Bloomfield.

From Taos in north-central New Mexico to just south of Albuquerque are numerous towns inhabited by contemporary Puebloan peoples. Many allow tours (often with a permit and a special fee for photographs), some have museums, and several allow visitors to native dances.

Bandelier National Monument northwest of Santa Fe encompasses the beautiful Frijoles Canyon. The large, late prehistoric pueblo of Tyuonyi lies on the canyon floor and nearby Long House was constructed against the canyon walls. The prehistoric occupants of the national monument also inhabited small caves carved into the soft volcanic tuff of the canyon walls. Several miles of trails provide access to other ruins, including a recon-structed kiva in Ceremonial Cave. Abundant rock art is another significant aspect of the national monument.

Alfred Kidder directed one of the most important excavations in the Southwest at Pecos Pueblo east of Santa Fe. **Pecos National Historical Park** includes the large pueblo which was visited by Coronado The Span-ish later constructed a mission at the settlement in their attempt to convert the Native Americans to Catholicism. The adobe foundation of an early church and the standing walls of a later mission provide a stark contrast with the ruins of the pueblo.

About half-an-hour's drive from Albuquerque are two noteworthy archaeological areas. **Petroglyph National Monument** lies on the north-western edge of the city and incorporates several discrete areas where vol-canic flows left boulders and cliff faces which the ancient Southwesterners used as canvases to depict animals, masks, anthropomorphs, and a variety of other symbols. The result is one of the most impressive concentrations of rock art anywhere in the Southwest. Northwest of Albuquerque is **Coronado State Monument** which includes the ruins of Kuaua, an adobe pueblo inhabited at the end of the prehistoric period and into the beginning of the historic era. Noteworthy at Coronado State Monument is a kiva with painted wall murals. These murals have been reconstructed and the originals are displayed in a museum. The **Pueblo Indian Cultural Center** and the **Maxwell Museum of Anthropology** at the University of New Mexico both illustrate the history of Native American settlement.

El Morro National Monument is best known for the signatures of Spanish and early American explorers, including Don Juan de Oñate in 1605, carved into Inscription Rock, but Native American prehistory also can be explored by visiting the ruins of Atsina on top of the mesa. Nearby **Zuni Pueblo** is the only remaining pueblo of the 'Seven Cities of Cibola' sought by Coronado. To the east is **Acoma Pueblo**, in a spectacular setting on top of an isolated mesa. Visitors can tour a small museum and walk through the pueblo and Spanish mission with a native guide.

Southeast of Albuquerque, **Salinas Pueblo Missions National Monument** includes three late prehistoric and historic pueblos – Quarai, Abó, and Gran Quivira – with well-preserved Spanish missions. The Visitors' Center in the small town of Mountainair is the best starting point and includes museum exhibits and an audiovisual program.

In southern New Mexico, **Three Rivers Petroglyph Site** north of Tularosa offers abundant examples of Mogollon rock art. North of Silver City is **Gila Cliff Dwellings National Monument**. Small Mogollon cliff dwellings above Cliff Dweller Canyon can be visited along a 1-mile self-guided trail.

Utah

See **Hovenweep National Monument** under Colorado section.

Notes to the Text

Preface (pp. 7–9)

1   Hill 1970; Leone 1968; Longacre 1970.

Chapter 1 (pp. 13–36)

1   Bolton 1963: 216–17.
2   Titiev 1992: 173–7.
3   Ortiz 1969: 105; Titiev 1992: 171–8.
4   Hale and Harris 1979: 170–77.
5   Lamphere 1979.
6   Hammond and Rey 1940: 73.
7   Hammond and Rey 1940: 172.
8   Hammond and Rey 1940: 223.
9   Kidder 1958: 322.
10 Judd 1968: 86.
11 Judd 1968: 65.
12 Smith 1992: 119.

Chapter 2 (pp. 37–45)

1   Haynes 1987.
2   Martin, Rogers, and Neuner 1985.
3   Anderson 1984: 59, 86; Shipman 1992: 85.
4   Haynes 1987: 85; Frison 1989: 771; Judge 1973: 251.
5   Haury 1959.
6   Wilmsen 1973: 23.
7   Wilmsen 1973: 26.
8   Judge 1973: 62–5.
9   Judge 1973: 126.
10 Judge 1973: 125, 196; Judge and Dawson 1972: 1212.
11 Downum 1989: 492; Roth 1993: 495.
12 Judge 1973: 308–09.
13 Frison 1989.
14 Judge, cited in Cordell 1979: 19–20.
15 Lundelius 1992: 46.
16 Shipman 1992: 77.
17 Shipman 1992: 86.
18 Shipman 1992: 87.
19 Guthrie 1984.
20 Fox and Smith 1992: 219.
21 Guilday 1984: 257; Marshall 1984: 787, 803.
22 Haynes 1984: 351.
23 Guthrie 1984.
24 Judge and Dawson 1972: 1212–14.
25 Judge 1982: 48–9.

Chapter 3 (pp. 46–55)

1   Berry 1982; Berry and Berry 1986; Bayham 1982; Huckell 1990; Matson 1991; Wills 1988a, 1988b; Wills and Huckell 1994.
2   Reher 1977.
3   Bayham 1982; Wills 1988a: 131.
4   Flannery 1968: 76–8; Steward 1938: 232, 254.
5   Flannery 1968: 77–8.
6   Martin, Rinaldo, Bluhm, Cutler, and Grange 1952: 221–5.
7   Flannery 1968: 74; Steward 1938.

8   Wills 1988a: 51.
9   e.g. Antevs 1949, 1955; Berry 1982; Hall 1985; Van Devender and Spalding 1979.
10 Judge 1992: 23–4.
11 We should note that 'continuity' in an archaeological sense is a relative term – there is certainly no area of the Southwest with excavated sites that have produced absolute dates for every single year of any 100-year period, even during eras when it is known that population levels were high. The issue thus becomes in part the type and amount of evidence that one needs to argue for 'continuity.'
12 Berry 1982; Berry and Berry 1986; Matson 1991.
13 At present we are unable to use dendrochronology in most parts of the Southwest during the centuries dating before Christ (BC), so the debate centers around radiocarbon dates and, in particular, how those dates are interpreted.
14 Wills 1988a: 58–69.
15 McBrinn 2005.
16 Hayden 1982: 115; Wills 1988a: 88.
17 Sites at which these early dates were collected were excavated in such a way that the association between the dates and cultigens is now questionable. Many of the sites were caves and rockshelters where archaeologists removed deposits in arbitrary blocks several centimeters thick and thus probably lumped together materials from temporally distinct occupations. Charcoal that was collected from one level within that arbitrary block, and subsequently radiocarbon dated, may have been from a different occupation than the cultigens with which it was grouped by the archaeologist.
18 Huber 2005.
19 Mabry 1999.
20 Huckell 1996.
21 The initial use of cultigens is correlated with changes in climatic conditions according to some proposals, but there are differences among these arguments for environmental causes. Some have suggested agriculture began during periods of increased precipitation that would have increased the likelihood of obtaining successful crops. Conversely, the Berrys (1986) argue that agriculture coincided with periods of decreased moisture and was brought by an influx of people from outside areas, although they do not explain why outside agricultural groups would have been attracted to the Southwest under such adverse climatic conditions.
22 Wills 1988b; Wills and Huckell 1994.
23 Wills 1988b: 449, 459; Wills and Huckell 1994: 35, 51.
24 Wills 1988a: 147–8.
25 Wills 1988a; 1988b.
26 Wills 1988a, 1988b; Wills and Huckell 1994: 49–52.
27 Huckell 1990; Wills and Huckell 1994: 40–41.
28 Roney and Hard 2002.
29 Wills 1988a; 1988b: 466–7.

30 Kidder and Guernsey 1919: 100–01.
31 Kidder and Guernsey 1919: 190–91.
32 Roth and Wellman 2001.
33 Haury 1957.
34 Wills 1988a: 130.

Chapter 4 (pp. 56–70)

1 Southwestern archaeologists traditionally have defined villages by physical characteristics such as houses, hearths, or middens (Wills 1988: 454), but here I depart from that pattern and emphasize physical characteristics *and* aspects of ritual, social, and economic behavior. House, hearths, and pits are necessary, but not sufficient conditions for the transformations that characterized Southwestern prehistory during the last 1,500 years.
2 Szuter and Gillespie 1994: 68.
3 Haury 1976: 45–71.
4 Gilman 1987.
5 DeBoer 1988; Wills and Windes 1989.
6 Roberts 1929; Wills and Windes 1989.
7 Wills and Windes 1989.
8 Martin 1940, 1943; Martin and Rinaldo 1947; Wills 1994.
9 Wills 1994: 6.
10 Doyel 1991: 239.
11 Ortiz 1972: 143.
12 Ortiz 1972: 143.
13 Ford 1972.
14 Wilmsen 1982.
15 Ford 1974.
16 Ford 1981: 14; Wills 1988a: 455.
17 Colton 1953: 9–13; Rogers 1936.
18 Kaplan 1965.
19 Ford 1968.
20 Ford 1968.
21 Binford and Chasko 1976: 138; Lee 1979: 329–30; Plog 1986.
22 Whiting, *Ethnobotany of the Hopi*, 1939: 85.
23 Doyel 1991: 240; Wills and Huckell 1994: 39.
24 Judge 1982: 55.

Chapter 5 (pp. 71–117)

1 Haury 1937: 282–8.
2 Haury 1976: 84–94.
3 Masse 1991: 216–23.
4 Schwartz 1989: 51; see also Schwartz, Chapman and Kepp 1980.
5 These figures must be regarded as minimum estimates because many were likely destroyed as the region became densely settled in the 19th and 20th centuries.
6 Doyel 1991: 239.
7 Although the terms 'social' and 'ritual' imply discrete, separate domains for these activities, in fact they are typically closely interrelated (along with economic and political relationships) in such societies. The simple terms represent an attempt to avoid cumbersome phrases (socio-political, socio-economic, etc.), but carry the danger of oversimplifying the complexity of cultural relationships and interaction.
8 Neitzel 1991: 194–8; Nicholas and Feinman 1989.
9 Wilcox 1991a: 261.
10 Haury 1976: 164–72.
11 Wilcox 1991a: 259–61; Fish and Fish 1991: 161.

12 Wilcox 1991a: 266.
13 Fish and Fish 1991: 158; Doyel 1991: 249.
14 Wilcox and Sternberg 1983: 212; Wilcox 1991a: 266.
15 Wilcox 1991b: 123–4.
16 Doyel 1991: 228–38, 247; Neitzel 1991: 177–230.
17 Crown 1991: 149–51; Gregory 1991: 182; Wilcox 1991a: 272.
18 Shafer and Taylor 1986: 43–68.
19 Shafer and Taylor 1986: 43–68.
20 Shafer and Taylor 1986: 43–68.
21 Anyon and LeBlanc 1980: 253–87; Blake, LeBlanc and Minnis 1986: 439–64; LeBlanc 1983: 110–11.
22 LeBlanc 1983: 118.
23 Gilman 1989: 457–69; LeBlanc 1983.
24 Thompson 1994.
25 LeBlanc 1983: 137, 139.
26 Shafer and Taylor 1986: 55.
27 Shafer and Taylor 1986: 65; Gilman 1989.
28 Shafer 1985.
29 LeBlanc 1983: 139.
30 Shafer and Taylor 1986: 67.
31 Shafer 1990.
32 Minnis 1985.
33 Shafer 1990.
34 Blake, LeBlanc and Minnis 1986.
35 Simmons 1942: 59.
36 Frazier 1979: 56–67.
37 Garfinkle 1992: 24.
38 Lekson 1984.
39 Vivian and Reiter 1960: 84.
40 Lekson 1984: 260.
41 Force et al. 2002.
42 Benson et al. 2003.
43 Fritz 1978.
44 Van Dyke 2004.
45 Fritz 1978: 41, 48.
46 Heitman and Plog 2006.
47 Fritz 1978: 53.
48 Wills 2001.
49 Heitman and Plog 2006.
50 Statements by explorers de Ribas and de Niza, quoted in Reff 1991a: 63, 74.
51 Akins 1986: 135–6; Palkovich 1984.
52 Whalen 1976: 75–9; Marcus 1989: 168; Welch 1991: 132–3, 179.
53 Roney 1992.
54 Plog 1986: 322–30.
55 Plog 1986: 310–36.
56 Crown 1991: 146.
57 Mathien 1986: 220–42.
58 Doyel 1991: 245.
59 Masse 1991: 218–19; Doyel 1991: 239.
60 Martin et al. 1991: 220, 227.
61 Plog 1986: 332–3; Plog and Hantman 1990: 448–51; Gregory 1991: 183; Masse 1991: 218–19.
62 Minnis 1985.
63 Wills et al. 1994: 314–15.
64 Rappaport 1979: 134.
65 Whiteley 1988: 289.
66 Palkovich 1984: 103–13; Shafer 1990; Martin, Piacentini, and Armelagos 1985: 104–14; Martin et al. 1991; Martin 1994.
67 Martin, Piacentini, and Armelagos 1985: 213.
68 Shafer, Marek, and Reinhard 1989.
69 Whiteley 1988: 235.

Chapter 6 (pp. 118–153)

1   Dean 1969.
2   Simmons 1942: 421.
3   Nordenskiöld 1973: 59.
4   Rohn 1991: 157.
5   Adler 1990: 264.
6   It should be emphasized that only six of the cliff dwellings have more than 30 rooms; the vast majority are thus small settlements.
7   Nordenskiöld 1973: 19.
8   Rohn 1971.
9   Erdman, Douglas and Marr 1969: 19.
10 Rohn 1971: 111–26; Osborne 1980: 317–67.
11 Adler 1990: 204.
12 Adler 1990: 272, 277.
13 Huber and Lipe 1992: 69–77.
14 Adler 1990: 342, 379.
15 Bradley 1992; Adler 1990.
16 Huber and Lipe 1992: 77.
17 Rohn 1991: 159.
18 Rohn 1971: 86.
19 Rohn 1991: 159.
20 Adler 1989: 35.
21 Adler 1990.
22 Michael Adler's examination of ethnographic evidence has shown that increases in community size are generally correlated with greater use of specialized ritual structures for community or intercommunity integration. Restrictions on public access, on the types of non-ritual activity allowed, and on the frequency of use are typical of such structures. Architecturally they are more formalized and construction is carefully planned.
23 Bradley 1992: 85, 87, 90.
24 Fewkes 1907.
25 Gregory 1987; Howard 1987; Fish and Fish 1994: 123.
26 Cordell, Doyel, and Kintigh 1994: 121.
27 Howard 1987.
28 Howard 1987: 214.
29 Fish 1989: 33; Fish and Fish 1994: 123; Cordell, Doyel, and Kintigh 1994: 121–2.
30 Doyel 1991: 267.
31 Neitzel 1991: 194.
32 Doyel 1991: 253; Fish 1989: 31.
33 Fish 1989: 34.
34 Doyel 1991: 255; Neitzel 1991: 209.
35 Gregory 1987: 186–91.
36 Fish 1989: 33; Mitchell 1992: 91.
37 Doyel 1991: 253.
38 Mitchell 1992.
39 Mitchell 1992.
40 Gregory 1987: 197–8.
41 Doyel 1991: 255.
42 Doyel 1991: 255; Fish 1989: 31.
43 Fish 1989: 31; Fish, Fish, and Madsen 1992; Fish and Fish 1994.
44 Fish, Fish, and Madsen 1992: 78–90.
45 Fish, Fish, and Madsen 1992: 85–6.
46 Fish, 1989: Fish and Fish 1992: 97–105; Fish and Fish 1994.
47 Rohn 1977: 104–09.
48 Fish and Fish 1991: 157.
49 Dean 1970.
50 Steward 1937.
51 Hill 1970: 72–73, 88–90.
52 Rohn 1971: 39–40.
53 Vivian 1970: 81–83.
54 Dean 1995.
55 Dean 1995.
56 Adler 1989; Adler 1990.
57 Adler 1990: 278; Varien et al. 1995.
58 Doyel 1991: 262.
59 Fish and Fish 1991: 161.
60 Abbott 1994: 385.
61 Fish and Fish 1991: 167.
62 Fish and Fish 1991: 167.
63 Fish 1989: 32.
64 Cordell, Doyel, and Kintigh 1991: 331.
65 McGuire 1991: 352.
66 Downum, Fish and Fish 1994.
67 Doelle and Wallace 1991: 330; Doyel 1991: 258; Cordell, Doyel, and Kintigh, 1994: 120; Haas and Creamer 1995.
68 Rohn 1971: 257.
69 Haas and Creamer 1993: 35.
70 Haas 1989: 502–03.
71 Haas and Creamer 1993: 31.
72 Haas and Creamer 1993: 124–5.
73 Gillmor and Wetherill 1953: 37.
74 Wilcox and Haas 1994: 211–38.
75 Nickens 1975.
76 White 1992.
77 White 1992: 341.
78 White 1992: 348.
79 White 1992; Turner and Turner 1992; Turner 1989.
80 Doelle and Wallace 1991: 330; Haas and Creamer 1993: 25, 136; Wilcox and Haas 1994: 225.
81 Haas 1989: 503–04.
82 Wilcox and Haas 1994: 236.
83 Doelle and Wallace 1991: 328–33; McGuire 1991: 352, 372.
84 Doelle and Wallace 1991: 331; Haas and Creamer 1995.
85 Van West 1990; Van West 1995.
86 Adler 1990; Varien et al. 1995.
87 *The Columbia Dictionary of Quotations* (Columbia University Press, New York, 1993).

Chapter 7 (pp. 154–179)

1   Crown 1991: 291–314.
2   Creamer 1993: 2–12, 134–48.
3   Creamer 1993: 40, 147–8.
4   Wetterstrom 1976: 3, 27, 403.
5   Nelson et al. 1994: 75–80; Palkovich 1980: 72–86; Palkovich 1987.
6   Wetterstrom 1976: 400.
7   Kintigh 1985: 86; LeBlanc 1989: 360.
8   Titiev 1944: 155.
9   Wilcox and Haas 1994: 222.
10 LeBlanc 1989.
11 Hammond and Rey 1940: 169.
12 LeBlanc 1989: 355.
13 LeBlanc 1989: 357–8; Martin 1994: 106; Wilcox and Haas 1994: 226–9.
14 LeBlanc 1989: 357.
15 Wilcox and Haas 1994: 234.
16 Adams 1991: 2–3.
17 Graves 1982, 1984; LeBlanc 1989: 359; Crown 1994.
18 Crown 1994.
19 Smith 1952; Dutton 1963; Hibben 1975.
20 Smith 1952.

21 Smith 1952: 239.
22 Adams 1991: 63, 90–91.
23 Miksicek 1991: 98; Adams 1989: 118–19.
24 Dean 1992.
25 Jones 1936: 51–2; Riley 1987: 186–7, 193.
26 Bolton 1908: 137.
27 Galle 1994: 25.
28 Hammond and Rey 1966: 192.
29 Bolton 1963: 186.
30 Riley 1987: 185.
31 Galle 1994.
32 Titiev 1944: 108.
33 Earle and Kennard 1938: 2.
34 Parsons 1936: 826.
35 Dean and Ravesloot 1993: 97.
36 Minnis and Whalen 1993: 42.
37 Minnis 1989: 274.
38 Wilcox 1991: 148.
39 Di Peso 1974: 422, 429.
40 Di Peso 1974, Vol. 2: 733.
41 Creel and McKusick 1994: 518.
42 Wyllys 1931: 129.
43 Smith 1952: 173.
44 Creel and McKusick 1994: 521.
45 Simmons 1942: 44, 239.
46 Minnis 1989: 287; Woosley and Olinger 1993: 120–21.
47 Bandelier 1890: 42, 61.
48 Minnis 1989: 295.
49 Minnis and Whalen 1993: 42.
50 Anawalt 1993; Galle 1994: 27–8.
51 Hammond and Rey 1940: 69–70; 74, 75, 188.
52 Ravesloot 1988: 69.
53 Di Peso 1974, Vol. 2: 419.
54 e.g. Levy 1992: 46.
55 Levy 1992.
56 Wilcox and Shenk 1977; Wilcox 1991.
57 Molloy 1969; Wilcox 1983: 150.

Chapter 8 (pp. 181–193)

1 Hammond and Rey 1940: 78–9.
2 Hammond and Rey 1940: 60.
3 Hammond and Rey 1940: 80.
4 Fish 1989: 34.
5 Doyel 1991: 233.
6 Haury 1976: 356; Doyel 1991: 267; Cordell, Doyel, and Kintigh 1994: 121.
7 Nials, Gregory, and Graybill 1986; Doyel 1991: 234, 262.

8 Fish 1989: 44.
9 Fish 1989: 44; Nelson *et al.* 1994: 100–03.
10 Wilcox 1991: 273.
11 Russell 1975: 227.
12 Martin 1994: 105–06; but see also Fink and Merbs 1991.
13 Martin 1994: 106.
14 Martin 1994: 106.
15 Doyel 1991: 266–7; McGuire 1991: 372–3.
16 McGuire 1991: 366–73.
17 Reff 1991a: 78–9, 1991b.
18 Reff 1991a: 78, 1991b: 645.
19 Reff 1991a: 74; 1991b.
20 Reff 1991a: 83.
21 Reff 1991: 100.
22 Reff 1991a: 237–40.
23 Lycett 1989: 118–19.
24 Reff 1991a: 100–02.
25 Reff 1991a: 1.
26 Dobyns 1983; Upham 1986.
27 Reff 1991a: 113–14, 131–2, 276.
28 Reff 1991a: 161, 167–8, 233.
29 Lycett 1989: 120–21; Reff 1991a: 142.
30 Reff 1991a: 244–5.
31 Reff 1991a: 278.
32 Kessell 1970: 21, 146.
33 Kessell 1970: 99.
34 Reff 1991a: 258.
35 Ezell 1983: 153.
36 Ezell 1983: 154.
37 Kessell 1979: 170.
38 Reff 1991a: 229.
39 Kessell 1970: 4.
40 Simmons 1979: 184.
41 Wilcox 1981.
42 Hammond and Rey 1940: 186.
43 Hammond and Rey 1953: 660.
44 Henderson 1994.
45 Wilcox 1981.
46 Wilcox 1981: 232.
47 Reeve 1956, 1957.
48 Courlander 1971: 179.

Epilogue (pp. 194–198)

1 Reff 1991a: 30.
2 Ezell 1983: 158–9.
3 Kidder 1924: 86–7.
4 Simmons 1942: 88.
5 Ecclesiastics 1: 4.

Further Reading

ABBOTT, DAVID R. 1994 *Hohokam Social Structure and Irrigation Management: The Ceramic Evidence from the Central Phoenix Basin*, Ph.D. dissertation, Arizona State University. Ann Arbor: University Microfilms.

—2000 *Ceramics and Community Organization among the Hohokam*. Tucson: University of Arizona Press.

—(ed.) 2003 *Centuries of Decline During the Hohokam Classic Period at Pueblo Grande*. Tucson: University of Arizona Press.

ADAMS, E. CHARLES 1991a *The Origin an Development of the Pueblo Katsina Cult*. Tucson: University of Arizona Press.

—1991b 'Homol'ovi in the 14th Century,' in *Homol'ovi II: Archaeology of an Ancestral Hopi Village Arizona*, eds. E.C. Adams and K.A. Hays. Anthropological Papers of the University of Arizona No. 55, Tucson.

ADAMS, E. CHARLES AND ANDREW DUFF 2004 *Protohistoric Pueblo World, AD 1275–1600*. Tucson: University of Arizona Press.

ADLER, MICHAEL A. 1989 'Ritual Facilities and Social Integration in Non-ranked Societies,' in *The Architecture of Social Integration in Prehistoric Pueblos*, eds. W.D. Lipe and M. Hegmon. Occasional Paper No. 1 of the Crow Canyon Archaeological Center, Cortez, Colorado.

—1990 *Communities of Soil and Stone: An Archaeological Investigation of Population aggregation among the Mesa Verde Region Anasazi, AD 900–1300* Ph.D. Dissertation, University of Michigan. Ann Arbor: University Microfilms.

—(ed.) 2000 *Prehistoric Pueblo World, AD 1150–1350*. Tucson: University of Arizona Press.

AKINS, NANCY J. 1986 *A Biocultural Approach to Human Burials from Chaco Canyon, New Mexico* National Park Service, Reports of the Chaco Center No. 9.

ANAWALT, PATRICIA RIEFF 1993 'Riddle of the Emperor's Cloth,' *Archaeology* 46(3):30–36.

ANDERSON, ELAINE 1984 'Who's Who in the Pleistocene: A Mammalian Bestiary,' in *Quaternary Extinctions: A Prehistoric Revolution*, eds. P.S. Martin and R.G. Klein. Tucson: University of Arizona Press.

ANTEVS, ERNST 1949 'Age of Cochise Artifacts on the Wet Legget,' in *Cochise and Mogollon Sites*, eds. P.S. Martin, J.B. Rinaldo, and E. Antevs. Fieldiana: Anthropology Vol. 38, No. 1. Chicago: Field Museum of Natural History.

—1955 'Geologic-Climatic Dating in the West,' *American Antiquity* 20:317–35.

ANYON, ROGER AND STEVEN A. LeBLANC 1980 'The Architectural Evolution of Mogollon-Mimbres Communal Structures,' *Kiva* 45:253–87.

BANDELIER, A.F. 1890 *Contributions to the History of the Southwestern Portion of the United States*. Papers of the Archaeological Institute of America, American Series V. Cambridge: John Wilson and Son.

BAYHAM, FRANK E. 1982 *A Diachronic Analysis of Prehistoric Animal Exploitation at Ventana Cave*. Ph.D. Dissertation, Arizona State University. Ann Arbor: University Microfilms.

BENSON, LARRY, LINDA CORDELL, KIRK VINCENT, HOWARD TAYLOR, JOHN STEIN, G. LANG FARMER,

AND KIYOTO FUTA 2003 'Ancient Maize from Chacoan Great Houses: Where was it Grown?' *Proceedings of the National Academy of Sciences* 100(22):13,111–15.

BERRY, MICHAEL 1982 *Time, Space, and Transition in Anasazi Prehistory*. Salt Lake City: University of Utah Press.

BERRY, CLAUDIA F. AND MICHAEL S. BERRY 1986 'Chronological and Conceptual Methods of the Southwestern Archaic,' in *Anthropology of the Desert West: Essays in Honor of Jesse D. Jennings*, eds. C.J. Condie and D.D. Fowler. University of Utah Anthropological Papers No. 10, Salt Lake City.

BINFORD, LEWIS R. AND W.J. CHASKO, JR. 1976 'Nunamiut Demographic History: A Provocative Case,' in *Demographic Anthropology*, ed. E.B.W. Zubrow. Albuquerque: University of New Mexico Press.

BLAKE, MICHAEL, STEVEN A. LeBLANC, AND PAUL E. MINNIS 1986 'Changing Settlement and Population in the Mimbres Valley, SW New Mexico,' *Journal of Field Archaeology* 13:439–64.

BOLTON, HERBERT EUGENE (ed.) 1948 *Kino's Historical Memoir of the Pimería Alta*. Berkeley: University of California Press.

—(ed.) 1963 *Spanish Exploration in the Southwest 1542–1706*. New York: Barnes & Noble, Inc.

BRADLEY, BRUCE A. 1992 'Excavations at Sand Canyon Pueblo,' in *The Sand Canyon Archaeological Project: A Progress Report*, ed. W.D. Lipe. Occasional Paper No. 2 of the Crow Canyon Archaeological Center, Cortez, Colorado.

CABLE, JOHN S., AND DAVID E. DOYEL 1987 'Pioneer Period Village Structure and Settlement Patterns in the Phoenix Basin,' in *The Hohokam Village: Site Structure and Organization*, ed. D.E. Doyel. Colorado: Southern and Rocky Mountain Division of the American Association for the Advancement of Science.

COLTON, HAROLD S. 1953 *Potsherds*. Flagstaff: The Northern Arizona Society of Science and Art.

The Columbia Dictionary of Quotations 1993. New York: Columbia University Press.

CORDELL, LINDA S. 1979 *Cultural Resources Overview of the Middle Rio Grande Valley, New Mexico*. Washington D.C.: U.S. Government Printing Office.

CORDELL, LINDA S., DAVID E. DOYEL, AND KEITH W. KINTIGH 1994 'Processes of Aggregation in the Prehistoric Southwest,' in *Themes in Southwest Prehistory*, ed. G.J. Gumerman. Santa Fe: School of American Research Press.

COURLANDER, HAROLD 1971 *The Fourth World of the Hopis*. New York: Crown Publishers, Inc.

CREAMER, WINIFRED 1993 *The Architecture of Arroyo Hondo Pueblo, New Mexico*. Santa Fe: School of American Research Press.

CREEL, DARRELL AND CHARMION McKUSICK 1994 'Prehistoric Macaws and Parrots in the Mimbres Area, New Mexico,' *American Antiquity* 59:510–24.

CROWN, PATRICIA L. 1991 'Evaluating the Construction Sequence and Population of Pot Creek Pueblo, Northern New Mexico,' *American Antiquity* 56:291–314.

—1991 'The Hohokam: Current Views of Prehistory and the Regional System,' in *Chaco & Hohokam*, eds. P.L. Crown and W.J. Judge. Santa Fe: School of American Research Press.

—1994 *Ceramics and Ideology: Salado Polychrome Pottery*. Albuquerque: University of New Mexico Press.

CROWN, PATRICIA L. AND RONALD L. BISHOP 1991 'Manufacture of Gila Polychrome in the Greater American Southwest: An Instrumental Neutron Activation Analysis,' in *Homol'ovi II: Archaeology of an Ancestral Hopi Village, Arizona*, eds. E. C. Adams and K.A. Hays. Anthropological Papers of the University of Arizona No. 55, Tucson.

DEAN, GLENNA 1992 'In Search of the Rare: Pollen Evidence of Prehistoric Agriculture,' paper presented at the Southwestern Agricultural Symposium, New Mexico Archaeological Council.

DEAN, JEFFREY S. 1969 *Chronological Analysis of Tsegi Phase Sites in Northeastern Arizona*, Papers of the Laboratory of Tree-Ring Research No. 3. Tucson: University of Arizona Press.

—1970 'Aspects of Tsegi Phase Social Organization: A Trial Reconstruction,' in *Reconstructing Prehistoric Pueblo Societies*, ed. W. A. Longacre. Albuquerque: University of New Mexico Press.

—1996 'The Kayenta Area,' in *The Prehistoric Pueblo World, AD 1150–1350*, eds. M. Adler and W. Lipe, in press. Tucson: University of Arizona Press.

DEAN, JEFFREY S., ROBERT C. EULER, G.J. GUMERMAN, FRED PLOG, RICHARD H. HEVLY, AND THOR N.V. KARLSTROM 1985 'Human Behavior, Demography, and Paleoenvironment on the Colorado Plateaus,' *American Antiquity* 50:537–54.

DEAN, JEFFREY S. AND JOHN C. RAVESLOOT 1993 'The Chronology of Cultural Interaction in the Gran Chichimeca,' in *Culture and Contact: Charles C. DiPeso's Gran Chichimeca*, eds. A.I. Woosley and J.C. Ravesloot. Dragoon: The Amerind Foundation.

DeBOER, WARREN R. 1988 'Subterranean Storage and the Organization of Surplus: The View From Eastern North America,' *Southeastern Archaeology* 7:1–20.

DiPESO, CHARLES C. 1974 *Casas Grandes: A Fallen Trade Center of the Gran Chichimeca*, Vol. 1–3 Dragoon: The Amerind Foundation.

DiPESO, CHARLES C., JOHN B. RINALDO, AND GLORIA J. FENNER 1974 *Casas Grandes: A Fallen Trading Center of the Gran Chichimeca*, Vols. 4 and 6–8. Dragoon: The Amerind Foundation.

—1974 *Casas Grandes: A Fallen Trading Center of the Gran Chichimeca*, Vol. 5. Flagstaff: Northland Press.

DOBYNS, HENRY F. 1983 *Their Number Became Thinned*. Knoxville: University of Tennessee Press.

DOELLE, WILLIAM H. AND HENRY D. WALLACE 1991 'The Changing Role of the Tucson Basin in the Hohokam Regional System,' in *Exploring the Hohokam*, ed. G.J. Gumerman. Albuquerque: University of New Mexico Press.

DOUGLAS, CHARLES L. 1972 'Analysis of Faunal Remains from Black Mesa: 1968–1970 Excavations,' in *Archaeological Investigations on Black Mesa, the 1969–1970 Seasons*, G.J. Gumerman, D. Westfall, and C.S. Weed. Prescott College Studies in Anthropology No. 4, Arizona.

DOWNUM, CHRISTIAN E. 1993 *Between Desert and River: Hohokam Settlement and Land Use in the Los Robles Community*. Anthropological Papers of the University of Arizona No. 57, Tucson.

—1993 'Evidence of a Clovis Presence at Wupatki National Monument,' *Kiva* 58:487–94.

DOWNUM, CHRISTIAN E., PAUL R. FISH, AND SUZANNE K. FISH 1994 'Refining the Role of *Cerros de Trincheras* in Southern Arizona,' *Kiva* 59:271–96.

DOYEL, DAVID E. 1987 'The Hohokam Village,' in *The Hohokam Village: Site Structure and Organization*, ed. D.E. Doyel. Colorado: Southern and Rocky Mountain Division of the American Association for the Advancement of Science.

—1991 'Hohokam Cultural Evolution in the Phoenix Basin,' in *Exploring the Hohokam*, ed. G.J. Gumerman. Albuquerque: University of New Mexico Press.

—1991 'Hohokam Exchange and Interaction,' in *Chaco & Hohokam*, eds. P.L. Crown and W.J. Judge. Santa Fe: School of American Research Press.

DOYEL, DAVID E. AND JEFFREY S. DEAN (eds.) 2006 *Environmental Change and Human Adaptation in the Ancient American Southwest*. Salt Lake City: University of Utah Press.

DUTTON, BERTHA P. 1963 *Sun Father's Way: The Kiva Murals of Kuaua*. Albuquerque: University of New Mexico Press.

EARLE, EDWIN AND KENNARD, EDWARD A. 1938 *Hopi Kachinas*. New York: J.J. Augustin.

ERDMAN, JAMES A., CHARLES L. DOUGLAS, AND JOHN W. MARR 1969 *Environment of Mesa Verde, Colorado*. National Park Service Archaeological Research Series 7B, Washington D.C.

EULER, ROBERT C., GEORGE J. GUMERMAN, THOR N.V. KARLSTROM, JEFFREY S. DEAN, AND RICHARD H. HEVLY 1979 'The Colorado Plateaus: Cultural Dynamics and Paleoenvironment,' *Science* 205:1089–1101.

EZELL, PAUL H. 1983 'History of the Pima,' in *Handbook of North American Indians*, Vol. 10, ed. A. Ortiz. Washington D.C.: Smithsonian Institution Press.

FEWKES, J. WALTER 1907 *Excavations at Casa Grande, Arizona, in 1906–1907*. Smithsonian Miscellaneous Collections, Vol. 50. Washington D.C.

FINK, T. MICHAEL, AND CHARLES F. MERBS 1991 'Paleonutrition and Paleopathology of the Salt River Hohokam: A Search for Correlates,' *Kiva* 56:293–318.

FISH, PAUL R. 1989 'The Hohokam: 1,000 Years of Prehistory in the Sonoran Desert,' in *Dynamics of Southwest Prehistory*, eds. L.S. Cordell and G.J. Gumerman. Washington D.C.: Smithsonian Institution Press.

FISH, PAUL R. AND SUZANNE K. FISH 1991 'Hohokam Political and Social Organization,' in *Exploring the Hohokam*, ed. G.J. Gumerman. Albuquerque: University of New Mexico Press.

—1992 'The Marana Community in Comparative Perspective,' in *The Marana Community in the Hohokam World*, eds. S.K. Fish, P.R. Fish, and J.H. Madsen. Anthropological Papers of the University of Arizona No. 56, Tucson.

—1994 'Multisite Communities as Measures of Hohokam Aggregation,' in *The Ancient Southwestern Community*, eds. W.H. Wills and R.D. Leonard. Albuquerque: University of New Mexico Press.

FISH, SUZANNE K., PAUL FISH, AND JOHN H. MADSEN (eds.) 1992 *The Marana Community in the Hohokam World*. Anthropological Papers of the University of Arizona No. 56, Tucson.

FLANNERY, KENT V. 1968 'Archaeological Systems Theory and Early Mesoamerica,' in *Anthropological Archaeology in the Americas*, ed. B.J. Meggers. Washington D.C.: Anthropology Society of Washington.

FORCE, ERIC R., R. GWINN VIVIAN, THOMAS C. WINDES, AND JEFFREY S. DEAN 2002 *The Relation of "Bonito" Paleo-channels and Base-level Variation to Anasazi Occupation in Chaco Canyon, New Mexico*. Tucson: University of Arizona Press.

FORD, RICHARD I. 1968 'Jemez Cave and Its Place in an Early Horticultural Settlement Pattern,' paper presented at the 33rd Annual Meeting of the Society for American Archaeology, Santa Fe, New Mexico.

—1972 'An Ecological Perspective on the Eastern Pueblos,' in *New Perspectives on the Pueblos*, ed. A. Ortiz. Albuquerque: University of New Mexico Press.

—1974 'Northeastern Archaeology: Past and Future Directions,' *Annual Review of Anthropology* 3:385–413.

—1981 'Gardening and Farming Before AD 1000: Patterns of Prehistoric Cultivation North of Mexico,' *Journal of Ethnobiology* 1:6–27.

FOX, JOHN W., AND CALVIN B. SMITH 1992 'Conclusion: Historical Perspectives,' in *Proboscidean and Paleoindian Interactions*, eds. J.W. Fox, C.B. Smith, and K.T. Wilkins. Waco: Baylor University Press.

FRAZIER, KENDRICK 1979 'The Anasazi Sun Dagger,' *Science* 801:56–67.

—2005 *People of Chaco*. New York: W.W. Norton & Co.

FRISON, GEORGE 1989 'Experimental Use of Clovis Weaponry and Tools on African Elephants,' *American Antiquity* 54:766–84.

FRITZ, JOHN M. 1978 'Paleopsychology Today: Ideational Systems and Human Adaptation in Prehistory,' in *Social Archaeology: Beyond Subsistence and Dating*, eds. C.L. Redman, M.J. Berman, E.V. Curtin, W.T. Langhorne, Jr., N.M. Versaggi, and J.C. Wanser. New York: Academic Press.

GALLE, JILLIAN E. 1994 'Haute Couture: Cotton, Class, and Culture Change in the Protohistoric Southwest,' senior Honors Thesis, University of Virginia, Charlottesville.

GARFINKLE, ROBERT A. 1992 'Supernova Linked to Indian Pottery,' *Astronomy* 20(2):24.

GIBSON, CHARLES 1964 *The Aztecs Under Spanish Rule*. Stanford: Stanford University Press.

GILLMOR, FRANCES, AND LOUISA WADE WETHERILL 1953 *Trader to the Navajos, the Story of the Wetherills of Kayenta*. Albuquerque: University of New Mexico Press.

GILMAN, PATRICIA A. 1987 'Architecture as Artifact: Pit Structures and Pueblos in the American Southwest,' *American Antiquity* 52:538–64.

—1989 'Social Organization and Classic Mimbres Period Burials in the SW United States,' *Journal of Field Archaeology* 17:457–69.

GLADWIN, HAROLD S., EMIL HAURY, E.B. SAYLES, AND NORA GLADWIN 1938 *Excavations at Snaketown: Material Culture*. Medallion Paper No. XXV, Gila Pueblo, Globe, Arizona.

GRAVES, MICHAEL W. 1982 'Breaking Down Ceramic Variation: Testing Models of White Mountain Redware Design Development,' *Journal of Anthropological Archaeology* 1:305–54.

—1984 'Temporal Variation Among the White Mountain Redware Design Styles,' *Kiva* 50:3–24.

GREGORY, DAVID A. 1987 'The Morphology of Platform Mounds and the Structure of Classic Period Hohokam Sites,' in *The Hohokam Village: Site Structure and Organization*, ed. D.E. Doyel. Colorado: Southwestern and Rocky Mountain Division of the American Association for the Advancement of Science.

—1991 'Form and Variation in Hohokam Settlement Patterns,' in *Chaco & Hohokam*, eds. P.L. Crown and W.J. Judge. Santa Fe: School of American Research Press.

GREGORY, DAVID A. AND DAVID WILCOX 2007 *Zuni Origins: Toward a New Synthesis of Southwestern Archaeology*. Tucson: University of Arizona Press.

GUERNSEY, SAMUEL J. 1931 *Explorations in Northeastern Arizona*. Papers of the Peabody Museum of American Archaeology and Ethnology Vol. XII, No. 1, Cambridge.

GUERNSEY, SAMUEL J. AND ALFRED V. KIDDER 1921 *Basket-Maker Caves of Northeastern Arizona*. Papers of the Peabody Museum of American Archaeology and Ethnology Vol. XII, No. 1, Cambridge.

GUILDAY, JOHN C. 1984 'Pleistocene Extinctions and Environmental Change: Case Study of the Appalachians,' in *Quaternary Extinctions: A Prehistoric Revolution*, eds. P.S. Martin and R.G. Klein. Tucson: University of Arizona Press.

GUMERMAN, GEORGE J. (ed.) 1988 *The Anasazi in a Changing Environment*. Cambridge: Cambridge University Press.

GUTHRIE, R. DALE 1984 'Mosaics, Allelchemics, and Nutrients: An Ecological Theory of Late Pleistocene Megafaunal Extinctions,' in *Quaternary Extinctions: A Prehistoric Revolution*, eds. P.S. Martin and R.G. Klein. Tucson: University of Arizona Press.

HAAS, JONATHAN 1989 'The Evolution of the Kayenta Regional System,' in *The Sociopolitical Structure of Prehistoric Southwestern Societies*, eds. S. Upham, K.G. Lightfoot, and R.A. Jewett. Boulder: Westview Press.

HAAS, JONATHAN AND WINIFRED CREAMER 1993 *Stress and Warfare Among the Kayenta Anasazi of the 13th Century AD*. Fieldiana Anthropology No. 21. Chicago: Field Museum of Natural History.

—1996 'The Role of Warfare in the Pueblo III Period,' in *The Prehistoric Pueblo World, AD 1150–1350*, eds. M. Adler and W. Lipe, in press. Tucson: University of Arizona Press.

HACK, JOHN T. 1942 *The Changing Physical Environment of the Hopi Indians of Arizona*. Papers of the Peabody Museum of Archaeology and Ethnology, Harvard University, 35(1), Cambridge.

HALE, KENNETH AND DAVID HARRIS 1979 'Historical Linguistics and Archaeology,' in *Handbook of North American Indians*, Vol. 9, ed. A. Ortiz. Washington D.C.: Smithsonian Institution Press.

HALL, STEPHEN A. 1985 'Quaternary Pollen Analysis and Vegetational History of the Southwest,' in *Pollen Records of Late-Quaternary North American Sediments*, eds. V. Bryant and R.G. Holloway. Dallas: American Association of Stratigraphic Palynologists.

HAMMOND, GEORGE P. AND AGAPITO REY (eds.) 1940 *Narratives of the Coronado Expedition 1540–1542*. Albuquerque: University of New Mexico Press.

—1966 *The Rediscovery of New Mexico 1580–1594*. Albuquerque: University of New Mexico Press.

—(eds.) 1953 *Don Juan de Oñate: Colonizer of New*

Mexico, 1596–1628. Albuquerque: University of New Mexico Press.

HARD, ROBERT J., JOSE E. ZAPATA, BRUCE K MOSES, AND JOHN R. RONEY 1999 'Terrace Construction in Northern Chihuahua, Mexico: 1150 BC and Modern Experiments,' *Journal of Field Archaeology* 26:129–46.

HARD, ROBERT J. AND JOHN R. RONEY 2004 'Late Archaic Hilltop Settlements in Northwestern Chihuahua, Mexico,' in *Identity, Feasting and the Archaeology of the Greater Southwest*, ed. Barbara. Mills, pp. 276–94. Boulder: University of Colorado Press.

HAURY, EMIL W. 1937 'A Pre-Spanish Rubber Ball from Arizona,' *American Antiquity* 4:282–8.

—1950 *The Stratigraphy and Archaeology of Ventana Cave.* Tucson: University of Arizona Press.

—1953 'Artifacts with Mammoth Remains, Naco, Arizona,' *American Antiquity* 19:1–24.

—1957 'An Alluvial Site on the San Carlos Indian Reservation,' *American Antiquity* 23:2–27.

—1976 *The Hohokam: Desert Farmers & Craftsmen.* Tucson: University of Arizona Press.

HAURY, EMIL W., E.B. SAYLES, AND WILLIAM W. WASLEY 1959 'The Lehner Mammoth Site, Southeastern Arizona,' *American Antiquity* 25:2–30.

HAYDEN, BRIAN 1982 'Interaction Parameters and the Demise of Paleo-Indian Craftsmanship,' *Plains Anthropologist* 27:109–123.

HAYS-GILPIN, KELLEY 2004 *Ambiguous Images: Gender and Rock Art.* Lanham: Altamira Press.

HAYNES, C. VANCE 1984 'Stratigraphy and Late Pleistocene Extinctions,' in *Quaternary Extinctions: A Prehistoric Revolution*, eds. P.S. Martin and R.G. Klein. Tucson: University of Arizona Press.

HAYNES, C. VANCE 1987 'Clovis Origin Update,' *Kiva* 52:83–93.

HEITMAN, CAROLYN AND STEPHEN PLOG 2005 'Kinship and the Dynamics of the House: Rediscovering Dualism in the Pueblo Past,' in *A Catalyst for Ideas: Anthropological Archaeology and the Legacy of Douglas W. Schwartz*, ed. Vernon L. Scarborough, pp. 69–100. Sante Fe: School of American Research Press.

HENDERSON, RICHARD 1994 'Replicating Dog Travois Travel on the Northern Plains,' *Plains Anthropologist* 39:145–59.

HIBBEN, FRANK C. 1975 *Kiva Art of the Anasazi at Pottery Mound.* Las Vegas: KC Publications.

HILL, JAMES N. 1970 *Broken K Pueblo: Prehistoric Social Organization in the American Southwest.* Anthropological Papers of the University of Arizona No. 19, Tucson.

HOWARD, JERRY B. 1987 'The Lehi Canal System: Organization of a Classic Period Community,' in *The Hohokam Village: Site Structure and Organization*, ed. D.E. Doyel. Colorado: Southwestern and Rocky Mountain Division of the American Association for the Advancement of Science.

HUBER, EDGAR K. 2005 'Early Maize at the Old Corn Site (LA 137258),' in *Fence Lake Project Archaeological Data Recovery in the New Mexico Transportation Corridor and First Five-Year Permit Area, Fence Lake Coal Mine Project, Catron County, New Mexico*, ed. Edgar K. Huber and Carla R. Van West, pp. 36.1–36.14. Technical Series 84, Statistical Research, Inc., Tucson.

HUBER, EDGAR K. AND WILLIAM D. LIPE 1992 'Excavations at the Green Lizard Site,' in *The Sand*

Canyon Archaeological Project: A Progress Report, ed. W.D. Lipe. Occasional Paper No. 2 of the Crow Canyon Archaeological Center, Cortez, Colorado.

HUCKELL, BRUCE B. 1990 *Late Preceramic Farmer-Foragers in Southeastern Arizona: A Cultural and Ecological Consideration of the Spread of Agriculture into the Arid Southwestern United States.* Ph.D. Dissertation, University of Arizona. Ann Arbor: University Microfilms.

—1995 *Of Marshes and Maize: Preceramic Agricultural Settlements in the Cienega Valley.* Tucson: University of Arizona Press.

—1996 'The Archaic Prehistory of the North American Southwest,' *Journal of World Prehistory* 10(3):305–73.

JONES, VOLNEY H. 1936 'A Summary of the Data on Aboriginal Cotton of the Southwest,' in *Symposium on Prehistoric Agriculture*, University of New Mexico Bulletin 296, Albuquerque.

JUDD, NEIL M. 1968 *Men Met Along the Trail.* Norman: University of Oklahoma Press.

—1964 *The Material Culture of Pueblo Bonito.* Smithsonian Miscellaneous Collections No. 124.

JUDGE, W. JAMES 1973 *PaleoIndian Occupation of the Central Rio Grande Valley in New Mexico.* Albuquerque: University of New Mexico Press.

—1982 'The Paleo-Indian and Basketmaker Periods: An Overview and Some Research Problems,' in *The San Juan Tomorrow*, eds. F. Plog and W. Wait. Santa Fe: School of American Research.

JUDGE, W. JAMES AND JERRY DAWSON 1972 'PaleoIndian Settlement Technology in New Mexico,' *Science* 176:1210–1216.

KAPLAN, LAWRENCE 1965 'Archaeology and Domestication in American Phaseolus (Beans),' *Economic Botany* 19:358–68.

KENT, KATE PECK 1983 *Prehistoric Textiles of the Southwest.* Santa Fe: School of American Research.

KESSELL, JOHN L. 1970 *Mission of Sorrows.* Tucson: University of Arizona Press.

—1979 *Kiva, Cross, and Crown.* Washington, D.C.: National Park Service, U.S. Department of Interior.

KIDDER, ALFRED V. 1924 *An Introduction to the Study of Southwestern Archaeology.* New Haven: Yale University Press.

—1958 *Pecos New Mexico: Archaeological Notes.* Papers of the Robert S. Peabody Foundation for Archaeology No. 5.

KIDDER, ALFRED V. AND SAMUEL J. GUERNSEY 1919 *Archaeological Explorations in Northeastern Arizona.* Smithsonian Institution, Bureau of American Ethnology Bulletin 65. Washington D.C.: Government Printing Office.

KINTIGH, KEITH W. 1985 'Settlement, Subsistence, and Society in Late Zuni Prehistory,' Anthropological Papers of the University of Arizona No. 44, Tucson.

KOHLER, TIMOTHY A. AND CARLA R. VAN WEST 1992 'The Calculus of Self Interest in the Development of Cooperation: Sociopolitical Development and Risk Among the Northern Anasazi,' manuscript, Department of Anthropology, Washington State University.

LAUB, RICHARD S. 1992 'On Disassembling an Elephant: Anatomical Observations Bearing on Paleoindian Exploitation of Probos-cidea,' in *Proboscidean and Paleoindian Interactions*, eds. J.W. Fox, C.B. Smith, and K.T. Wilkins. Waco: Baylor University Press.

LAMPHERE, LOUISE 1979 'Southwestern Ceremonialism,'

in *Handbook of North American Indians*, Vol. 10, ed. A. Ortiz. Washington D.C.: Smithsonian Institution Press.

LEBLANC, CATHERINE J. 1977 'Design Analysis of Mimbres Pottery,' paper presented at the 42nd annual meeting of the Society for American Archaeology, New Orleans.

LEBLANC, STEVEN A. 1983 *The Mimbres People.* London: Thames & Hudson.

—1989 'Cibola,' in *Dynamics of Southwest Prehistory*, eds. L.S. Cordell and G.J. Gumerman. Washington D.C.: Smithsonian Institution Press.

—1999 *Prehistoric Warfare in the American Southwest.* Salt Lake City: University of Utah Press.

LEE, RICHARD B. 1979 *The !Kung San.* New York: Cambridge University Press.

LEKSON, STEPHEN H. 1984 *Great Pueblo Architecture of Chaco Canyon, New Mexico* National Park Service Publications in Archeology 18B, Chaco Canyon Studies, Albuquerque.

—(ed.) 2006 *The Archaeology of Chaco Canyon: An Eleventh-Century Pueblo Regional Center.* Santa Fe: SAR Press.

—(ed.) 2007 *The Architecture of Chaco Canyon, New Mexico.* Salt Lake City: University of Utah Press.

LEKSON, STEPHEN H., THOMAS C. WINDES, JOHN R. STEIN, AND W. JAMES JUDGE 1988 'The Chaco Canyon Community,' *Scientific American* 259 (1): 100–9.

LEONARD, ROBERT D. 1989 *Anasazi Faunal Exploitation: Prehistoric Subsistence on Northern Black Mesa Arizona* Southern Illinois University Center for Archaeological Investigations Occasional Paper No. 18, Carbondale.

LEONE, MARK 1968 'Neolithic Autonomy and Social Distance,' *Science* 162:1150–51.

LEVY, JERROLD E. 1992 *Orayvi Revisited.* Santa Fe: School of American Research Press.

LONGACRE, WILLIAM A. 1970 *Archaeology as Anthropology: A Case Study.* Anthropological Papers of the University of Arizona No. 17, Tucson.

LUNDELIUS, E. L., JR. 1992 'Quaternary Paleofaunas of the Southwest,' in *Proboscidean and Paleoindian Interactions*, eds. J.W. Fox, C.B. Smith, and K.T. Wilkins. Waco: Baylor University Press.

LYCETT, MARK T. 1989 'Spanish Contact and Pueblo Organization: Long-term Implications of European Colonial Expansion in the Rio Grande Valley, New Mexico,' in *Columbian Consequences: Archaeological and Historical Perspectives on the Spanish Borderlands*, ed. D.H. Thomas. Washington D.C.: Smithsonian Institution Press.

MABRY, JONATHAN B. 1999 'Las Capas and Early Irrigation Farming,' *Archaeology Southwest* 13(1):14.

—2002 'The Role of Irrigation in the Transition to Agriculture and Sedentism in the Southwest: A Risk Management Model' in *Traditions, Transitions and Technologies*. ed. Sarah H. Schlanger, pp. 178–99. Boulder: University of Colorado Press.

MARCUS, JOYCE 1989 'Zapotec Chiefdoms and the Nature of Formative Religions,' in *Regional Perspectives on the Olmec*, eds. R.J. Sharer and D.C. Grove. Cambridge: Cambridge University Press.

MARSHALL, LARRY G. 1984 'Who Killed Cock Robin? An Investigation of the Extinction Controversy,' in *Quaternary Extinctions: A Prehistoric Revolution*, eds. P.S. Martin and R.G. Klein. Tucson: University of Arizona Press.

MARTIN, DEBRA L. 1994 'Patterns of Health and Disease Stress Profiles for the Prehistoric Southwest,' in *Themes in Southwest Prehistory*, ed. G.J. Gumerman. Santa Fe: School of American Research Press.

MARTIN, DEBRA L., ALAN H. GOODMAN, GEORGE J. ARMELAGOS, AND ANN L. MAGENNIS 1991 *Black Mesa Anasazi Health: Reconstructing Life from Patterns of Death and Disease.* Southern Illinois University Center for Archaeological Investigations Occasional Paper No. 14, Carbondale.

MARTIN, DEBRA L., CAROL PIACENTINI, AND GEORGE J. ARMELAGOS 1985 'Paleopathology of the Black Mesa Anasazi: A Biocultural Approach,' in *Health and Disease in the Prehistoric Southwest*, eds. C.F. Merbs and R.J. Miller. Arizona State University Anthropological Research Papers No. 34, Tempe.

MARTIN, L.D., R.A. ROGERS, AND A.M NEUNER 1985 'The Effect of the End of the Pleistocene on Man in North America,' in *Environments and Extinctions: Man in Late Glacial North America*, eds. J.I. Mead and D.J. Meltzer. Orono: Center for the Study of Early Man, University of Maine.

MARTIN, PAUL S. 1940 *The SU Site: Excavations at a Mogollon Village, Western New Mexico, 1939.* Anthropology Series, Field Museum of Natural History, Vol. 32, No. 1. Chicago.

—1943 *The SU Site: Excavations at a Mogollon Village, Western New Mexico, Second Season, 1941.* Anthropology Series, Field Museum of Natural History, Vol. 32, No. 2. Chicago.

—1959 *Digging into History.* Chicago Natural History Museum Popular Series No. 38, Chicago.

MARTIN, PAUL S. AND FRED PLOG 1973 *The Archaeology of Arizona.* New York: Doubleday/Natural History Press.

MARTIN, PAUL S. AND JOHN B. RINALDO 1947 *The SU Site: Excavations at a Mogollon Village, Western New Mexico, Third Season, 1946.* Anthropology Series, Field Museum of Natural History, Vol. 32, No. 3. Chicago.

MARTIN, PAUL S., JOHN B. RINALDO, ELAINE BLUHM, HUGH C. CUTLER, AND ROGER GRANGE JR. 1952 *Mogollon Cultural Continuity and Change: The Stratigraphic Analysis of Tularosa and Cordova Caves.* Fieldiana: Anthropology Vol. 40. Chicago: Chicago Natural History Museum.

MARTIN, PAUL S. AND ELIZABETH S. WILLIS 1940 *Anasazi Painted Pottery in the Field Museum of Natural History.* Anthropology Memoirs No. 5 Field Museum of Natural History, Chicago.

MASSE, W. BRUCE 1991 'The Quest for Subsistence Sufficiency and Civilization in the Sonoran Desert,' in *Chaco & Hohokam*, eds. P.L. Crown and W.J. Judge. Santa Fe: School of American Research.

MATHIEN, FRANCES J. 1986 'External Contacts and the Chaco Anasazi,' in *Ripples in the Chichimec Sea*, eds. F. J. Mathien and R. H. McGuire. Carbondale: Southern Illinois University Press.

MATSON, R.G. 1991 *The Origins of Southwestern Agriculture.* Tucson: University of Arizona Press.

MCBRINN, MAXINE 2005 *Social Identities Among Archaic Mobile Hunters and Gatherers in the American Southwest.* Arizona State Museum Archaeological Series 197, Tucson.

MCGUIRE, RANDALL H. 1991 'On the Outside Looking in: The Concept of Periphery in Hohokam Archaeology,' in *Exploring the Hohokam*, ed. G.J. Gumerman. Albuquerque: University of New Mexico Press.

McNITT, FRANK (ed.) 1964 *Navaho Expedition: Journal of a Military Reconnaissance from Santa Fe, New Mexico to the Navajo Country Made in 1849 by Lieutenant James H. Simpson.* Norman: University of Oklahoma Press.

MIKSICEK, CHARLES H. 1991 'Paleoethnobotany,' in *Homol'ovi II: Archaeology of an Ancestral Hopi Village, Arizona,* eds. E. Charles Adams and Kelley Ann Hays. Anthropological Papers of the University of Arizona No. 55, Tucson.

MINDELEFF, VICTOR 1891 *A Study of Pueblo Architecture in Tusayan and Cibola.* Eighth Annual Report of the Bureau of Ethnology, Washington D.C.: U.S. Government Printing Office.

MILLS, BARBARA (ed.) 2000 *Alternative Leadership Strategies in the Prehispanic Southwest.* Tucson: University of Arizona Press.

—(ed.) 2004 *Identity, Feasting, and the Archaeology of the Greater Southwest.* Boulder: University of Colorado Press.

MINNIS, PAUL E. 1985 *Social Adaptation to Food Stress: A Prehistoric Southwestern Example.* Chicago: University of Chicago Press.

—1989 'Prehistoric Diet in the Northern Southwest: Macroplant Remains from Four Corners Feces,' *American Antiquity* 54:543–63.

—1989 'The Casas Grandes Polity in the International Four Corners,' in *The Sociopolitical Structure of Prehistoric Southwestern Societies,* eds. Steadman Upham, Kent G. Lightfoot, and Roberta A. Jewett. Boulder: Westview Press.

MINNIS, PAUL AND MICHAEL WHALEN 1993 'Grandes, Archaeology in Northern Mexico,' *Expedition* 35:34–43.

MINNIS, PAUL E., MICHAEL E. WHALEN, JANE H. KELLEY, AND JOE D. STEWART 1993 'Prehistoric Macaw Breedings in the North American Southwest,' *American Antiquity* 58(2):270–76.

MITCHELL, DOUGLAS R. 1992 'Burial Practices and Paleodemographic Reconstructions at Pueblo Grande,' *Kiva* 58:91.

MITCHELL, DOUGLAS R. AND JUDY L. BRUNSON-HADLEY (eds.) 2004 *Ancient Burial Practices in the American Southwest: Archaeology, Physical Anthropology, and Native American Perspectives.* Albuquerque: University of New Mexico Press.

MOLLOY, J. 1969 'The Casa Grande Archaeological Zone: Pre-Columbian Astronomical Observation,' manuscript, Western Archaeological Center, National Park Service, Tucson.

NEITZEL, JILL (ed.) 1988 *Great Towns and Regional Polities in the Prehistoric American Southeast and Southwest.* Albuquerque: University of New Mexico Press.

—1991 'Hohokam Material Culture and Behavior: The Dimensions of Organizational Change,' in *Exploring the Hohokam,* ed. G.J. Gumerman. Albuquerque: University of New Mexico Press.

—(ed.) 2003 *Pueblo Bonito: Center of the Chacoan World.* Washington D.C.: Smithsonian Institution.

NELSON, BEN A., DEBRA L. MARTIN, ALAN C. SWEDLUND, PAUL R. FISH, AND GEORGE J. ARMELAGOS 1994 'Studies in Disruption: Demography and Health in the Prehistoric American Southwest,' in *Understanding Complexity in the Prehistoric Southwest,* eds. G.J. Gumerman and M. Gell-Mann. Reading, MA: Addison-Wesley Publishing Co.

NIALS, FRED, D.A. GREGORY, AND D.A. GRAYBILL 1989 'Salt River Streamflow and Hohokam Irrigation Systems,' in *The 1982–1984 Excavations at Los Colinas: Environment and Subsistence,* eds. D.A. Graybill, D.A. Gregory, F.L. Nials, S.K. Fish, R.E. Gasser, C.H. Miksicek, and C.R. Szuter. Archaeological Series No. 162(5), Arizona State Museum, Tucson.

NICHOLAS, LINDA M. AND GARY M. FEINMAN 1989 'A Regional Perspective on Hohokam Irrigation in the Lower Salt River Valley, Arizona,' in *The Sociopolitical Structure of Prehistoric Southwestern Societies,* eds. S. Upham, K.G. Lightfoot, and R.A. Jewett. Boulder: Westview Press.

NICKENS, PAUL R. 1975 'Prehistoric Cannibalism in the Mancos Canyon, Southwestern Colorado,' *Kiva* 40:283–93.

NOBLE, DAVID G. (ed.) 2004 *In Search of Chaco: New Approaches to an Archaeological Enigma.* Sante Fe: SAR Press.

NORDENSKIÖLD, GUSTAF 1973 *The Cliff Dwellers of the Mesa Verde, Southwestern Colorado, Their Pottery and Implements.* New York: AMS Press Inc.

ORTIZ, ALFONSO 1969 *The Tewa World.* Chicago: University of Chicago Press.

—1972 'Ritual Drama and the Pueblo World View,' in *New Perspectives on the Pueblos,* ed. A. Ortiz. Albuquerque: University of New Mexico Press.

OSBORNE, CAROLYN M. 1980 'Objects of Perishable Materials,' in *Long House, Mesa Verde National Park, Colorado,* G.S. Cattanach Jr. National Park Service, Archaeological Research Series No. 7H, Washington D.C.

PALKOVICH, ANN M. 1980 *The Arroyo Hondo Skeletal and Mortuary Remains.* Santa Fe: School of American Research Press.

—1984 'Disease and Mortality Patterns in the Burial Rooms of Pueblo Bonito: Preliminary Considerations,' in *Recent Research on Chaco Prehistory,* eds. W.J. Judge and J.D. Schelberg. National Park Service, Report of the Chaco Center No. 8, Albuquerque.

—1987 'Endemic Disease Patterns in Paleopathology: Porotic Hyperostosis,' *American Journal of Physical Anthropology* 74:527–37.

PARSON, E.C. (ed.) 1936 *Hopi Journal of Alexander M. Stephen.* Columbia University Contributions to Anthropology Vol. 23. New York: Columbia University.

PEPPER, GEORGE H. 1909 'The Exploration of a Burial-Room in Pueblo Bonito, New Mexico,' in *Putnam Anniversary Volume,* ed. by his friends and associates. G. E. Stechert, New York.

PLOG, FRED 1974 *The Study of Prehistoric Change.* New York: Academic Press.

PLOG, STEPHEN 1986 'Understanding Southwestern Culture Change,' in *Spatial Organization and Exchange: Archaeological Survey on Northern Black Mesa,* ed. S. Plog. Carbondale: Southern Illinois University Press.

PLOG, STEPHEN AND JEFFREY L. HANTMAN 1990 'Chronology Construction and the Study of Prehistoric Culture Change,' *Journal of Field Archaeology* 17(4):448–51.

PLOG, STEPHEN AND CAROLYN HEITMAN 2006 'Understanding Chaco: A Digital Archive Approach,' *Archaeology Southwest* 20(3):17–18.

PLOG, STEPHEN AND JULIE SOLOMETO 1996 'Alternative Pathways in the Evolution of Western Pueblo Ritual,' in *Proceedings of the Chacmool Conference*, in press.

POWELL, SHIRLEY AND G.J. GUMERMAN 1987 *People of the Mesa*. Carbondale: Southern Illinois University Press.

POWERS, ROBERT P. (ed.) 2005 *Peopling of Bandelier: New Insights from the Archaeology of the Pajarito Plateau*. Sante Fe: SAR Press.

PRUDDEN, T. MITCHELL 1918 *A Further Study of the Small House Ruins*. Memoirs of the American Anthropological Association, No. 50, Lancaster, Pennsylvania.

RAPPAPORT, ROY 1979 *Ecology, Meaning, and Religion*. Berkeley: North Atlantic Books.

RAVESLOOT, JOHN C. 1988 *Mortuary Practices and Social Differentiation at Casas Grandes, Chihuahua, Mexico*. Anthropological Papers of the University of Arizona No. 49, Tucson.

REED, PAUL R. (ed.) 2000 *Foundations of Anasazi Culture: The Basketmaker-Pueblo Transition*. Salt Lake City: University of Utah Press.

REFF, DANIEL 1991a *Disease, Depopulation, and Culture Change in Northwestern New Spain 1518–1764*. Salt Lake City: University of Utah Press.

—1991b 'Anthropological Analysis of Exploration Texts: Cultural Discourse and the Ethnological Import of Fray Marcos de Niza's Journey to Cibola,' *American Anthropologist* 93:636–55.

REEVE, FRANK D. 1956 'Early Navaho Geography,' *New Mexico Historical Review* 31:290–309.

—1957 'Seventeenth Century Navaho-Spanish Relations,' *New Mexico Historical Review* 32:36–52.

REHER, C. A. (ed.) 1977 *Settlement and Subsistence Along the Lower Chaco River*. Albuquerque: University of New Mexico Press.

RICE, GLEN E. AND STEVEN A. LEBLANC (eds.) 2001 *Deadly Landscapes: Case Studies in Prehistoric Southwestern Warfare*. Salt Lake City: University of Utah Press.

RILEY, CARROLL L. 1987 *The Frontier People: The Greater Southwest in the Protohistoric Period*. Albuquerque: University of New Mexico Press.

ROBERTS, FRANK H.H. 1929 *Shabik'eschee Village, A Late Basket Maker Site in the Chaco Canyon New Mexico*. Bureau of American Ethnology Bulletin 92. Washington D.C.: Government Printing Office.

ROGERS, MALCOLM J. 1936 *Yuman Pottery Making*. San Diego Museum Papers No. 2.

ROHN, ARTHUR H. 1971 *Mug House: Mesa Verde National Park – Colorado*. National Park Service, Archaeological Research Series No. 7D, Washington D.C.

—1977 *Cultural Change and Continuity on Chapin Mesa* Lawrence: The Regents Press of Kansas.

—1991 'Northern San Juan Prehistory,' in *Dynamics of Southwest Prehistory*, eds. L.S. Cordell and G.J. Gumerman. Washington D.C.: Smithsonian Institution Press.

RONEY, JOHN R. 1992 'Roads and Regional Integration in the Chacoan System,' in *Anasazi Regional Organization and the Chaco System*, ed. D.E. Doyel. Maxwell Museum of Anthropology Anthropological Papers No. 5, Albuquerque.

RONEY, JOHN R. AND ROBERT J. HARD 2002 'Early Agriculture in Northwestern Chihuahua,' in *Traditions, Transitions, and Technologies*, ed. Sarah S. Schlanger, pp. 160–77. Boulder: University of Colorado Press.

ROTH, BARBARA J. 1993 'A Clovis Point from East-Central Arizona,' *Kiva* 58:495–8.

ROTH, BARBARA J. AND KEVIN WELLMAN 2001 'New Insights into the Early Agricultural Period in the Tucson Basin: Excavations at the Valley Farms Site (AZ AA:12:736),' *Kiva* 67:59–79.

RUSSELL, FRANK 1975 *The Pima Indians*. Tucson: University of Arizona Press.

SAYLES, E. B. 1938 'Houses,' in *Excavations at Snaketown: Material Culture*, Harold S. Gladwin, Emil W. Haury, E.B. Sayles, and Nora Gladwin. Medallion Paper No. XXV, Gila Pueblo, Globe, Arizona.

SCHAAFSMA, CURTIS F. AND CARROLL L. RILEY (eds.) 1999 *Casas Grandes World*. Salt Lake City: University of Utah Press.

SCHAAFSMA, POLLY (ed.) 2007 *New Perspectives on the Pottery Mound Pueblo*. Albuquerque: University of New Mexico Press.

SCHLANGER, SARAH H. (ed.) 2002 *Traditions, Transitions, and Technologies: Themes in Southwestern Archaeology*. Boulder: University of Colorado.

SCHROEDER, ALBERT H. 1972 'Rio Grande Ethnohistory,' in *New Perspectives on the Pueblos*, ed. A. Ortiz. Albuquerque: University of New Mexico Press.

SCHWARTZ, DOUGLAS W. 1989 *On the Edge of Splendor: Exploring Grand Canyon's Human Past*. Santa Fe: School of American Research Press.

SCHWARTZ, DOUGLAS W., RICHARD C. CHAPMAN, JANE KEPP 1980 *Archaeology of the Grand Canyon, Unkar Delta*. Santa Fe: School of American Research Press.

SHAFER, HARRY J. 1985 'A Mimbres Potter's Grave: An Example of Mimbres Craft-Specialization?' *Bulletin of the Texas Archaeological Society* 56:185–99.

—1990 'Life Among the Mimbres: Excavating the NAN Ruin,' *Archaeology*, 1990 Nov./Dec., 48–51.

SHAFER, HARRY J., MARIANNE MAREK, AND KARL J. REINHARD 1989 'A Mimbres Burial with Associated Colon Remains from the NAN Ranch Ruin, New Mexico,' *Journal of Field Archaeology* 16(1):17–30.

SHAFER, HARRY J. AND ANNA J. TAYLOR 1986 'Mimbres Mogollon Pueblo Dynamics and Ceramic Style Change,' *Journal of Field Archaeology* 13:43–68.

SHIPMAN, PAT 1992 'Body Size and Broken Bones: Preliminary Interpretations of Proboscidean Remains,' in *Proboscidean and Paleoindian Interactions*, eds. J.W. Fox, C.B. Smith, and K.T. Wilkins. Waco: Baylor University Press.

SIMMONS, LEO W. (ed.) 1942 *Sun Chief: The Autobiography of a Hopi Indian*. New Haven: Yale University Press.

SIMMONS, MARC 1979 'History of Pueblo-Spanish Relations to 1821,' in *Handbook of North American Indians*, Vol. 9, ed. A. Ortiz. Washington D.C.: Smithsonian Institution Press.

SIRES, EARL W., JR. 1983 'Excavations at El Polvoron.,' in *Hohokam Archaeology Along the Salt-Gila Aqueduct, Central Arizona Project*, eds. L.S. Teague and P.L. Crown. Arizona State Museum Archaeological Series 150(9), Tucson.

SMILEY, FRANCIS EDWARD 1985 *The Chronometrics of Early Agricultural Sites in Northeastern Arizona: Approaches to the Interpretation of Radiocarbon Dates*. Ph.D. dissertation, University of Michigan. Ann Arbor: University Microfilms.

SMITH, WATSON 1952 *Kiva Mural Decorations at Awatovi*

and Kawaika-a with a Survey of Other Wall Paintings. Papers of the Peabody Museum of Archaeology and Ethnology No. 37, Cambridge.

—1992 'One Man's Archaeology,' *Kiva* 57(2).

STEWARD, JULIAN 1937 'Ecological Aspects of Southwestern Society,' *Anthropos* 32: 87–104.

—1938 *Basin-Plateau Aboriginal Sociopolitical Groups.* Smithsonian Institution, Bureau of American Ethnology Bulletin 120. Washington D.C.: Government Printing Office.

STUART, DAVID E. AND RORY P. GAUTHIER 1984 *Prehistoric New Mexico* (2nd ed). Albuquerque: New Mexico Archaeological Council.

SZUTER, CHRISTINE R. AND WILLIAM B. GILLESPIE 1994 'Interpreting Use of Animal Resources at Prehistoric American Southwest Communities,' in *The Ancient Southwest Community*, eds. W.H. Wills and R.D. Leonard, 67–76. Albuquerque: University of New Mexico Press.

TITIEV, MISCHA 1992 *Old Oraibi: A Study of the Hopi Indians of Third Mesa.* Albuquerque: University of New Mexico Press.

TURNER, CHRISTY G. II 1989 'Teec Nos Pos: More Possible Cannibalism in Northeastern Arizona,' *Kiva* 54:147–52.

TURNER, CHRISTY G. II AND JACQUELINE TURNER 1992 'The First Claim for Cannibalism in the Southwest: Walter Hough's 1901 Discovery at Canyon Butte Ruin 3, Northeastern Arizona,' *American Antiquity* 57:661–82.

TURNER, VICTOR 1969 *The Ritual Process.* Ithaca: Cornell University Press.

UPHAM, STEADMAN 1986 'Smallpox and Climate in the American Southwest,' *American Anthropologist* 88:115–28.

VAN DEVENDER, THOMAS R., AND W. GEOFFREY SPAULDING 1979 'Development of Vegetation and Climate in the Southwestern United States,' *Science* 204:701–10.

VAN DYKE, RUTH M. 2004 'Memory, Meaning, and Masonry. The Late Bonito Chacoan Landscape,' *American Antiquity* 69(3):413–31.

VAN POOL, CHRISTINE S. AND TODD L. VAN POOL (eds.) 2007 *Religion in the Prehispanic Southwest.* Lanham: Altamira Press.

VAN WEST, CARLA R. 1990 *Modeling Prehistoric Climatic Variability and Agricultural Production in Southwestern Colorado: A GIS Approach.* Ph.D. dissertation, University of Colorado. Ann Arbor: University Microfilms.

—1996 'Agricultural Potential and Carrying Capacity in Southwestern Colorado, AD 901–1300,' in *The Prehistoric Pueblo World, AD 1150–1350*, eds. M. Adler and W. Lipe, in press. Tucson: University of Arizona Press.

VARIEN, MARK D., WILLIAM D. LIPE, BRUCE A. BRADLEY, MICHAEL A. ADLER, AND IAN THOMPSON 1996 'Southwest Colorado and Southeast Utah, Mesa Verde Region Settlement AD 1100 to 1300,' in *The Prehistoric Pueblo World, AD 1150–1350*, eds. M. Adler and W. Lipe, in press. Tucson: University of Arizona Press.

VARIEN, MARK D. AND RICHARD H. WILSHUSEN (eds.) 2002 *Seeking the Center Place: Archaeology and Ancient Communities in the Mesa Verde Region.* Salt Lake City: University of Utah Press.

VIVIAN, GORDON, AND PAUL REITER 1960 *The Great Kivas of Chaco Canyon and Their Relationships.* School of American Research Monograph No. 22, Santa Fe.

VIVIAN, R. GWINN 1970 'An Inquiry into Prehistoric Social Organization in Chaco Canyon, New Mexico,' in *Reconstructing Prehistoric Pueblo Societies*, ed. W.A. Longacre. Albuquerque: University of New Mexico Press.

—1974 'Conservation and Diversion: Water-Control Systems in the Anasazi Southwest,' in *Irrigation's Impact on Society*, eds. T.E. Downing and M. Gibson. Anthropological Papers of the University of Arizona No. 25, Tucson.

—1990 *The Chacoan Prehistory of the San Juan Basin.* New York: Academic Press.

VIVIAN, R. GWINN, DULCE N. DODGEN, AND GAYLE H. HARTMANN 1978 *Wooden Ritual Artifacts from Chaco Canyon New Mexico: The Chetro Ketl Collection.* Anthropological Papers of the University of Arizona No. 32, Tucson.

WELCH, PAUL D. 1991 *Moundville's Economy.* Tuscaloosa: University of Alabama Press.

WETTERSTROM, WILMA ELAINE 1976 *The Effects of Nutrition on Population Size at Pueblo Arroyo Hondo, New Mexico.* Ph.D. dissertation, University of Michigan. Ann Arbor: University Microfilms.

WHALEN, MICHAEL 1976 'Zoning Within an Early Formative Community in the Valley of Oaxaca,' in *The Early Mesoamerican Village*, ed. K.V. Flannery. New York: Academic Press.

WHALEN, MICHAEL E. AND PAUL E. MINNIS 2001 *Casas Grandes and its Hinterland: Prehistoric Regional Organization in Northwest Mexico.* Tucson: University of Arizona Press.

WHITE, TIMOTHY 1992 *Prehistoric Cannibalism at Mancos.* New Jersey: Princeton University Press.

WHITELEY, PETER M. 1988 *Deliberate Acts.* Tucson: University of Arizona Press.

WIESSNER, POLLY 1977 *Hxaro: A Regional System of Reciprocity for Reducing Risk Among the !Kung San.* Ph.D. dissertation, University of Michigan. Ann Arbor: University Microfilms.

—1983 'Style and Information in Kalahari San Projectile Points,' *American Antiquity* 49:253–76.

WILCOX, DAVID R. 1981 'The Entry of Athapaskans into the American Southwest: The Problem Today,' in *The Protohistoric Period in the North American Southwest, AD 1450–1700*, eds. D.R. Wilcox and W.B. Masse. Arizona State University Anthropological Papers No. 24.

—1991a 'Hohokam Social Complexity,' in *Chaco & Hohokam*, eds. P.L. Crown and W.J. Judge. Santa Fe: School of American Research Press.

—1991b 'The Mesoamerican Ballgame in the American Southwest,' in *The Mesoamerican Ballgame*, eds. V.L. Scarborough and D.R. Wilcox. Tucson: University of Arizona Press.

WILCOX, DAVID R. AND JONATHAN HAAS 1994 'The Scream of the Butterfly, Competition and Conflict in the Prehistoric Southwest,' in *Themes in Southwest Prehistory*, ed. G.J. Gumerman. Santa Fe: School of American Research Press.

WILCOX, DAVID R. AND LYNETTE O. SHENK 1977 *The Architecture of Casa Grande and its Interpretation.* Arizona State Museum Archaeological Series No. 115, Tucson.

WILCOX, DAVID R. AND CHARLES STERNBERG 1983

Hohokam Ballcourts and Their Interpretation. Arizona State Museum Archaeological Series No. 160, Tucson.

WILLS, WIRT. H. 1988a *Early Prehistoric Agriculture in the American Southwest.* Santa Fe: School of American Research Press.

—1988b 'Early Agriculture and Sedentism in the American Southwest: Evidence and Interpretations,' *Journal of World Prehistory* 2:445–88.

—1994 'The Transition from the Preceramic to the Ceramic Period in the Mogollon Highlands of Western New Mexico,' manuscript, Department of Anthropology, University of New Mexico.

—1996 'The Preceramic to Ceramic Transition in the Mogollon Highlands,' *Journal of Field Archaeology* 23:335–59.

—2001 'Ritual and Mound Formation During the Bonito Phase in Chaco Canyon,' *American Antiquity* 663:433–51.

—2006 'Review of "The Late Archaic Across the Borderlands,"' *Kiva* 73:119–127.

WILLS, WIRT H. AND BRUCE HUCKELL 1994 'Economic Implications of Changing Land-Use Patterns in the Late Archaic,' in *Themes in Southwest Prehistory*, ed. G.J. Gumerman. Santa Fe: School of American Research Press.

WILLS, W. H. AND THOMAS C. WINDES 1989 'Evidence for Aggregation and Dispersal During the Basketmaker III Period in Chaco Canyon, New Mexico,' *American Antiquity* 54:347–69.

WILLS, W.H. , P.L. CROWN, J. S. DEAN, AND C. G. LANGSTON 1994 'Complex Adaptive Systems and Southwestern Prehistory,' in *Understanding Complexity in the Prehistoric Southwest,* eds. G.J. Gumerman and M. Gell-Mann. New York: Addison-Wesley.

WILMSEN, EDWIN N. 1973 'Interaction, Spacing Behavior, and the Organization of Hunting Bands,' *Journal of Anthropological Research* 29:1–31.

—1982 'Biological Variables in Forager Fertility Performance: A Critique of Bongaarts' Model,' *African Studies Center, Working Papers* 60, Boston University.

WILSHUSEN, RICHARD H. 1989 'Unstuffing the Estufa: Ritual Floor Features in Anasazi Pit Structures and Pueblo Kivas,' in *The Architecture of Social Integration in Prehistoric Pueblos*, eds. W.D. Lipe and M. Hegmon. Occasional Paper No. 1 of the Crow Canyon Archaeological Center, Cortez, Colorado.

WOODBURY, RICHARD B. 1979 'Prehistory: Introduction,' in *Handbook of North American Indians*, Vol. 9, ed. A. Ortiz, pp. 22–30. Washington D.C.: Smithsonian Institution Press.

WOODBURY, RICHARD B. AND EZRA B.W. ZUBROW 1979 'Agricultural Beginnings, 2000 BC–AD 500,' in *Handbook of North American Indians*, Vol. 9, ed. A. Ortiz. Washington D.C.: Smithsonian Institution Press.

WOOSLEY, ANNE I. AND BART OLINGER 1993 'The Casas Grandes Ceramic Tradition: Production and Interregional Exchange of Ramos Polychrome,' in *Culture and Contact: Charles C. DiPeso's Gran Chichimeca*, eds. A.I. Woosley and J.C. Ravesloot. Dragoon: The Amerind Foundation.

WYLLYS, RUFUS K. 1931 'Padre Luis Velarde's *Relación* of Pimería Alta, 1716,' *New Mexico Historical Review* 6:111–57.

Sources of Illustrations

I want to thank several people for their indispensable assistance in collecting many of the photographs: Nina Cummings at the Field Museum, Paula Fleming and Vyrtis Thomas at the National Anthropology Archives, Maureen O'Neil of the Amerind Foundation, Tony Thibodeau and Baylor Chapman of the School of American Research, and Cathy Hubenschmidt at the Arizona State Museum.

Color illustrations

1 Photo © Chuck Place, 1996.
4 Photo Stephen Plog.
5 Photo Stephen Plog.
6 Photo Stephen Plog.
7 Photo Stephen Plog.
78 Photo © Mick Sharp.
81 Photo © Jean Williamson/Mick Sharp.
84 Photo © Mick Sharp.
85 Photo © Mick Sharp.
96 Photo © Mick Sharp.
98 Photo Stephen Plog.
99 Photo Stephen Plog.
104 Photo © Mick Sharp.
121 Photo Dennis Tedlock. University of New Mexico, Albuquerque, Maxwell Museum of Anthropology.
126 Photo Steadman Upham.
127 Photo Steadman Upham.
131 Photo Werner Forman Archive, Peabody Museum Harvard University, Cambridge MA.

Black and white illustrations

Frontispiece: Photo Dennis Tedlock. University of New Mexico, Albuquerque, Maxwell Museum of Anthropology.
2 Amy Elizabeth Grey after Woodbury 1979, figure 1
3 Photo Stephen Plog.
8 Amy Elizabeth Grey after Trimble 1993:4–5.
9 After James W. Abert courtesy Amon Carter Museum of Western Art, Texas.
10 Photo courtesy of the National Anthropology Archives, Smithsonian Institution, negative no. 41831.
11 Amy Elizabeth Grey after Titiev 1944, figures 7, 8, and 9.
12 Amy Elizabeth Grey after Ortiz 1969, figure 11.
13 Amy Elizabeth Grey after Ortiz 1969, figure 10.
14 Photo Sumner W. Matteson, 1900, courtesy of the National Anthropology Archives, Smithsonian Institution.
15 Amy Elizabeth Grey after Mindeleff 1891, figure 22.
16 Photo Stephen Plog
17 Photographer unknown, courtesy of the National Anthropology Archives, Smithsonian Institution, negative no. 47-983-A.
18 Photo Daniel Boone Linderman, 1912, courtesy of the Arizona State Museum.
19 Amy Elizabeth Grey after Ferguson and Hart 1985, map 15.
20 Photo Stephen Plog.
21 Photo Neil Judd, courtesy of the National

Anthropology Archives, Smithsonian Institution, negative no. 254.
22 Photo Neil Judd, courtesy of the National Anthropology Archives, Smithsonian Institution.
23 Amy Elizabeth Grey.
24 Amy Elizabeth Grey.
25 Amy Elizabeth Grey after Billings 1970, figure 7–12.
26 Photo Stephen Plog.
27 Simon S. S. Driver in Brian M. Fagan *Ancient North America* 2nd edition (1995, Thames and Hudson).
28 Photo courtesy of the National Anthropology Archives, Smithsonian Institution, negative no.786.
29 Photo O. C. Havens, courtesy of the National Anthropology Archives, Smithsonian Institution, negative no. 11962-A.
30 Amy Elizabeth Grey after Judge 1973: figure 8.
31 Amy Elizabeth Grey after Frison 1989: figures 2 and 3.
32 Photo courtesy of the Arizona State Museum, University of Arizona, negative no. 3155-X-55.
33 Amy Elizabeth Grey after Judge 1973: figures 1 and 4.
34 Amy Elizabeth Grey after Judge and Dawson 1972: figure 2A.
35 Amy Elizabeth Grey after Guernsey 1931: plate 50 and Woodbury and Zubrow 1979: figure 2.
36 Simon S. S. Driver in Brian M. Fagan *The Great Journey* (1987, Thames and Hudson).
37 Amy Elizabeth Grey after Martin *et al.* 1952: figures 78 and 79 and Guernsey and Kidder 1921: plate 32; Guernsey 1931: plate 31.
38 Amy Elizabeth Grey after Powell and Gumerman 1987: figure 2.18.
39 Amy Elizabeth Grey after Guernsey and Kidder 1921: plate 26d.
40 Amy Elizabeth Grey after Guernsey and Kidder 1921: plate 20.
41 Photos © The Field Museum, Chicago IL., negative nos. A93639 and A93644.
42 Amy Elizabeth Grey after Guernsey and Kidder 1921: plate 19.
43 Amy Elizabeth Grey after Sayles 1938: figure 36.
44 Amy Elizabeth Grey after Martin 1959: 60.
45 Amy Elizabeth Grey after Roberts 1929: plate 1.
46 Amy Elizabeth Grey after Roberts 1929: figure 2.
47 Photo courtesy of the National Anthropology Archive, Smithsonian Institution.
48 Photo © The Field Museum, Chicago IL., negative no. A88136.
49 Amy Elizabeth Grey after Doyel 1991: figure 6.2.
50 Amy Elizabeth Grey.
51 Photo James Mooney, courtesy of the National Anthropology Archive, Smithsonian Institution, negative no. 1876-A.
52 Photo © The Field Museum, Chicago IL., negative no. 94042.
53 Photo J. H. Bratley, courtesy of the National Anthropology Archive, Smithsonian Institution, negative no. 53,445.

220

54 Amy Elizabeth Grey after Doyel 1991: figure 6.6.
55 Amy Elizabeth Grey after Gladwin *et al.* 1938:
plate CXLIIb.
56 Amy Elizabeth Grey after Masse 1991: figure 9.2.
57–59 Photos © The Field Museum, Chicago IL.,
negative nos. 102501, 97809, 94810.
60 Photo © The Field Museum, Chicago IL.,
negative no. 94830.
61 Amy Elizabeth Grey after Prudden 1918: figure 1
and plate V.
62 Photo courtesy of the National Anthropology
Archive, Smithsonian Institution, negative no.
37617a.
63 Photo © The Field Museum, Chicago IL.,
negative no. 85402.
64 Amy Elizabeth Grey after Wilcox and Sternberg
1983: figure 5.5.
65 Photo Helga Teiwes, courtesy of the Arizona State
Museum, University of Arizona.
66 Photo Emil Haury, courtesy of the Arizona State
Museum, University of Arizona.
67 Amy Elizabeth Grey after Gladwin *et al.* 1938:
plates LXV, CII, CXXIV, CXCV.
68 Amy Elizabeth Grey after Wilcox 1983: figure 6.1.
69 Amy Elizabeth Grey after Shafer and Taylor 1986:
figure 6.
70 Amy Elizabeth Grey after LeBlanc 1983: figures
56, 71, and 77.
71 Photo courtesy Colorado Springs Fine Art Centre
– Taylor Museum Collection.
72, 73 Photos Werner Forman Archive, Maxwell
Museum of Anthropology, Albuquerque.
74 Thomas W. Gatlin, courtesy of Southern Illinois
University Press.
75 Amy Elizabeth Grey after Hack 1942: figure 15.
76 Amy Elizabeth Grey after Lekson *et al.* 1988: 102
77 Photo © Chuck Place, 1996.
79 Amy Elizabeth Grey after Lekson 1984: figure
4.17.
80 From Lewis H. Morgan *Houses and House Life of
the American Aborigines*, 1881: figure 37.
82 Amy Elizabeth Grey after Canby 1982: 580.
83 Photo Stephen Plog.
86 Amy Elizabeth Grey after Lekson 1984: figure
4.72.
87 Amy Elizabeth Grey after Lekson 1984: figure
4.12.
88 Photo probably by O. C. Havens, courtesy of the
National Anthropology Archives, Smithsonian
Institution, negative no. 22673-A.
89 Amy Elizabeth Grey after Vivian and Reiter 1965:
figure 29.
90 Photo courtesy of the National Anthropology
Archive, Smithsonian Institution, negative no.
130113a.
91 Amy Elizabeth Grey after Vivian 1974: figure 9.4.
92 Photo Stephen Plog.
93 Stephen Plog.
94 Amy Elizabeth Grey.
95 Photo Stephen Plog.
97 Photo Stephen Plog.
100 Amy Elizabeth Grey after Rohn 1971: figure 2.
101–103 Photos Stephen Plog.
105 Photo Stephen Plog.
106 Photo © The Field Museum, Chicago IL.,
negative no. 75659.

107 Amy Elizabeth Grey after Rohn 1971: figure 38.
108 Amy Elizabeth Grey after Bradley 1992: figure 7.1.
109 Amy Elizabeth Grey after Howard 1987: figure 1.
110 Amy Elizabeth Grey after Doyel 1991: figure 6.8.
111 Photo Stephen Plog.
112 Amy Elizabeth Grey after Doyel 1991: figure 6.5.
113 Photo Stephen Plog.
114 Amy Elizabeth Grey after Downum 1993: figure 4.1.
115 Amy Elizabeth Grey after Haas and Creamer
1993: figure 2-7.
116 Photo Fred Plog.
117 Photo Stephen Plog.
118, 119 Photos David Grant Noble, School of
American Research, Santa Fe.
120 Photo John K. Hillers, courtesy of the National
Anthropology Archives, Smithsonian Institution,
negative no. 1859-b-a.
122 Photo A. C. Vroman, courtesy of the National
Anthropology Archives, Smithsonian Institution,
negative no. 42,189F.
123 Photo Hillel Burger, Peabody Museum, Harvard
University, photo no. N24068. Copyright ©
President and Fellows of Harvard College. All
rights reserved.
124 Photo courtesy of the Museum of Archaeology
and Anthropology, Cambridge.
125 Amy Elizabeth Grey after Martin and Willis 1940.
128 Photo Peabody Museum, Harvard University,
photo no. N20305. Copyright © President and
Fellows of Harvard College. All rights reserved.
129 Photo Stephen Plog.
130 Amy Elizabeth Grey after Smith 1952: figure 52b.
132 Photo Peabody Museum, Harvard University,
photo no. N20258. Copyright © President and
Fellows of Harvard College. All rights reserved.
133 Amy Elizabeth Grey after Kent 1983: figures 133,
147 and 149.
134 Amy Elizabeth Grey after Kent 1983: figure 58c.
135 Photo J. H. Bratley, courtesy of the National
Anthropology Archive, Smithsonian Institution,
negative no. 53458.
136 Amy Elizabeth Grey after Di Peso, Rinaldo, and
Fenner 1974: figure 285-5.
137, 138 Photos courtesy of the Amerind Foundation
Inc., Dragoon, Arizona.
139 Photo Stephen Plog.
140 Amy Elizabeth Grey after Ravesloot 1988: figure 7.1.
141 Photo Cosmos Mindeleff, courtesy of the National
Anthropology Archive, Smithsonian Institution,
negative no. Az-99.
142 Amy Elizabeth Grey after Reff 1991: figure 1.
143 Episode of Conquest of America by Jan Mostaert,
© Frans Halsmuseum.
144 Photo William H. Jackson, courtesy of the
National Anthropology Archive, Smithsonian
Institution, negative no. 1827.
145 Photo courtesy of the Colorado Springs Fine
Arts Centre.
146 After H. B. Mollhausen from Ives 'Report Upon
the Colorado River' 1861, courtesy of the Amon
Carter Museum, Fort Worth, Texas.
147 Photo Fred Mang Jr, National Park Service, US
Department of the Interior.
148 Photo courtesy fo the Museum of New Mexico.
149 Amy Elizabeth Grey after Martin and Plog 1973,
inside cover.

Index